In Flux: American Jewelry and the Counterculture

Susan Cummins
Damian Skinner
Cindi Strauss

arnoldsche
art publishers

Contents

Ken Cory holding a balsawood boat in the shape of a pencil, which he made and raced in the Gaylen Hansen Regatta in Pullman, Washington, 1975. The engine was powered by two D cell batteries, and the boat "cruised through the water with authority," according to Cory's friend, Leslie LePere. Courtesy of Cory Estate.

Acknowledgments	04	Chapter Five The Politics of American Jewelry	97
Introduction American Jewelry in Turbulent Times	07	Chapter Six Civil Rights and Body Politics	125
Chapter One Objects and Politics	13	Conclusion The End of an Era	153
Chapter Two Making in the Counterculture	33	Further Readings	158
		Notes	160
Chapter Three Counterculture Jewelers	47	Copyright and Photo Credits	168
Chapter Four Funk Jewelry	75	Index	170

Acknowledgments

To create this book, we relied on the generosity of many people and institutions, those who remember and preserve the history of contemporary jewelry in America. We would like to thank the following individuals who agreed to be interviewed, sharing with us their memories and ideas, and in many cases hosting us in their homes and studios: Mark Baldridge, Harriete Estel Berman, Jan Brooks, Sharon Church, Jim Cotter, Justin Klocke, Lane Coulter, Robin Cust, Helen Drutt, Robert Ebendorf, Arline Fisch, Laurie Hall, Lloyd Herman, Mary Lee Hu, Matthew Kangas, Susan Kingsley, Janet Koplos, Kathleen Kriegman, Diane Kuhn, David LaPlantz, Leslie LePere, Keith Lewis, Marcia Lewis, Karen Lorene, Karen McCreary, Thomas Mann, Richard Mawdsley, Bruce Metcalf, Larry Metcalf, Randy Milhoan, Eleanor Moty, Louis Mueller, Albert Paley, Joyce J. Scott, Christina Smith, Paul Smith, Lori Talcott, Merrily Tompkins, Lynda Watson, Pat Wheeler, Nancy Worden, and Sandie Zilker.

We would also like to acknowledge Linda Shearer and Anne Tucker, who in the early stages of this project attended an informal workshop in Houston, where they listened to presentations about key themes and jewelers and responded with ideas drawn from their extensive knowledge of fine art and photography in the 1960s and 1970s. Having this opportunity to test our ideas and fit them into the wider field of American art was a great privilege and pleasure.

A number of colleagues have provided essential research assistance in helping us track down information, articles, and illustrations: Rachel Arauz; Nora Atkinson, Renwick Gallery of the Smithsonian American Art Museum; Kara Bargmann; David Driskell; Beth Goodrich, American Crafts Council librarian; Barbara Gifford, Museum of Arts and Design; Toni Greenbaum; Diana Greenwold, Portland Museum of Art; Ron Porter; Perry Price, Houston Center for Contemporary Craft; Paul Sacaridiz, Haystack School of Crafts; Anna Walker, the Museum of Fine Arts, Houston; Alvia Wardlaw; Elizabeth Williams, Rhode Island School of Art Museum; Marilyn Zapf, Center for Craft; and Emily Zilber.

William Dunn, Marguerite Durling, and Madison Rendall transcribed hours of interviews and, along with Atiyah Curmally, completed valuable research, and we greatly appreciate their contributions to this book.

We are also extremely grateful to the following institutions and individuals who have facilitated our access to their records of American jewelry in the 1960s and 1970s: Jon Evans, chief librarian, Lynn Wexler, former associate librarian, and Jamie Teich, former library associate, at the Museum of Fine Arts, Houston; former librarian Jessica Shaykett, current librarian Beth Goodrich, and library assistants Rachel Kirchgasler and Alexandra Alisauskas at the American Craft Council; Mary Savig, curator of manuscripts, and the reading room staff at the Archives of American Art; Jennine Scarboro, library technician, Serials, Conservation, Archives, at the California College of Arts and Crafts library; and Amy Spencer, exhibitions director at the Richmond Art Center.

Thank you to the following individuals who have provided permissions for the illustrations in this book: Dr Robert Aibel, Executor of Brent Kington Estate, Harriete Estel Berman, Sharon Church, Beverly Cory, Executor of Ken Cory Estate, Jim Cotter, Helen Drutt, Arline Fisch, John Griebsch, Executor of Barry Merritt Estate, Lynda Merritt Hutchinson, Alexandra Jacopetti, Martha Jackson Jarvis, Arthur Korb, Nancy Cain Krassner, Kathleen Kriegman, Daniel Kron/Laurie Seniuk, Diane Kuhn, Executor of William Clark Estate, Stanley Lechtzin, Leslie LePere, Thomas Mann, Richard Mawdsley, Karen McCreary, Bruce Metcalf, Larry Metcalf, Executor of the Ramona Solberg Estate, Randy Milhoan, Evangeline J. Montgomery, Louis Mueller, Jim Nutt and Gladys Nilsson, Albert Paley, Roberta Price, Senghor Reid, Deedie Rose, Chad Redmon, Charles Russell, Executor of Art Smith Estate, Joyce Scott, Baunnie Sea, Executor of Merry Renk Estate, Ruth and Rich Synderman, Cledie Collins Taylor, Paul Tompkins and the Don Tompkins family, Betty Tompkins, Arlo Tompkins, Executor of Merrily Tompkins Estate, Rimas VisGirda, Lynda Watson, Nancy Worden, and Pat Wheeler.

The following institutions have kindly given us permission to reproduce jewelry in their collections: American Craft Council Archives, Artists Rights Society, Art Resource, Cantor Arts Center Collection, Center for the Study of Political Graphics, Dallas Museum of Art, Des Moines Art Center, Detroit Institute of Art, Georgia Museum of Art, Getty Images, Honolulu Museum of Art, Los Angeles County Museum of Art, Mills College Library, the Museum of Fine Arts, Houston, Museum of Fine Arts, Boston, Museum of Arts and Design, Philbrook Museum of Art, Smithsonian American Art Museum, and Tacoma Museum of Art.

We owe a huge debt to the Rotasa Fund, which provided the funding and support to research, write, and publish this book. This is another example of Rotasa's dedication to promoting serious scholarship about the contemporary jewelry field in the United States and internationally. Thanks, too, to Art Jewelry Forum, which was the fiscal sponsor for this project.

Finally, we want acknowledge everyone involved in the publication process: Heather Brand and Wendy Brouwer, who edited the book, Kay Banning, who created the index, Benjamin Kivikoski and Philipp Staege from Bureau Progressiv, Stuttgart, who designed the book, and Dirk Allgaier, from Arnoldsche, who published this book. Thank you.

Susan Cummins
Damian Skinner
Cindi Strauss

AMERICAN JEWELRY IN TURBULENT TIMES

Introduction

American Jewelry in Turbulent Times

From the mid-1960s onward, a small group of jewelers working in different parts of the United States began to make jewelry and other objects connected to the turbulent social and political currents that rocked America in the sixties and seventies. Often deeply invested in the struggle to assert contemporary jewelry as a professional practice, these jewelers opened their work to the issues of the day, commenting on or taking part in the significant discussions that were upending the certainties and status quo in the post-World War II era.

The 1960s were an extraordinary period. Protestors marched to end the Vietnam War; women threw mops, high heels, lipsticks, and bras into a "Freedom Trash Can" to show their disgust with sexist standards; and civil rights activists were viciously beaten and tear-gassed by the police as they walked between Selma and Montgomery in Alabama, in what became known as "Bloody Sunday." It was a time of fear and paranoia stemming from the threats of the Cold War between America and the Soviet Union during the 1950s. Presidents, politicians, and visionary leaders were assassinated. Equal rights for women, civil rights for African Americans, and gay rights for queer Americans were also challenging the long-standing discrimination embedded in the U.S. legal and political systems, as well as in everyday life. The fragility of the environment and the effects of industrial society on nature and biodiversity were increasingly publicized in books and the media.

Some Americans dropped out, living off the grid in communes where life was in tune with the seasons, and depended on growing food and making things by hand, repurposing the discarded consumer waste of the suburbs they had left behind. Others gathered in the cities, as in 1967, when thousands of Americans flooded into San Francisco to be part of the "Summer of Love." They were enticed by regular media coverage of the "heads," "freaks," and "hippies" and the growing popularity of psychedelic rock. Teenagers and college students who wanted to create a utopia, along with curious middle-class tourists and even military personnel on leave from nearby bases looking for a party, found their way to the Bay Area for a memorable few months. Happenings, be-ins, and festivals sometimes included music and light shows, which were enhanced by the use of drugs. People were searching for what it meant to be an authentic human being, living in harmony with each other and with the natural world.

For any American jeweler working in the 1960s and 1970s, these events were part of life, perhaps experienced up close and in person, or perhaps at a distance through the news headlines. For some, these events and values found their way into the studio. They shared a desire to comment on contemporary issues in their jewelry, and in this way they contributed to the social, cultural, and political movements that were challenging the certainties of mainstream American society.

American studio jewelry emerged from the American studio craft movement, which had experienced explosive growth after World War II. Often this growth is traced to the G.I. Bill, the Serviceman's Readjustment Act, passed in 1944 by the U.S. government to provide — in addition to hospitalization for wounded veterans, unemployment benefits, and low-cost loans to buy houses and businesses — free tuition for education. By 1951 more than eight million former soldiers had studied at university level, and colleges and art schools sprung up or expanded to fill the need. Many of these mature and motivated students wanted courses with practical benefits, a substantial minority did not want to work in bureaucracies or with big business, and many thousands had visual aptitude and manual skills. Becoming a craftsperson was a great way to participate in the arts and earn a living.[1]

By the 1960s and 1970s, the jewelers who graduated from university programs were openly challenging traditional ideas of jewelry by invoking trends from architecture, fine art, and popular culture. By placing their work within larger artistic movements as well as engaging with the political, economic, and cultural issues of the time, they found a welcoming and cohesive structure in which to express their individuality. University programs in jewelry and metalsmithing also afforded teaching positions and studio space in which to explore new ideas. Along with these programs, an increase in visibility for jewelers in America through magazines such as *Craft Horizons*, national organizations such as the American Craft Council and the Society for North American Goldsmiths, commercial galleries, and exhibition opportunities in museums and alternative venues encouraged the interest in jewelry as an art form. The burgeoning studio craft movement, of which jewelry was a part, includes ceramics, textiles, woodworking, furniture, glass blowing, and casting. Each craft has its own specific history, but the years between 1965 and 1980 were transformational for the promotion and acceptance of handmade objects in the United States.

Some of these artistically progressive American jewelers were also part of the counterculture. The most typical association with that term is the hippies of the 1960s, with their long hair, flowers, flowing clothes, and ethnic beads. Yet the term stands for more than just this one group. The counterculture of the 1960s and 1970s was a mix of politically active protesters, alternative-living advocates, hippie drug culture, peaceniks, environmental advocates, commune participants, anti-government and pro-individual activists, folk and pop musicians, and technology pioneers, all of whom wanted to experiment with new ways of living, each in a different way. They could be identified by their clothing, living arrangements, by the choices they made about work and employment, and their political and social concerns.

Members of the counterculture were opposed to war, which included the Vietnam War in Southeast Asia and the threat of nuclear war. They believed in personal freedom, and they often expressed it through recreational drugs and sexual liberation. They cared about the environment and took seriously the responsibilities of humans to nature and the ecosystem. They embraced Eastern spirituality and mysticism and rejected the organized religions in which they had been raised. They wanted society to be more equal, open, and transparent. They believed in the individual on the one hand, and in communal living on the other; they were passionately interested in politics and protest, but they also wanted to live peaceful lives full of love, poetry, music, and meditation. They were young, restless, and conflicted.

The counterculture was a reaction to what Theodore Roszak called, in 1968, the "technocracy," a society that believed in modernizing, updating, rationalizing, and planning — a system that could only be understood by specially trained experts who were the ultimate authorities over all aspects of life. Young Americans looked at their parents' generation and saw citizens who had given up responsibility for making hard moral decisions, or generating ideas, or taking control of public authority and keeping social institutions safe against those who would ruin them. All of this had been sacrificed in exchange for prosperity and wealth, for the improved material quality of life in the years after World War II. In response, the counterculture was fighting for America's soul. Roszak understood that sometimes the counterculture seemed outlandish, but he also appreciated what became possible when hippies and others dropped out of mainstream society and tried to find other ways to live. As he described in his book *The Making of the Counter Culture*:

> The tribalized young gather in gay costume on a high hill in the public park to salute the midsummer sun in its rising and setting. They dance, they sing, they make love as each feels moved, without order or plan. Perhaps the folklore of the affair is pathetically ersatz at this point — but is the intention so foolish after all? There is the chance to express passion, to shout and stamp, to caress and play communally. All have equal access to the event: no one is misled or manipulated. Neither kingdom, nor power, nor glory is desperately at stake. Maybe, in the course of things, some even discover in the commonplace sun and the ordinary advent of summer the inexpressible grandeur that is really there and which makes those who find it more authentically human.[2]

American jewelry, and American studio craft more widely, grew to maturity in the same years that diverse countercultural experiments were seeking to transform American society. The relationship between jewelry and the counterculture was in flux over the decades of the 1960s and 1970s, sometimes close and sometimes distant. Like the American population in general, some American jewelers did not have a lot to do with the counterculture, while others embraced its values and aims, in their lives and in their work.

The jewelers featured in this book were part of a larger field of American studio jewelry that was looking for an identity in the 1960s and 1970s, and experiencing an intense process of self-discovery and development. Jewelers were forming organizations, staging exhibitions, establishing educational programs to teach skills and techniques, building markets for their work, and connecting with craftspeople around the world. Like their colleagues in other countries, American jewelers were part of a postwar trend in contemporary jewelry that embraced new and sometimes commonplace materials that had little or no monetary value. This revolutionary gesture freed contemporary jewelry from the ideas of preciousness that equated the value of an object with the economic value of the materials from which it was made. In its place, there was room for creativity and innovation as markers of value.

The history of American jewelry has been convincingly told from the perspective of the field's internal development, a story of innovations in the use of materials and techniques, and the ever-increasing ambitions of jewelers to make wearable objects that would challenge artistic preconceptions as well as the social and cultural expectations of wearers and viewers. American jewelry—along with the studio craft movement to which it belonged—came of age in the 1960s and 1970s, which was also an extraordinary time in American history. What new understandings become possible when American jewelry and the counterculture become the focus of research? Were American jewelers listening to the news and joining protests, supporting causes, and referring to contemporary events in their work? Were they armchair travelers jumping on an aesthetic bandwagon? Did they ignore political and cultural struggles in favor of materials and techniques? Was the decision to make craft itself a political or social response to the dramatic times in which American jewelers lived and worked? These and other questions are at the heart of *In Flux: American Jewelry and the Counterculture*.

Objects and Politics

Chapter One

Objects and Politics

In the 1960s, artists grappling with the dramatic cultural and political transformations in America faced a particular challenge: how best to deal with the country's social problems and horrific events such as the assassinations of politicians and civil rights leaders, and the mounting death toll of the Vietnam War? One artistic approach, Social Realism, had been discredited due to its political associations with fascism and communism, and it seemed old-fashioned compared to exciting new developments such as Abstract Expressionism. Some artists found a solution in the methods of collage and assemblage, which became very popular in the early 1960s. Found images, texts, and objects provided a way for artists to reflect the struggles and values of the counterculture, and they gave these material facts of American society new and surprising meanings.

Collage was especially useful as a type of activist engagement. By including newspaper photographs or clippings from articles and advertisements, artists could introduce "reality" into an artwork and make direct reference to cultural and political issues. Evidence of what was happening in the world at large could thereby be strategically contrasted with materials that might suggest moods, emotions, or actions; an artwork could offer open-ended interactions rather than certain and often one-sided interpretations.[3]

The Museum of Modern Art's 1961 exhibition *The Art of Assemblage* generated a lot of critical discussion, showcasing the work of artists who were revisiting the historical precedents of Cubism, Dada, and Surrealism and adapting the technique for their own cultural and political moment. The curator of the exhibition, William C. Seitz, wrote, "In thought-provoking ways assemblage is poetic rather than realistic, for each constituent element can be transformed. Physical materials and their auras are transmuted into a new amalgam that both transcends and includes its parts."[4]

According to Seitz, assemblage had become "the language for impatient, hypercritical, and anarchistic young artists." It could deal with the squalor of reality as well as express mystical and moral hopes for humanity. At the time, symbols of democracy, power, and authority (such as flags, shields, and eagles) began appearing in the work of American artists such as Jasper Johns and Robert Rauschenberg, among others, who used them with mild amusement, irony, unconcealed resentment, scatological bitterness, or simply as banal images.[5] For those who wanted to get involved with the struggles of the sixties, assemblage proved to be extremely useful.

Artists did not always turn to assemblage because they had something political to say; sometimes their turn to assemblage is what provoked a more political point of view in their work. This was the case with J. Fred Woell, who began using found objects in his jewelry in the mid-1960s. Born in 1934 in Evergreen Park, Illinois, Woell first encountered metalsmithing while completing a BFA in art education at the University of Illinois in Champaign-Urbana. There, he was required to take two semesters of craft, which meant a choice between ceramics and metals. Woell chose clay, thinking it would bring him a little closer to his goal of becoming

Fig. 1.1

Fig. 1.2

a sculptor. His first semester with the ceramics professor Don Frith went very well, and Woell was keen to complete a second semester in the ceramics department, but Frith had other ideas. He recommended that Woell take a metals course with Robert von Neumann, who was internationally respected for his work. Woell followed Frith's advice, and it changed his life. Later Woell said, "Robert von Neumann got me so turned on to metals and jewelry in one semester that I wanted to continue."[6] After graduating with a BFA in 1959, Woell went on to pursue an MFA in metals at the University of Wisconsin–Madison, where von Neumann had completed his graduate studies.[7] There, Woell studied under Art Vierthaler, whom Woell remembers as having strong social and political convictions. For example, Vierthaler told his students about the diamond cartels and the miseries experienced by the Black men who labored in the South African mines. After that lesson, Woell never used diamonds again.

Vierthaler also encouraged his students to experiment with materials. Over the course of his graduate work, Woell played around with rare woods, plastic resins, plexiglass, silver amalgam, pewter, and square aluminum tubing, which he colored with liver of sulfur.[8] Yet Woell still clung to a traditional ideal of jewelry. "I left college with the impression that metals (ART METALS) had a strong tradition in using precious metals and stones, and that it was about jewelry (personal adornment) or functional objects to use, such as flatware and hollowware," he recalled in 1994. "So I left college making jewelry to wear. It was mostly made of silver (because I could afford silver)."[9]

After graduation, Woell got a job as a grade-school art teacher in rural Wisconsin, but he only lasted a couple of years. Woell had read Henry David Thoreau's book *Walden*, first published in 1854, and like thousands of Americans before him, he was beguiled by Thoreau's narrative of living a simple, spiritual, and self-reliant life in nature. In September 1964, he left the security of teaching for a journey of self-discovery. Friends had offered him the use of a remote summer cottage on a sand dune overlooking Lake Michigan, and he planned to live there during winter, reading, making jewelry, and pursuing his version of the American dream. Two months into his stay, his blue Volkswagen bus (nicknamed BB) broke down, requiring a big chunk

Fig. 1.1
Tamara Karla Surendorf, *Pendant*, no date
Purse frame, toy gun part, tintype photograph, and metal
Courtesy American Craft Council Library & Archives

Fig. 1.2
J. Fred Woell, *Fetish Pendant*, 1966
Wood, brass, copper, glass, steel, paper, and silver
3½ × 3½ × ⅝ inches
Detroit Institute of Art, Founders Society Purchase with funds from the Modern Decorative Arts Group, Andrew L. and Gayle Shaw Camden Contemporary and Decorative Arts Fund, Jean Sosin, Dr. and Mrs. Roger S. Robinson, Mr. and Mrs. Marvin Danto, Dorothy and Byron Gerson, and Dr. and Mrs. Robert J. Miller

Objects and Politics

Fig. 1.3

of his savings to fix and bringing his quest to an abrupt end.[10] He ended up living back in Champaign-Urbana, where he met the sculptor Frank Gallo and began working in his studio. To prove that he knew how to work with his hands, Woell showed Gallo his jewelry, and he proposed a trade: he would work in Gallo's studio, casting his sculptures, and in exchange Gallo would give him one of his works. In the evenings and on weekends, Woell made his own jewelry in Robert von Neumann's classroom at the University of Illinois.[11]

In 1965 Frank Gallo was offered a solo show at the Graham Gallery in New York City, and he asked Woell to transport the work. Woell set off in a station wagon filled with sculpture and used the opportunity to show his own sterling-silver jewelry to various shops in New York City. The news was not good: Scandinavian silver jewelry, which was well designed and inexpensively priced, had cornered the market, and he was told that the only way to stand out and sell would be to make jewelry in gold.[12] The message left Woell feeling disheartened.

But the trip to New York City also involved a second experience that would prove essential in answering the challenge of what kind of jewelry to make. Woell saw *The Art of Personal Adornment*, a sprawling exhibition at the Museum of Contemporary Crafts that displayed wearable objects made by different societies across centuries and, in some cases, millennia. One of the featured contemporary makers, the American jeweler Tamara Karla Surendorf, left a big impression on Woell.(Fig. 1.1) She had five pendants in the show, with wacky names like *Re-Aul*, *Robbery*, and *Warf*, made from various found objects including a broken funeral plaque, a toy gun, a fork, a champagne tag, a tintype photograph, antique beads, and the metal frame from a coin purse.[13] To Woell's eyes, her jewelry appeared crude, and very inventive.[14] When he returned home to Illinois, his memory of Surendorf's work played a part in his turn to "junk" as the perfect raw material for his own jewelry.

The breakthrough was a work called *Fetish Pendant*,(Fig. 1.2) completed soon after his trip, in which Woell staked everything on the total rejection of refined and commercially appealing materials. He recounted:

> I remember finding a piece of scrap wood splotched with paint, which I further corrupted by burning with a torch and proceeded to drive staples into it with my brand-new Duo-Fast staple gun. "No traditional goldsmiths techniques, no precious materials,"... my mind kept muttering. I was mad and "Fetish" provided me with an object to vent my anger. I never intended it to go any further than that. I had no grand plan to create a series of found objects or "Pop Art" or "Anti-Jewelry" jewelry, but I suddenly found myself creating more. I liked non-precious materials and the found object. Also my feelings about social-political-ecological issues began to surface. "Hell," I told myself, "this isn't jewelry. I can do or say anything I want!"[15]

In anthropology, the term "fetish" applies to an inanimate object that is imbued with religious or supernatural powers. Woell's pendant is a fetish against the attitudes he encountered in New York City, a way to exorcise and ward off their power; it is also a comment on the fetishizing of precious materials in jewelry. In making *Fetish*, Woell placed a used, torn one-cent postage stamp printed with an image of the American president George Washington against some shards of broken mirror and then used staples to create a kind of decorative frame, with a star capping each corner. As a final touch, he varnished the pendant and then set it on fire to give it an antique appearance, or what he called a "rusticated" look.[16]

Fetish kicked off an extraordinary period for Woell as he explored the potential of assemblage. Perhaps his most famous work, *Come Alive, You're in the Pepsi Generation* (1966), was made a few months later.(Fig. 1.3) At the time, Woell was working in Robert von Neumann's basement classroom on the university campus, and the radio kept playing Pepsi's latest jingle, which he adopted as the title. In a magazine, Woell saw a photograph of one of the young actors from the ABC prime-time soap opera *Peyton Place* running down a hill with a joyous expression on her face, all white teeth and glossy dark hair, a perfect embodiment of the "whole new way of living" that Pepsi promised its customers.[17] Originally, Woell intended to float the young woman's face on a black background, but the copper support on which the glass photo lens would sit would not oxidize to a flat black. Woell eventually gave up and painted the metal red, white, and blue, applying a final overcoat of Japan Gold Size (a liquid adhesive for gilding) to make the surface appear old. He rusticated the Pepsi bottle caps with a blowtorch, and then gave them a coating of Japan Gold Size as well. The silver frame was dented and the glass shattered when it fell to the floor while Woell was trying to solder it to the copper support, which had warped with the heat. Rather than trying to fix or replace the damage, Woell incorporated it into the final piece, seeing it as an improvement. As he wrote much later, "This attitude allowed the piece to end up being much freer and 'alive' than I am sure it might have ever been had all gone well throughout the construction."[18]

Come Alive, You're in the Pepsi Generation was a breakthrough for Woell. This brooch represents the moment he threw off the conventions of jewelry making that he had absorbed during his education and surrendered himself to the grungy, exciting world of found-object assemblage. Two external factors helped him make this leap. The first was his time spent working with the sculptor Frank Gallo, who would torch the surfaces of his epoxy sculptures to discolor and crack them, and then poorly fix the breaks to create a kind of spontaneous embellishment.[19] The second was his admiration for the avant-garde American composer John Cage. He was famous for compositions such as *4'33"*, in which no sounds were played by the musician for a period of time (4 minutes and 33 seconds in the first performance in 1952), making the ambient sounds of the venue the focus of the audience's attention and highlighting the important role of duration in music. Cage composed music using the *I Ching*, an ancient Chinese text that became popular in the 1960s as a divination manual among Americans who subscribed to New Age spirituality. Three coins tossed six times would designate one of sixty-four hexagrams that could be interpreted using the text of the *I Ching*. The process channeled the seemingly random forces of the universe, and it was particularly appealing because it did not involve experts; everyone interpreted their own results.

Fig. 1.3
J. Fred Woell
Come Alive, You're in the Pepsi Generation, 1966
Brooch
Sterling silver, copper, brass, steel, glass, and found objects
4 × 4 × ¼ inches
Smithsonian American Art Museum, gift of Kathleen Kriegman, 2006.34.1

Fig. 1.4

Cage and Woell met in person in the 1960s, when Cage gave a lecture at the University of Illinois, which Woell attended. In a self-described "fan letter" that Woell sent to Cage in 1987, he wrote that he could "still remember vividly you sitting on the stage at a table with an amplifier and microphone hooked to it. When you wanted to give emphasis to what you wanted the audience to hear, you'd reach over and turn up the volume. You read from your 'new' book on music entitled 'Silence.'" Published in 1961, *Silence* included essays by Cage on musical history, examples of his own work, and even a text about the artist Robert Rauschenberg. Despite being an introvert and somewhat shy, Woell joined the queue of people who wanted to speak to Cage afterward, and he became increasingly nervous as the queue got shorter. When he reached Cage, Woell blurted out "Thank you" and then turned to leave, but Cage drew Woell out, taking the time to ask him what he was studying and looking him in the eye. For the young jeweler, it was a powerful personal lesson on how to treat people, as well as a profound encounter with an aesthetic that embraced and celebrated chance and spontaneity.[20]

Come Alive, You're in the Pepsi Generation could be interpreted as a subversive take on the problems of capitalism. The reference to an all-American soda brand and the smiling, attractive young woman are undercut by the shape of the top part of the brooch, which resembles the silhouette of a military helmet, and the modified bullet casings from which the battered Pepsi tokens hang, mimicking the appearance of a row of military medals lined up on a uniform. The work employs these particular found objects to offer a commentary on the industrial–military complex, and on the intricate links between capitalism and imperialism that put profits first and people last.[21] The shiny world of consumer goods and advertising are presented battered and broken and turned into a medal that mocks rather than confers distinction or honor.

In 1966, the year this brooch was made, the United States was ramping up its bombing of North Vietnam. In February, public hearings led by Senator William Fulbright challenged the justifications for the war given by the government and the way the conflict was being conducted, and a public outcry about the use of the flammable gel napalm in the Vietnam War led to public protests at Dow Chemical Company factories and U.S. naval bases. Woell later suggested that he was annoyed by the claims made by Pepsi and other soft-drink manufacturers that their products were a kind of miraculous tonic promoting good health, whether physical or emotional: "I was tired of seeing on TV and hearing over the radio the Pepsi ads touting the idea that by drinking Pepsi you'd 'come alive' and be happy and even look young and full of life."[22] The material poetry of the brooch, especially its rusticated surfaces and beat-up forms, undercuts the pleasure of the young woman's laughter, transforming it into an emotional display tinged with a darker, more ambiguous mood.

Kathleen Kriegman, who married Woell in 1966, just after he made this brooch, does not agree that *Come Alive, You're in the Pepsi Generation* is a comment on war, commercialism, or anything else. As she remembers it, Woell was eagerly exploring the possibilities of assemblage and found objects, gleefully rusticating his surfaces, and willingly accepting the accidents of making as an aesthetic improvement.[23] Perhaps these early works had less calculated meanings, being fueled primarily by the mad rush of artistic experimentation. However, material choices also matter, and bullet casings are not an innocent addition.

By the late 1960s, assemblage had become a method for Woell to address a surprisingly diverse range of topics. During the second half of that decade, Woell made work about consumerism, the environment, political events and beliefs, the unjust treatment of Native Americans, and religion. A lot of it was funny, much of it was satirical, and all of it demonstrated Woell's assured use of found objects in combination with techniques and processes that mask the maker's skill and aesthetic delicacy with a kind of good-natured faux amateurism. "My work is partly satire and tries to mimic ... with such things as campaign badges, fan-club buttons, awards, medals, etc.," he wrote in an artist statement from that time. "It also provides me with a tool to express my thoughts and reactions about the conditions and situations that exist. I make things I hope people can laugh at and yet take seriously. I use my work as a platform to express my reactions to the things I see around me; I use humor in my work to make the serious nature of those things bearable."[24]

Woell was not the only American jeweler playing around with the idea of medals in the mid-1960s. Don Tompkins produced an entire series of so-called *Commemorative Medals* between 1965 and 1975, made at a time of increasing militarization with the growing commitment of American troops and resources in the Vietnam War. Tompkins, who was born in Everett, Washington, in 1933, came to jewelry through Russell Day. Day had been his art teacher both at Everett High School and then later at Everett Junior Community College, where Tompkins studied drawing, painting, and design and worked as Day's teaching assistant. Noticing his interest in jewelry, Day had given Tompkins some tools, silver, and other materials so he could experiment. However, Tompkins's breakthrough came when he raided his family home for unusual materials (spoons, bottle caps, broken glass) and tools (a blowtorch) and used them to create two pendants and a ring that were accepted for the second annual Northwest Craftsman's Exhibition in Seattle in 1954. That same year, Tompkins transferred to study with Ruth Penington at the University of Washington; her philosophy of using a minimum of tools to allow invention and creativity was perfectly suited to Tompkins's own artistic discoveries. Tompkins graduated with a BA in art education in 1956, and in 1958 he completed an MFA in design, with specialties in metal, jewelry, and sculpture. Having completed the first phase of his education, Tompkins moved back to Everett, where he taught alongside Day at Everett Junior Community College.[25]

Tompkins traveled to Syracuse University in 1963 on a teaching fellowship to study art education, which allowed him to spend time in New York City. By that time, Pop Art was ascendant, led by artists such as Jasper Johns, Robert Rauschenberg, and Andy Warhol, among others, who used everyday life in the city as source material. While in New York, Tompkins began making his series of *Commemorative Medals*, which ultimately encompassed portraits of key political figures, artists, writers, and musicians of the period. His treatment of these figures resonates with Pop sensibilities, in particular with Warhol's representation of Hollywood film stars, combining glamour and pathos. In these works, Tompkins used both traditional and untraditional materials along with found objects arranged in a series of interrelated but compartmentalized geometric forms. He also masterfully employed carefully selected quotes to parody or satirize the figures. Tompkins was also a great experimenter with novel processes such as photo-etching. (Fig. 1.4)

Fig. 1.4
Don Tompkins
Pendant, c. 1965
Sterling silver, semiprecious stones, pearls, and coin
2 3/4 × 2 1/2 × 3/8 inches
Collection of the Tompkins family

Fig. 1.5

What is likely to be Tompkins's first *Commemorative Medal* includes a metal cast of a toy Native American figure owned by Tompkins's son, a cast of wax paper, lettering from a newspaper etched into metal, some pearls, two unfaceted stones set in silver, and a Canadian penny. This tableau suggests a short story that has been jumbled, a series of narrative beginnings that tail off just as the story gets underway. By embracing the detritus of consumer culture, Tompkins conclusively breaks with modernist jewelry, replacing po-faced good taste with eccentricity, satire, and humor.[26]

An important moment in the development of the *Commemorative Medals* came in 1966, when Tompkins worked for the commercial jeweler Wesley Emmons in Philadelphia. Tompkins was hired to buff and repair jewelry, and he hated his job as a repairman and production-line drone. Recognizing his frustration, Emmons suggested that Tompkins play around with a group of cast-metal charms and other discarded production objects; a couple of the results became popular designs.[27]

A teaching position at Central Washington University in Ellensburg, Washington, brought Tompkins back to the West Coast in 1966 at the behest of jeweler Ramona Solberg. She had met Tompkins when he was working with Russell Day, and over the years she had kept an eye on his work. Ellensburg was a small town on the other side of the Cascade Mountains from Seattle, in the dry, sparsely populated ranching country of the Kittitas Valley. It was as far from the sophistication, energy, and dense urban environment of the East Coast as you could get, and Tompkins's wife, Betty, hated it immediately. The job, however, proved to be good. Tompkins got along well with Solberg, and his attitudes and personality made him a popular teacher. "As long as you understand your tools, you can make anything," he would tell his students, and at school and during social events at his home, he encouraged them to explore the technical and intellectual dimensions of making jewelry. In 1969, when Solberg left to teach at the University of Washington in Seattle, Tompkins became head of the program at Central Washington.

Tompkins's *Patriotic (Fuck Communism)*,(Fig. 1.6) from about 1969, is a pendant in three parts: the red, white, and blue stripes of the American flag at the top; a tintype photograph of a gentleman with "friendly muttonchops," probably from the second half of the nineteenth century, in the middle; and, at the bottom, a woman's lips, slightly parted, with a metallic speech bubble that says, "Fuck Communism." The colors of the flag evoke conservative notions of patriotism, which are supported by the aggressive dismissal of Communism (if not the coarse use of the swear word), while the gentleman in the tintype seems to stand in for the prototypical patrician and conservative American who loves the flag and hates the commies. The semiprecious stone that ornaments the planished silver of the speech bubble is like a jewelry in-joke, since the swear, the most profane part of the brooch, gets the valuable adornment.

In the late 1960s, the role of the United States in the Vietnam War was couched in the rhetoric of Communism. U.S. leaders argued that military force was necessary to defend South Vietnam from external Communist aggression. Protesters rejected this interpretation and saw it as an imperialist counterrevolution to crush a movement of national liberation. When Tompkins was making this pendant, President Lyndon B. Johnson was arguing to the American public that the Communists in Vietnam were supported and guided by the Soviet Union and China, and that the war in Vietnam was a critical part of the struggle to contain the threat of further Communist expansion. The "domino" theory favored by policymakers of the time proposed that if South Vietnam fell to Communism, neighboring countries would not be far behind. "Fuck Communism" is what the authorities proposed to do through their military intervention.

Tompkins was not the first to use this phrase, and his pendant follows in the footsteps of a banner and car bumper sticker designed by art director John Francis Putnam and based on a concept by Putnam and the magazine editor Paul Krassner. Published in 1963 by Krassner's magazine *The Realist*, a celebrated source of countercultural satire and humorous political commentary, the graphic features the word "Fuck" in the red, white, and blue and stars and stripes of the American flag, and the word "Communism" in solid red, the top of each letter featuring the hammer and sickle of the Russian revolution.(Fig. 1.5) It was the perfect example of cognitive dissonance, a sort of poetry bomb designed to explode in the minds of everyone who believed in the Cold War slogan "better dead than red" but could not bring themselves to say such a filthy swear word.[28] "At the beginning of the 1960s, FUCK was believed to

Fig. 1.5
Paul Krassner and John Francis Putnam
Fuck Communism!, 1963
Offset lithograph on paper
8 ½ × 22 inches
Center for the Study of Political Graphics, Culver City, accession no. 15998

Fig. 1.6
Don Tompkins
Patriotic (Fuck Communism), c. 1969
Pendant
Sterling silver, tintype photograph, and semiprecious stone
8 × 3 inches
Collection of Betty Tompkins

Fig. 1.6

be so full of bad magic as to be unprintable," wrote the author Kurt Vonnegut in 1996. "COMMUNISM was to millions the name of the most loathsome evil imaginable. To call an American a communist was like calling somebody a Jew in Nazi Germany. By having FUCK and COMMUNISM fight it out in a single sentence, Krassner wasn't merely being funny as heck. He was demonstrating how preposterous it was for so many people to be responding to both words with such cockamamie Pavlovian fear and alarm."[29] Tompkins embraced this strategy as well, and his medal mocks the spurious invocations of patriotism that sustained the war effort.

Tompkins could be aggressively political in his jewelry, getting stuck in the messy and controversial issues of the day. The same was true of Woell, who never shied away from addressing events of national significance and shame. Between 1967 and 1969, Woell made a series of three brooches that tackled the brutal legacy of political assassinations in the 1960s. At the time, he was completing his MFA in sculpture at the Cranbrook Academy of Art in Bloomfield Hills, Michigan, developing an artistic language of heads, torsos, and reliefs in cast bronze and epoxy resin. He applied the lessons he had learned in Frank Gallo's studio. The sculptures featured the creamy glow of resin, the figures often staring off into the distance as if in a trance, the surfaces sometimes etched and impressed with the silhouettes of the found objects that had taken over his jewelry.[30]

Woell's education in sculpture affected the way he chose to display his brooches. "I like to think of my work as objects of art not just jewelry, not just a thing to be worn," he wrote in 1967. "Thus by mounting them on bases I am attempting to make that kind of statement. Jewelry usually is thrown in the drawer when not in use — I like the idea of a base that would enable a person to display and enjoy it when it is not being worn."[31] This strategy suits the elegiac subject matter of some of his brooches, turning them into memorials, with frames that add gravitas and different materials to evoke poetic moods.

Objects and Politics

Fig. 1.7

Fig. 1.7
J. Fred Woell
November 22, 1963 12:30 p.m., 1967
Brooch, mounted
Copper, silver, brass, gold leaf, newspaper photo, walnut, velvet, and glass
6 ¼ × 5 × ⅞ inches
Smithsonian American Art Museum, gift of Rose Mary Wadman, 1991.57.1

Fig. 1.8
J. Fred Woell
Requiem, 1968
Brooch, mounted
Silver, bronze, glass, photo, wood, and putty
4 ¾ × 4 ⅝ × ¾ inches
Smithsonian American Art Museum, gift of Rose Mary Wadman, 1991.57.2

Fig. 1.9
J. Fred Woell
The American Way, 1969
Brooch, mounted
Copper, silver, brass, and glass
4 ½ × 4 ½ × ¾ inches (frame)
Collection of Olga de Amaral

Fig. 1.8

Fig. 1.9

Objects and Politics

November 22, 1963 12:30 p.m. (1967) takes its title from the precise moment when Lee Harvey Oswald shot President John F. Kennedy as the presidential motorcade drove through Dealey Plaza in Dallas, Texas.(Fig. 1.7) Americans experienced the assassination firsthand through the so-called "Zapruder" film, a home movie shot by a member of the public. Kennedy's assassination is an indelible series of images: the President and his wife, Jacqueline, waving from the Lincoln convertible with its top down; Kennedy pitching forward after being hit by the first bullet; Jacqueline Kennedy trying to crawl out of the back of the car, her pink Chanel suit covered with blood.

None of this horror is reflected in Woell's brooch. A newspaper photograph of John F. Kennedy, youthful and smiling, sits behind cracked glass, set in an ornately shaped but simply decorated metal frame. A single spent bullet casing hangs from the curlicues of metal wire at the base, while the top of the brooch is capped with a single star, representing the Lone Star State, where Kennedy lost his life. The base that displays the brooch when it is not being worn is dominated by a rectangle of gold leaf with four decorative metal studs at each corner, surrounded by a sober frame of dark velvet and walnut. It is a curiously old-fashioned-looking work, with its muted colors and ornate scrolls and flourishes, more nineteenth century than swinging sixties. Perhaps this elegiac mood is intentional, an indication that the optimism of the early 1960s, with its aspirational vision of Camelot (as Kennedy's presidency came to be known), would seem very far away only three years later.

In June 1968, Senator Robert Kennedy was shot and killed in Los Angeles while he was campaigning to become the Democratic Party's nominee for the upcoming presidential election. After finishing a televised address at the Ambassador Hotel, Kennedy was making his way back to his room through a kitchen hallway when he was shot multiple times by Sirhan Sirhan, a Palestinian born in Jerusalem who claimed he acted because of Kennedy's support for Israel against its Arab neighbors in the Middle East. Photographs of a wounded Kennedy, lying on the ground with his head cradled by Juan Romero, a busboy at the hotel, became the defining images of the event. Rushed to a nearby hospital, Kennedy went straight into surgery, but he never recovered.

Requiem is the name that Woell gave to his brooch marking the second Kennedy assassination.(Fig. 1.8) It refers to a mass performed in the Catholic Church to guide the soul of the deceased and is named for the first word of the Latin liturgy, which in English begins "Eternal rest grant them, O Lord." A photograph behind glass of the dead man as a smiling, handsome youth is warped, as if it had been distorted during printing, a visual analogue of Kennedy's traumatic end. Kennedy's portrait is mounted in a beveled square metal frame; the sloping sides are stamped four times with the phrase "Jesus Saves," while four *X*s occupy the corners of the front face, and four stars protrude from the edges of the brooch, one on each side. The base in which the brooch can be displayed is a stained square timber frame with a circle cut dead center.

The individual elements of *Requiem*, though impossible to pin down, are very suggestive. The phrase "Jesus Saves" might be a reference to the Catholic faith of the Kennedy clan, but it could just as easily be a kind of melancholy satire, as God's omnipotence clearly failed in this situation. The four stars could be a nod to Kennedy's burial site in Arlington Cemetery, where America's war dead are laid to rest. Yet they might also reference J.F.K.'s assassination five years earlier, or point to the cult of celebrity and film-star glamour that accompanied the Kennedys. Whatever the case, they are balanced out — canceled out — by the four *X*s that also adorn the frame.

The third work in Woell's trinity of assassination-themed jewelry is the brooch titled *The American Way* (1969).(Fig. 1.9) Two photographs ground the theme in an actual and specific death, in this case the shooting of the civil rights leader Dr. Martin Luther King, Jr. The face in the smaller round frame is definitively that of King, who was killed in April 1968 while he stood on the balcony of the Lorraine Motel in Memphis, Tennessee. The larger figure may represent James Earl Ray, the man who fired the single shot from a boarding house across the street. Whereas King is shown with a serious, pensive look on his face, the figure above is laughing.

The sequence of Woell's brooches is out of step with historical events, since King was assassinated two months before Robert Kennedy in 1968, although King's murder was once again front-page news in March 1969, when Ray decided to plead guilty to avoid a jury trial and the possibility of receiving the death penalty. Even though *The American Way* explicitly invokes King's murder, the brooch's title and individual elements show that Woell is striving to say something larger. (The title brings to mind Superman's battle for "truth, justice, and the American way," a phrase repeated at the start of each episode of *Adventures of Superman*, televised weekly on American TV in the 1950s.) At the base of the work, Woell has hung twelve spent bullet cartridges, echoing the device used in his brooch *November 22, 1963 12:30 p.m.* for President Kennedy; the trophy row of spent bullets is an acknowledgement that more killings would, inevitably, follow. A badge sarcastically declaring "pro-marksman" crowns the top of the brooch, while an honors-student pin is both patently false in what it says about American values and melancholic in its longing for Americans to live up to the standards of conduct on which their society is supposedly based. A single star and a blood-red heart complete Woell's lament on the awful history of those Americans who have paid the ultimate price for their beliefs.

Woell was not a hippie, nor was he a fully subscribed member of any other visually distinctive countercultural group — no long hair and beard, no string of beads around his neck, denim bell-bottoms, or fringed leather jacket over a paisley shirt. He was a lanky, clean-cut Midwesterner, with black glasses and a shy smile. He was handsome with a somewhat nerdy vibe. The artist's photo for his 1967 exhibition at the Museum of Contemporary Crafts in New York City shows him in a button-down shirt, with a white T-shirt underneath — all very respectable.(Fig. 1.10) Yet his shirt is stained with paint, and Woell stands before a jury-rigged contraption that includes a circular mirrored surface held in place with bulldog clips, doubling his portrait to show another Fred Woell, looking off to the right.

Fig. 1.10

Fig. 1.11

Although he did not dress the part, Woell shared many of the values of the counterculture tribes in reevaluating what it meant to live an authentic life. His work, made out of the detritus of American consumerism, was a plea against waste and environmental degradation. He drove a Volkswagen bus, and his interest in buying food from natural health food stores challenged the corporate model of the food industry. His themes, tackling the self-serving myths of American society, were designed to challenge the status quo, although always with a sense of humor to provide a little relief. Sometimes he got serious, and the hopelessness that he felt about the future of humanity would come out unvarnished. "Nothing is precious to man," he wrote in a 1969 artist statement. "We waste. We have little respect for anything.... Nature has been raped by our greed. Our endless orgy leaves its scar along every inch of our path.... Man is a disaster. We can't save ourselves. So, we laugh and make fun of our plight.... Life is like a joke, a bad joke. I join in the telling of it. The bad joke. It's the humor in my work. It ain't funny, but somehow it helps. It helps me feel a little better. And I can go on at least a little longer without feeling the pain quite so much."[32] However, his work never reflects such bleakness. Even when it deals with horrible truths, it revels in the poetry of materials and found objects. Ultimately, Woell's jewelry is a joy to behold, no matter how sobering the message.

The same can be said of Don Tompkins, (Fig. 1.11) who was no hippie. As his sister and fellow jeweler Merrily Tompkins recalled, "His wonderful and mischievous humor, his wit, talent, intelligence, warmth and generosity as well as his great enthusiasm for bad-smelling cheese, horseradish, raw oysters, New York City, electric knives and strong perfume, were part of his genuine delight at the subtle beauties and little ironies of life."[33]

Encouraged by his wife, Betty, and following his own inclinations, Tompkins got out of sleepy, rodeo-loving Ellensburg as soon as he could in the early 1970s. He headed back to the Big Apple and the sophisticated East Coast culture that so often turned up in his jewelry through references to famous artists (Jackson Pollock) and authors (Norman Mailer). His *Commemorative Medals* could be funny, sentimental, and culturally literate — but they could also be white hot in their satirical takedown of pompous political figures. Like Woell, Tompkins would never be caught dead in a pair of bell-bottoms and beads, but his attitude toward politics and contemporary society made him a bona fide member of the counterculture.

By the late 1960s, the American jewelry movement had produced its own homegrown version of the radical new ideas that had resulted in the international contemporary jewelry movement. As J. Fred Woell wrote in 1970, "I have certain feelings regarding what jewelry has become, and what jewelry can be.... jewelry doesn't have to be made of precious stones and metals to be valuable. I like to think that an object gets its value from what you make of it, and not of what it is made."[34] Jewelers were free to dispense with precious materials, and to make their work from almost anything; found objects, industrial materials such as resin and plastic, and common materials like leather, paper, and rubber all found their way into wearable objects. This new material palette called for either new techniques (some borrowed from the fine arts, some from industry or artisan craft) or traditional techniques and processes (such as enameling) to be used in contemporary and even provocative ways. It also ushered in fresh subject matter, ranging from the cartoons and logos of popular culture and the myths of national identity, such as the Wild

Fig. 1.10
Portrait of J. Fred Woell from the back cover of the exhibition catalogue *Jewelry by Fred Woell*.
Courtesy American Craft Council Library & Archives

Fig. 1.11
Don Tompkins, in front of a rented storefront, 1980
Courtesy Tompkins family

Fig. 1.12
Olaf Skoogfors
Brooch, 1966
Gold-plated sterling silver, round pearls, and Biwa pearls
2 × 2 × ½ inches
The Museum of Fine Arts, Houston, Helen Williams Drutt Collection, museum purchase funded by the Caroline Wiess Law Foundation, 2002.4089

West, to the contemporary political questions that were tearing great rifts in the social fabric. American jewelers were innovative and iconoclastic, challenging the conventions of jewelry with wearable objects that channeled the spirit of the times in which they were made.

Yet alongside the trends represented by Woell and Tompkins, another group of jewelers simultaneously pursued a different kind of experimentation. They were largely involved with the explosive growth of university programs in jewelry and metalsmithing during the 1960s. Jewelers such as Hans Christensen, Alma Eikerman, Philip Fike, Arline Fisch, L. Brent Kington, Stanley Lechtzin, John Paul Miller, Earl Pardon, Ron Pearson, Jack Prip, Richard Reinhardt, Heikki Seppä, and Olaf Skoogfors, among others, led these dynamic programs, ultimately indoctrinating the next generation of American jewelers in their artistic philosophies. Although each of these jewelers had their own individual styles, they shared overwhelming commonalities in their choice of materials and techniques. Gold and silver dominated the field, often punctuated by natural materials such as pearls, semiprecious stones, or geodes. They employed color through the use of enamel or niello and achieved texture through the use of historic techniques such as reticulation, granulation, engraving, lost-wax casting, forging, chasing, or other means of metal manipulation. Often, their forms were based on historical examples such as the fibula or torque, or on the organic shapes of Scandinavian metalwork, with a focus on wearable scale.

Nowhere is the primacy of these aesthetics, materials, and techniques seen more fully than in the jewelry and metalsmithing programs in Philadelphia, one of the most important centers for jewelry and the larger American craft movement in the 1960s. Stanley Lechtzin at the Tyler School of Art and Olaf Skoogfors at the Philadelphia College of the Arts (PCA, later the University of the Arts) not only led their own programs but also were considered the de facto leaders of the American jewelry movement during this period. Through their connections, a steady stream of jewelers, including the likes of Hans Christensen, Philip Fike, L. Brent Kington, John Paul Miller, and Ronald Pearson, visited the city, gave lectures, and exhibited their work there, thereby strengthening the local students' knowledge and appreciation of the dominant influences of the time. Richard Reinhardt, another Philadelphia-based jeweler and a close friend of Lechtzin and Skoogfors who took over the PCA program after Skoogfors's death, was also a regular presence in exhibitions and discussions around the city.

Considered one of the deans of American jewelry, Olaf Skoogfors was renowned for his sculptural forms, which are at once formal and organic.[Fig. 1.12] He championed skills and creativity, saying, "I have strong feelings about the relationship of organic forms to rigid mechanical forms, the desire to combine them in a complementary way to enrich each other."[35] He drew inspiration from a variety of sources, including pre-Columbian, Viking, and Celtic cultures, the Art Nouveau style, and nature. Yet organic form was his primary style, achieved through the use of lost-wax casting, forging, chasing, and folding. In his *Brooch* from 1966, Skoogfors has created a visually rich composition, complete with inset and hanging natural pearls.

Jewelry such as Skoogfors's was celebrated by his American and international colleagues for its technical superiority as well as its seriousness in artistic intent. In these ways, his jewelry was held up as embodying the ideals of American studio jewelry at the time, as promulgated by his peers as well as by the Society of North American Goldsmiths (SNAG), of which he was part. In a testament to its acceptance, Skoogfors's jewelry was also commercially successful, so much so that he sold both production jewelry, such as easily fabricated belt buckles, and one-of-a-kind studio pieces such as complex necklaces, brooches, and rings.

Fig. 1.13

Fig. 1.14

In the late 1960s, Skoogfors's friend and colleague Stanley Lechtzin began translating his ponderous cast forms into lighter-weight jewelry, leading him to the late nineteenth-century industrial technique of electroforming. Electroforming is a process by which metal deposits itself on a removable substrate by way of a chemical bath. The technique also allowed Lechtzin to incorporate stones and other natural materials into his compositions without having to resort to using traditional goldsmithing settings. In shifting from casting organic forms to utilizing electroforming, Lechtzin set new standards for American jewelry, as he was able to increase the scale of his jewelry while still making it wearable. In essence, he designed objects to work with the body, not merely to decorate it.

Lechtzin's use of electroforming opened the door for American jewelers to consider new directions in their work. (Fig. 1.13) The reasonably large scale of *Brooch 64-B3* (1969), and the use of mica and pearls as natural foils to the electroformed structure, telegraphed that American jewelers could embrace technical virtuosity and precious materials while pushing the boundaries of the field. In comparison with the narrative and found-object assemblage jewelry being made by some of his peers, such as Woell and Tompkins, Lechtzin's jewelry still appeared as part of the accepted norm. Yet his dramatic shift from straightforward casting to technical innovation during this time renders his jewelry a type unto itself.

Albert Paley was a student of Lechtzin's at Tyler and was brought, along with his fellow student Eleanor Moty, into Lechtzin and Skoogfors's inner circle. He remembers being invited into their homes, where the three debated problem-solving, scale, and techniques, yet each retained their individual aesthetics. As Paley recalled, "Olaf came out of a Scandinavian tradition. [His jewelry] was much more geometric, much more regimented ... very singular. Stanley was doing a lot of investigation — technical investigation for all of us was very important because if in fact the technique was the basis of design and form development, the greater technique you had, the greater vocabulary you had .... I was more in line with the aspect of art for art's sake .... I was trying to find my own voice."[36]

Paley began first casting then chasing gold and silver, his preferred materials. Soon he began using forging techniques and increased the scale of his forms. Forging allowed him to achieve an aesthetic that is best described as abstract lyricism, with flowing curves and an otherworldly nature reminiscent of Art Nouveau. His technique could be linked to the spontaneous working methods of the Abstract Expressionists. *Brooch*, from 1969, exemplifies these tendencies in its shape as well as its use of kinetics in the hanging gold elements. (Fig. 1.14)

Fig. 1.13
Stanley Lechtzin
Brooch 64-B3, 1969
Silver-gilt, mica, and baroque pearls
4 ¼ × 3 ½ × 1 ¾ inches
The Museum of Fine Arts, Houston,
Helen Williams Drutt Collection,
museum purchase funded by Mr.
and Mrs. John W. Mecom Jr., by
exchange, 2002.3913

Fig. 1.14
Albert Paley
Brooch, 1969
14k gold, sterling silver, freshwater pearls, and baroque pearls
3 ¼ × 5 ¼ × 1 ½ inches
The Museum of Fine Arts, Houston,
Helen Williams Drutt Collection,
museum purchase funded by Mr.
and Mrs. John W. Mecom, Jr., by
exchange, 2002.4000

Despite its forward-looking conception, Paley employed the historical fibula form for the pin back. This signaled his understanding of and connection to the larger interests of American jewelers during the period as well as his desire to pursue his own individual style.

The main priorities of American jewelers were on full display when, in March 1970, *Goldsmith '70* opened at the Minnesota Museum of Art in St. Paul during the first national conference of the newly formed SNAG. The exhibition made clear that one group was to be institutionally sanctioned as the torchbearers of American jewelry; featuring 133 works by 70 jewelers, it was a who's who of metalsmiths leading academic programs around the country. Many of these individuals were among the founders of SNAG, such as Hans Christensen, Robert Ebendorf, Philip Fike, Arline Fisch, Michael Jerry, L. Brent Kington, Ron McNeish, Philip Morton, Ron Pearson, and John Prip, in addition to Lechtzin and Skoogfors. They were among the 23 jewelers invited to participate in the exhibition; a jury selected an additional 47 from among 1,500 submissions.

For all its ambitions to assert American jewelry and metalsmithing as an important part of the studio craft movement, *Goldsmith '70* was focused only on the metals community and did not take into consideration the broader world of studio craft and its makers, critics, or consumers. Lechtzin's juror's statement was purely about the basic characteristics of the submissions and how they did or did not dovetail with his vision of the field at that moment. "Generally, there was not enough attention to detail," he wrote. "The jeweler today has reached a level of sophistication in his craft which precludes the use of commercially manufactured chain or nylon cord for hanging pendants—there are better solutions."[37] Lechtzin also praised the important role that academic programs had in raising standards. Just five years ago, American metalsmithing had not demonstrated a high degree of skill, but he had been pleasantly surprised and encouraged by the technical competence displayed by the submissions to the exhibition. "This can be directly attributed, I feel, to the numerous excellent metalsmithing and jewelry programs presently being offered in the universities and colleges …. It is apparent that a tradition of excellence is developing."[38] John Prip, in his own juror's statement, made it clear that American jewelry would be judged on its formal and technical innovation. "Considering the wealth of new materials and processes available," he wrote, "there were few signs of any real experimentation in the

Fig. 1.15
J. Fred Woell
Mother/Family Icon, 1967
Brooch, mounted
Silver, brass, copper, tin, and glass
5 ¾ × 3 ⅝ × 1 ¼ inches
Courtesy American Craft Council Library & Archives

Fig. 1.16
L. Brent Kington
Pull Toy, no date
Bronze
12 ½ inches high
Courtesy American Craft Council Library & Archives

Fig. 1.17

Fig. 1.18

work submitted. In the use of traditional techniques, entire areas seem to have been overlooked or disregarded entirely. With few exceptions, no acceptable entries made use of such techniques as niello, engraving, chasing, or inlaying."[39]

Despite its overwhelming focus, Goldsmith '70 did feature some examples of jewelry involving found objects and narrative content, quirky objects with a bit of humor and satire. J. Fred Woell was represented by a single work called *Mother/Family Icon*,[Fig. 1.15] which included a found photographic portrait of a woman behind cracked glass and a Den Mother scout badge, all set within an ornate metal frame with a faceted bead suspended from the base. L. Brent Kington's cast bronze *Pull Toy* [Fig. 1.16] is an absurd figure with elongated arms and legs sitting on a two-wheeled cart, like something out of a fantasy novel or dark children's tale. David LaPlantz's *Real American Male Pendant*[Fig. 1.17] is all arrows and pointing fingers, with a label from a wedge of Laughing Cow cheese and a cartoon U.S. postal worker speedily delivering a letter, clearly a sardonic take on American masculinity. Richard Mawdsley had four neckpieces in the exhibition, showcasing his meticulous technique of fabricating miniature elements from metal tubing and then constructing them into narrative compositions with high and low cultural references, from Calliope, the Greek muse of epic poetry, in one piece to the space-faring adventures of the popular cartoon hero Flash Gordon in another.[Fig. 1.18] These works demonstrated that there was more going on in American jewelry than technical skill and the rejuvenation of historical processes. Yet even though Goldsmith '70 included these examples in its survey of American jewelry, it did not especially promote them.

In October 1969, six months before *Goldsmith '70*, another survey exhibition, called *Objects: USA*, had opened at the National Collection of Fine Arts of the Smithsonian Institution in Washington, D.C. While *Objects: USA* took stock of American jewelry, it was also a broad survey of craft in all media. Massively ambitious, with a huge touring program and a lavishly illustrated catalogue, the exhibition was curated by the gallerist Lee Nordness and Paul Smith, the director of the Museum of Contemporary Crafts in New York.

Fig. 1.17
David LaPlantz
Real American Male Pendant,
no date
Brass and bronze
Courtesy American Craft Council
Library & Archives

Fig. 1.18
Richard Mawdsley
Gordon's Flash, no date
Necklace
Silver, pearls, and enamel
Courtesy American Craft Council
Library & Archives

Fig. 1.19

Objects: USA was a sprawling show of 308 objects by 258 makers. The exhibition and its accompanying publication were extraordinarily influential: the show traveled to twenty venues in the United States and ten in Europe, and the catalogue quickly became a key reference for the American studio craft movement. *Objects: USA* was not the first studio craft exhibition organized by medium, nor was it the first to try to characterize a national identity for American studio craft. But it was the most impressive, funded by the largesse of the Johnson Wax Company and based on the earlier model of *Art USA Now*, a survey of 102 painters. It was a grand undertaking, bringing the achievements of American craft to a broad new audience.[40]

Most jewelers featured in the pages of the catalogue were involved in the experimentation that has become the dominant focus of craft history: a story of innovation in techniques and materials, of makers finding new expressions for old techniques, introducing new techniques and materials, or by testing the limits of scale and wearability. Jewelers, like most studio craftspeople, wanted to make work that spoke to the times in which it was made, but as *Objects: USA* demonstrates, this was commonly articulated through individual expression of aesthetics, materials, and techniques rather than through an engagement with narrative.

However, some jewelers in *Objects: USA* went further. J. Fred Woell was represented by his pendant *The Good Guys* (1966),(Fig. 1.19) which includes three buttons featuring comic-strip heroes—Superman, Dick Tracy, and Little Orphan Annie—mounted on a large circle of wood edged with a copper band and divided into three equal segments by a pattern of staples roughly applied to the gold-leaf surface "as if they were sacred icons."[41]

A red cross—more like the Red Cross symbol than a Christian cross—occupies the center of the pendant. It is both a symbol of rescue and a witty play on the trinity of cartoon characters that appears in this secular, pop-cultural medallion.

Woell made *The Good Guys* at a time when it was becoming increasingly unclear whether the United States could still claim to be a force for good on the world stage. America's reputation was becoming tarnished by the messy realities of the Cold War with the Soviet Union and the Vietnam War in Southeast Asia. Although the worn gold-leaf surface was no doubt a dig at fine jewelry conventions, the title conveys another reading of the material: that the gloss had been knocked off America's claims to greatness, and that this icon of "truth, justice, and the American way" had seen better days. The work is populated by Superman, with his unassailable morality and superhuman abilities; Dick Tracy, a hard-boiled detective fighting crime on the mean streets of the big city; and Little Orphan Annie, an innocent scamp having serial adventures in a corrupt and uncaring world, but who always seemed to come out on top.

Despite its topical content, *The Good Guys* pendant was selected for *Objects: USA* because Woell played a key role in the story of innovation and originality that the project and its backers were keen to promote. Paul Smith appreciated Woell's jewelry because of his startling use of found objects. What stood out for Smith was not the narrative potential of this jewelry, or the way it allowed jewelers to grapple with political and social issues, but instead the contribution that found objects and assemblage made in challenging the association of jewelry with precious and valuable materials.[42]

In his lengthy introduction to the *Objects: USA* catalogue, Lee Nordness explored the connection between studio craft and the big questions facing society, but not in relation to the counterculture of the late 1960s. Rather, Nordness focused on the years directly after World War II, when makers "were concerned with the solutions to social problems, seeking to create 'universally understood forms' that expressed the contemporary moment in which they made art…. For the creative person seeking spiritual harmony, working by hand in craft media was an answer."[43] Studio craft had moved on from this kind of thinking, and by the time of *Objects: USA* the dominant urge driving the studio craft movement in America was a striving for professionalism, for equality with fine art, and for a robust infrastructure of critics, galleries, collectors, and museums that could support and validate the finest work by the best makers. According to Nordness, American studio craft was no longer an amateur activity, or a panacea for social ills; it was a professional practice, informed by higher education, exploring ideas and concepts that went far beyond the functional roots of studio craft.

From some perspectives, *Objects: USA* was deeply implicated in its times. Robert Simmons, in his review of the exhibition in *Craft Horizons* in 1969, noted that the tenor of the 1960s found its way into the objects on display: "The bizarre, the misshapen, the caricature. The func part of function. The spectacular, the exciting, the chic. The useless. The experimental, the mistaken, the discarded. The found, the lost, the free. The pure. The multi. The involved." His list reads like a prose poem in celebration of the wild freedom of the counterculture, but Simmons did not mean it as praise. He continued: "The successful, the moneymaking, the publicity-invoking, the publicity-seeking, the resident-industrial-revolutionizing, the gold-shaking, the hundred-dollar-bill-imprinted, the televised, the famous. The very, very famous, well-off, almost wealthy. The highly successful. The useless."[44]

In his opinion, *Objects: USA* was full of makers whose works were contemporary statements, full of ideas and social commentary, and this was a problem because it involved studio craft turning its back on tradition. He thought that the radical objects in the exhibition shared a quality of deliberate distortion, one directly connected to the moment of the late 1960s: "If the spirit most commonly manifest in the products of traditional crafts over the past thousands of years is quiet and balance, it is perhaps appropriate that movement and distortion are typical of the far-out present. The walking cabinet, the enamel swimming across a panel, glass spilling toward the floor, textiles seething across the wall—all are part of the squirming and uncomfortable human situation today."[45]

That uncomfortable human situation was precisely what jewelers like Woell and Tompkins and others were evoking in their work. They addressed the urgent concerns of the counterculture, and the feeling of rage that was growing among young Americans. In 1969 and 1970, many Americans were being drafted into a war that they did not believe in, were fighting discrimination against African Americans and other non-white Americans, were demanding equal rights for women, and were grieving their heroes who had been shot down in the struggle to change the world. Some of them, seeking spiritual harmony and an alternative to the social and environmental destruction wrought by American consumer society, strongly believed that making things by hand was indeed an answer, a pathway to an honest life and an expression of what it meant to be authentically human. This was the world in which *Objects: USA* and *Goldsmith '70* took place and what their audiences and the participating American jewelers were dealing with in their daily lives. Some jewelers decided that these political and social issues would become the subject of their work. Sometimes the institutions of American jewelry decided to join the revolution; more often than not, they looked the other way entirely.

Fig. 1.19
J. Fred Woell
The Good Guys, 1966
Pendant
Wood, steel, copper, plastic, sterling silver, and found objects
4 inches diameter
Museum of Arts and Design, New York, 1977.2.102

Making in the Counter culture

Chapter Two

Making in the Counterculture

In 1979 the nonprofit organization California Design published a book called *Craftsman Lifestyle: The Gentle Revolution*. It documented many of the craftspeople who had been accepted into the annual *California Design* exhibition, which had been showcasing the latest developments in craft and design in the Golden State since 1954. Its untreated cardboard cover was decorated with hand-painted dots and calligraphic brushstrokes that represented the creamy froth of waves where land meets sea on the California coast. The pages in between featured eighty-five potters, basket makers, woodworkers, needle workers, blacksmiths, glassblowers, furniture makers, weavers, and jewelers, who were interviewed and photographed in their studios and homes. The result was a composite picture of studio craft as a way of life.

Most of the jewelers featured in *Craftsman Lifestyle* were steeped in the values of the counterculture. Arthur Korb, a jeweler making mostly commissions in precious metals and semiprecious stones, had his jeweler's bench in one room of the house that he rented with his family at El Capitan on the coast just north of Santa Barbara. (Fig. 2.1) Like many young Americans in the 1960s, the mind-altering visions he experienced while tripping on LSD opened him up emotionally. Turning his back on the rat race, where he had worked in the aeronautical industry making helicopter blades used in the Vietnam War, he started making jewelry, meditating, practicing Surat Shabd Yoga, and eating natural health foods. Korb's journey changed his work as a jeweler and affected how he approached commissions. As he explained, "My sensitivities, my intuitive flow have allowed me to tune in on that person and translate the energy in terms of form relationships, mental relationships, stone relationships." Each commission involved an astrological chart for the client, revealing important information such as whether they had a lot of earth or air signs, and not enough water or fire. "Certain stones can help bring about a balance, so the chart suggests the materials I use."[46]

Other jewelers featured in the book were not as mystical in the way they talked about their jewelry, but their home and studio environments revealed deep connections to countercultural values. Merry Renk, a jeweler and sculptor, had her studio in a Victorian house in the Castro district of San Francisco. She and her family

Fig. 2.1

Fig. 2.2

had renovated the interior into an open-plan dwelling. They converted individual rooms into one big space and painted the walls yellow, orange, and purple. They installed a bathtub outside on the porch, and the studio was upstairs in a loft. (Fig. 2.2) Renk and her family were eager participants in the hippie social experiment of San Francisco in the 1960s; she had traded her jewelry and her husband's pottery for health care and education, and they taught craft skills in their children's school. The ideals of community living, most often realized in a move to a rural commune, could also be realized in the city. As Renk said at the time, "We have a ranch right here, so we don't have to flee to the country as many of our friends have."[47]

The variety of the jewelers interviewed in *Craftsman Lifestyle* reveals that some were devotees of craft technique, in love with intricate processes and specific materials; a few prioritized education, taking teaching positions in universities and supporting the professional studio-jewelry movement of highly skilled craftspeople; and others made jewelry because it satisfied deep emotional and spiritual needs. Common themes emerged, despite these differences. In her introduction to the book, Eudorah M. Moore, the director of *California Design*, identified four. First, these makers all made "a conscious and considered choice" to become a craftsperson, to pursue a life of making things with their hands. "The desire for freedom is ubiquitous, even at material cost," Moore remarked. Second, they shared the belief that the process of making was as important or more important than the end result: "In short, for these people, art and life are a single fabric, and the quality of living is the monument." Third, Moore observed how "manifestations of love of nature and identification with the unity of all things runs like a refrain through the interviews." Fourth, these makers had reevaluated the standard American priorities of the so-called good life. Moore concluded, "Old ideas of 'suffer now for ultimate rewards,' are replaced by, 'extract from every moment the joy it offers; whether pleasure in one's work, in visual perceptions, in good food, or in quiet repose. LIVE IT.'"[48]

Clearly, these sentiments and values relate to those of the counterculture, yet they were instead seen as deriving from the Arts and Crafts movement of the late nineteenth and early twentieth century, which promoted the handmade as an antidote to the horrors of industrialization. "Reading the literature of the Arts and Crafts movement and the thinking which generated it, reading the formulations of the ideal of living as expressed in publications of that time," wrote Moore, "the thought repeatedly and urgently recurred to us that many of today's craftspeople whose work had been in our shows, and whom we had come to know, were, in fact, now living that ideal articulated at the turn of the century."

Even when explaining why the West Coast of America, and California in particular, had more than its fair share of studio craftspeople, Moore still made no mention of the counterculture that was so prevalent there. According to her, the region's particular social structure, educational facilities, and climate were what mattered. The West Coast was a place of freedom compared to the rigid hierarchies of the East Coast, and it contained top-tier universities, a number of state-run universities, and tuition-free community colleges to boot. The environment, too, set it apart; Moore remarked on its "odd, brilliant light, so different from the softer glow of eastern days." The beauty of the landscape and the mild climate offered easy living, inducing a kind of hedonism. The result was a population of individuals rather than assembly-line robots, free to pursue personal identity and personal possibility, to ask "why not?" and see where it led.[49]

Fig. 2.1
Arthur Korb brooch and an image of the interior of his house, published in *Craftsman Lifestyle*, 1976

Fig. 2.2
Merry Renk's porch with tub, published in *Craftsman Lifestyle*, 1976

Fig. 2.3
Thomas Mann, 1974
Collection of the artist

Fig. 2.4
Thomas Mann
Rainbow Winged Heart Pin, 1974
Laminated acrylic, bronze, and silver
1½ × 3 inches

Fig. 2.3

Moore might have been cagey about the strong link between studio craft and the counterculture, but for others this was something to be celebrated. Donald Willcox, who wrote the 1973 book *Body Jewelry: International Perspectives*, connected it with the quest to find new values—human values as well as artistic, technical, and material values. Hippies hoped to wake from the nightmare of their parents' dreams and find a renewed reason for existence. At the same time, jewelers were rejecting the values of conventional jewelry—what Willcox referred to as "the precious and semiprecious globs of material that we used to fasten or stick onto people like warts or like cancerous growths that the human body would instinctively reject," "the doodad, gimcrack, and sugar-frosted forms of the past thirty years"—and embracing new ideas and materials.[50] Jewelry was coming alive once again, and becoming expansive and ambitious. For Willcox, the rush of experimentation in contemporary jewelry was equivalent to what was happening in the counterculture. The celebration of craftsmanship and technology (craft's particular version of the technocratic society) was giving way to creativity and humanity. "Our rediscoveries are in harmony with similar value rediscoveries going on all around us," he observed. "For many of us, it's as if we've just come through (and thankfully survived) a kind of sleeping sickness, an artistic lethargy, or an extraordinarily over delayed birth-giving within our medium."[51]

Craftspeople had to face up to the same search for meaning and relevance as everyone else. As Willcox wrote:

> We are asking questions. We are asking where we are, and who we are. And some of us don't like our answers. We find ourselves creating expensive frills at a time when our world shows signs of falling apart. When the bellies of children remain empty, can an "exclusive" necklace help to fill them? When men are engaged in destroying each other and their environment, can a hand-made finger ring become a voice? Can body adornment really contribute to problem-solving? Is jewelry perhaps unnecessary? Is it in fact a contradiction? And are we not also contradicting the things we feel?[52]

Crazy and not-so-crazy ideas had convulsed the visual arts in the 1960s, and these spilled over into jewelry. A few makers experimented with Optical Art, with Pop Art, with protest, with using junk and collage. Many of these experiments did not last long, according to Willcox, but they did break open traditional ideas about materials and recover techniques that could be used to incorporate the new materials that jewelers increasingly brought into their work. Silver and acrylic, gold and wood, amber and iron, diamonds and granite, amethyst and leather, pearls and hemp—every combination imaginable was tried out in the studio. At the same time, questions arose about what parts of the body could be adorned. The counterculture was freeing the body from the myriad restrictions of American society, and jewelry followed suit with adornments for previously overlooked parts like the chest, back, breasts, face, legs, and hair. The male body was also new territory to be claimed. Men, who formerly had played it safe with tie clips, cuff links, and rings, began to embrace breast pendants, then belt buckles, clasps, and leather bags. For Willcox, the spirit animating contemporary jewelry was part of the counterculture, with all the same possibilities and problems. There was no place for conventional thinking—in jewelry or in life.

In the 1960s and 1970s, studio craft offered an answer to Americans who were seeking to reject the structures of work and patterns of consumption fostered by capitalism. Updating the nineteenth-century notion of craft as a conscious life choice that fostered honesty, integrity, and self-sufficiency, the counterculture found a type of labor that supported the creative development of the self. Through craft, work life and everyday life could fuse into an indivisible, organic whole.[53]

The counterculture had lots of radical ideas when it came to new—and better—ways to live. For example, "ecofreaks" believed that they could heal the earth by keeping their needs to a minimum and scavenging everything they required from the waste produced by "Fat City," the mainstream American consumer lifestyle they rejected.[54] Overall, members of the counterculture prized practical skills and the ability to make things as essential to survival. However, they also saw them as a means of creativity and self-actualization, a pathway to becoming a well-rounded and fulfilled individual.

Long-lasting, well-made objects were an alternative to the cult of built-in obsolescence that demanded consumers replace last season's model with this season's latest fashion, which helped to address the environmental impact of American society. Studio craft was also an answer to the hunger for authentic and individual objects that showed the trace of the hand and the personality of the maker. To be a studio craftsperson was to embody many of the traits that the counterculture idealized. Making pots, jewelry, or furniture could support a kind of alternative moral lifestyle: living simply, sometimes in a rural location in close proximity to nature, making functional objects for people to use in their daily lives that were well designed, well made, and modestly

Fig. 2.4

Fig. 2.5

priced, and being pacifist, anti-war, or committed to other causes seeking to transform American society.[55]

One jeweler who did exactly this is Thomas Mann. (Fig. 2.3) He had been politically active in the anti-war movement during his college years at East Stroudsburg University in Pennsylvania, yet when it came time to graduate, he wondered, what was the point? Protesting the war in Vietnam had not made a difference, and he was profoundly frustrated and disillusioned. So he retreated, renting a country farmhouse outside of East Stroudsburg in the fall of 1972 that came with a hundred acres of land and a forty-foot waterfall. His home was heated with wood harvested from local state parks. He planted gardens, composted, and canned food. He staged large "Back to the Earth" festivals on the property and worked hard to become a successful jeweler.[56]

One of Mann's best-selling pieces of jewelry was his *Rainbow Winged Heart Pin*, (Fig. 2.4) which he made in 1974 as a personal response to the failure of the anti-war movement and the popular sentiment that Americans should "make love not war." It was his attempt to get in touch with the sweeter side of the counterculture, to go back to 1967 and the Summer of Love, where "flower power" prevailed. At the time, Mann was practicing transcendental meditation and reading about other spiritual practices such as Universal Sufism. Mann had learned about this mystical practice derived from Islam in the book *The Sufi Message* by Hazrat Inyat Khan, and it had a profound effect on his thinking. For him, the winged heart represented ascension toward the heavens and spiritual attainment. Mann added rainbow colors in laminated acrylic to the brooch to symbolize the cosmos. "We are stardust / We are golden," Joni Mitchell sang in her 1970 song "Woodstock," one of Mann's favorites, "And we've got to get ourselves / Back to the garden."[57] That sentiment is what Mann's brooch represented.

Mann recalls recognizing a strong connection between being a studio craftsperson and the ideals of the counterculture:

> Many of us who'd been so active in resisting the Vietnam War, and who were so disillusioned post-1970, and who had nascent artistic intentions, would eventually find a home in the burgeoning crafts world and market. In this micro-world the combination of lifestyle and occupation would grant us sanctuary and support. Natural organic foods, back-to-the-land homesteading and learning survival skills from the previous century, alternative energy sources, handmade utilitarian objects, and material and skill sets would deliver an alternative lifestyle that could salve our souls.[58]

Mann was also deep into the drug culture that fueled the counterculture experiment. Beginning in college, he used the income from selling his jewelry to buy bricks of marijuana, which he broke down into "lids" and sold to his fellow students. In 1967 a friend of his went to San Francisco for the Summer of Love and came back with some Daffy Duck and Mickey Mouse blotter acid. After a couple of trips on LSD, Mann was certain he was never going back to the straight world. He marched against the Vietnam War and registered as a conscientious objector so that, if drafted, he would be assigned as a noncombatant. Ultimately, he was dismissed from service for having flat feet. Mann became a vegetarian, which led him to start a natural foods

Fig. 2.5
Richard Wehrman's house
at Libre Commune, c. 1971

store, Earthlight Supply Natural Foods, with his brother. By 1973 he owned and operated two additional businesses as well: Mountain Gallery, which sold art and craft and had a metalsmithing studio in the back, and Solar Wind Silversmiths, which sold jewelry at retail fairs and wholesaled to craft shops and galleries. In 1978 Mann ended his direct involvement with these enterprises and focused on making his own assemblage jewelry, which he called Techno-Romantic© Jewelry Objects. The romantic aspect came from the counterculture ideals of love and peace, while the "techno" aspect pointed to the rise of technology and its impact on humanity.[59]

Another jeweler who sought an alternative way to live was Richard Wehrman. In 1970 he and his family moved to Libre, a community located in the Huerfano Valley in southwest Colorado that had been founded two years earlier. Libre, a Spanish word meaning "free," consisted of couples and families who had no individual ownership of the land but otherwise maintained their own finances. They committed to building their own homes, with the residents collectively vetting proposed building projects to make sure they fit into the aesthetic sensibility of the group. Having seen the disastrous effects of an open-door policy on other communes, Libre carefully selected new members of the community, approving them by unanimous decision at the regular council meetings. As an artist-centered community, Libre preferred individuals who had creative pursuits, recognizing that artistic activities were an important way to maintain community in such an isolated location, as well as a potential way to generate income. The community jealously guarded space and time for creativity, which is why new arrivals were expected to build their own homes, rather than relying on the resources of the other residents.[60]

By the time Wehrman and his family came to build at Libre, the dome homes that had been popular in the late 1960s had given way to creative experiments with traditional building forms and techniques, informed by extensive handicraft and often incorporating recycled materials. It was an improvisational process, relying on elementary building methods and allowing architectural form to emerge from the selection of materials. The Wehrmans designed and built a star-shaped structure, with faceted forms that derived from the construction of geometric solids and that echoed the surrounding mountains and evoked the gemstones of his jewelry. (Fig. 2.5) Roberta Price, one of the Libre residents, wrote in her memoir that Wehrman "has designed a house that looks kind of like four joined A-frames and says it's a model of a garnet crystal ... *really* cool."[61] They built it in four months using inexpensive lumber, plywood, shingles, and fifty-gallon drums to collect water from the roof.[62] The wood-paneled walls and timber floor laid in a modified chevron pattern created a serene interior, finished with handmade furniture that sat low to the ground, Japanese style.[63] The space was divided into a living room, kitchen, jeweler's workshop, and children's room on the ground floor, and two lofts above, one for sleeping and one for meditation. Wehrman used his new studio to continue making silver jewelry that he sold through private commissions to fund his lifestyle and express his creativity.

The high value that the counterculture placed on making is perhaps best represented by the *Whole Earth Catalog*, first published in 1968. This hippie almanac featured an image of the Earth on the cover and offered "Access to Tools," which ran the gamut from looms for weaving to personal computers. The *Whole Earth Catalog* was published by Stewart Brand, who in 1968 toured communes across America with his first wife, Lois Jennings, in their Whole Earth Truck Store, a vehicle that was a mixture of mobile library and education center. The publication, originally 64 pages long, had grown to 452 pages by the time the last edition was published in 1972. It was organized into sections such as "Understanding Whole Systems," "Shelter," "Land Use," and "Community." The *Whole Earth Catalog* did not sell products directly but offered reviews and information on how to acquire almost any item or skill a person could want: maps, tools for gardening, carpentry and house building, outdoor gear, synthesizers, and other books on self-realization and self-fulfillment.[64]

By 1972 the section in the *Whole Earth Catalog* devoted to craft was so large it had to be divided into sections. These were wood furniture, reed craft, frontier crafts, country crafts and antiques, craft design, philosophy and craft access, craft supplies, jewelry supplies, jewelry, glass, sculpture, candles and bonsai, pottery, kilns and throwing, potters wheels, ceramic supplies, weaving, spinning, dyeing, looms, wool and yarn, knitting, sewing, embroidery and quilts, macramé, tie dye, and leather. Two books about jewelry were included in its pages: Oppi Untracht's *Metal Techniques for Craftsmen* (1968) and Augustus F. Rose and Antonio Cirino's *Jewelry Making and Design*, a reprint of a book originally published in 1918. The review of Untracht's book was effusive: "This is one of those rare and super books written by someone that wanted to lay his trip on others. Well worth the money. The 'definitive text,' as they say." The review of the much earlier *Jewelry Making and Design* was briefer: "Super-floral middle finger rock rings, grandma's brooches. ... Studies in geometrical patterns and better yet, suggestions for lifting design from shell, bud, leaf, bug, snow crystal, finger, and so forth." Cheap too, the review concluded.[65]

The do-it-yourself, home craft, and studio craft books that appeared in the pages of the *Whole Earth Catalog* demonstrate the sheer variety of how-to guides that were published in the late 1960s and early 1970s. Thomas Gentille's *Step-by-Step Jewelry* (1968), Philip Morton's *Contemporary Jewelry: A Craftsman's Handbook* (1970), Ramona Solberg's *Inventive Jewelry Making* (1972), and Arline Fisch's *Textile Techniques in Metal for Jewelers, Sculptors, and Textile Artists* (1975) encouraged those with an interest to explore the creative possibilities of making their own adornment. These books varied in their approach and audience. Morton's publication was grand and comprehensive, requiring a serious commitment of study as well as technology and materials, and Fisch's book had a tight focus on particular techniques that could transform metal into wearable objects, whereas Solberg's book was a manual for making jewelry without any elaborate technical skills or tools, using found objects and materials widely available in suburban America.

Fig. 2.6

Making by hand was practical and cheap but it was also aspirational, a key to self-actualization and authentic self expression. While all of the how-to jewelry guides published in the late 1960s and early 1970s shared this belief in a general way, none of them made the point so explicitly as Paulus Berensohn's *Finding One's Way with Clay: Pinched Pottery and the Color of Clay*, published in 1972. For the author, the simple act of making a pot through pinching clay was a healing and centering process. His book featured exercises as well as techniques, including one that was titled "A Way of Being with Clay/A Way of Attention: Being in the Here and Now/A Way of Practice." The pots that resulted from this exercise were less important than what Berensohn described as "the quality of the act of the practicing itself."[66] Making was meditation, more about the journey than the destination.

The values and ideas—and especially the language—of the counterculture began to turn up in the studio craft movement in the late 1960s. "Insight '69" a conference organized by the Northeast Region of the American Craft Council (ACC) in July 1969 and held on the bucolic Bennington College campus in Bennington, Vermont, featured two days of "contact" sessions, during which attendees were assigned to instructors and encouraged to explore new ways of thinking that stretched beyond the typical boundaries of craft. In one session held in a barn on campus, the dancer Carolyn Bilderback and the stage designer Shirley Kaplan used movement around constructed forms to lead participants toward a greater awareness of their bodies in relation to the world around them. Another session run by Janice Lourie, from the pioneering computer company IBM, introduced craftspeople to the psychedelic wonders of liquid graphics and light environments controlled by state-of-the-art IBM technology. Other attendees took part in an intense two-day talk fest with the Cleveland architect Jerry Weiss, who wanted to move beyond the personal search for insight to address social questions that looked outward, beyond the jeweler's bench and the studio.

The clamor of political and social change could be heard at other times during the conference as well. "Monday night's recap session kept returning to the problem of black craftsmen, for instance," wrote Jane Holtz Kay in her *Craft Horizons* magazine review. "The all-white entourage widely applauded Virginia West's efforts in a craft festival and demonstrations for impoverished black and white students in Baltimore. 'The irrelevance of what we're doing to what's going on in the nation today,' disturbed silversmith-teacher Kurt Matzdorf and several others in these big bull sessions and in the private meetings about the campus. 'We can waddle in the words but it's the every-day gesture that counts,' Stanley Walters told the group."[67]

Sometimes the tone was serious, but at other times craftspeople were just out to have fun. Members of the South Central Region of the ACC organized a "primitive craft-in" at Steamboat Springs, Colorado, in July 1971. The name was a nod to the "Human Be-In" held in Golden Gate Park in January 1967, a hippie pun on "human being," which in turn was an adaptation of the "teach-in" and "sit-in," consciousness-raising events pioneered by anti-war activists at college campuses around the country in the mid-1960s. The subtitle of the Human Be-In was "a gathering of the tribes," and indeed a huge crowd gathered: barefoot women in madras saris, shamans, men in Edwardian jackets and velvet cloaks, others dressed like cowboys or Native Americans. Some men had long hair, past their shoulders, while the women wore long flowing dresses, or miniskirts and see-through tops. The poet Allen Ginsberg was one of the speakers, as was the LSD guru Timothy Leary, who tucked yellow flowers behind his ears and told the crowd, "We have to get Western man out of the cities and back into tribes and villages. The only way out is in." He also tried out his phrase "turn

Fig. 2.7

on, tune in, drop out" for the first time. Bands including Jefferson Airplane and the Grateful Dead played music for the crowd. Be-ins quickly followed in other parts of the country, gatherings of outrageously dressed people who danced, played musical instruments, and got high.[68]

Colorado in 1971 may not have had as many flowers, beads, and feathers as California, but it provided a gathering of the studio craft tribes. The craft-in took place at a local lodge, and the attendees stayed at a nearby federal campground. The cost was ten dollars for ACC members and twelve dollars for non-members. Children and pets were welcome.[69] Like a survival course for hippies heading back to the land, the craft-in covered almost everything that a person needed to know to survive in aesthetic harmony with nature. Amateur and experienced craftspeople dug clay and threw, glazed, and fired pots, learned how to tan cowhide, made chairs from the timber they gathered, foraged for the food they ate, and dyed wool from the wildflowers they collected from nearby meadows. They spun fiber and then wove it into textiles, using looms and macramé techniques.(Fig. 2.6) They cast jewelry. They learned how to make wine.[70]

The event was such a success that it was restaged the following year in the old mining town of Breckenridge, Colorado. One group, led by Bill Alexander, Paul Soldner, Jean and Russ Peterson, and Elise McGuire, transformed local clay into pots, glazed them using local ore, and fired them on site. Another group learned metal casting under Nilda Getty and Ken Hendrie using a basic cuttlebone technique, and another adapted an African method to produce aluminum sculptures with exquisite details. Mary Sartor demonstrated how to make elaborate jewelry without soldering, Kay Gonzalez led a batik workshop, Phyllis Clemmer instructed participants in how to make looms from tree branches, and Kathryn Wertenberger showed them how to weave using only their fingers. Grace Bitz, a Navajo weaver, taught a group how to make rugs, and Lorissa Payne, of the Tohono O'odham people native to the Sonoran Desert, demonstrated how to weave baskets from yucca. Even glass blowing was included, with Charles Litner attracting an enthusiastic audience. As Clotilde Barrett reported in *Craft Horizons* magazine, "The cordial atmosphere was further enhanced by folk dancing, beer making, guitar playing, and by the Pete Aquino family of Pueblo Indians who enlivened the 'Craft-in' with their many skills, such as bread baking in an adobe oven, the weaving of sashes, pottery making, and by their traditional dances."[71]

Aside from the events organized by the ACC, other places also provided craft-making experiences and served as studio craft communes. The Haystack Mountain School of Crafts in Deer Isle, Maine, the Penland School of Craft, in Penland, North Carolina, and the Arrowmont School of Arts and Crafts in Gatlinburg, Tennessee, are three of the most famous craft schools in the United States that offered professionals and amateurs alike the opportunity to take classes taught by esteemed makers. Their rural and beautiful locations promoted a convening with nature, an escape from the concerns of daily life, and a utopian atmosphere. Those attending lived in basic accommodations, ate locally harvested food, and talked intensely with their peers. This kind of community activity involving collaboration and knowledge sharing was already part of studio craft culture; in the 1960s and 1970s, it became overlaid

Fig. 2.6
Participants at a craft-in held by the American Craft Council South Central Conference on July 21–25, 1971, in Steamboat Springs, Colorado

Fig. 2.7
Earth, Air, Fire, Water gathering, 1974

with the countercultural ideals of communal activities. For craftspeople, these occasions offered temporary exposure to the kinds of alternative communal environments that many Americans were trying to establish by dropping out and living in intentional communities according to a different set of values.

The jeweler Christina Smith recalls attending a mind-blowing ceramics summer school in Grass Valley, California, in 1974 called Earth, Air, Fire, Water. (Fig. 2.7) The name was a witty play on the forces that potters harness in their work and the popularity of astrological signs among members of the counterculture. Attendees would dig their own raw materials and make pots that were fired in a six-chambered climbing kiln that the organizers had built at a local Quaker school. Everyone had chores, so the responsibility for the daily running of the event was communal. There was skinning-dipping in the nearby lake, as well as sex and drugs. The poet Gary Snyder, a key member of the Beat literary movement who lived nearby on Rainbow Ridge, remembers seeing a pig roasting on a spit there, and dancing around the fire. In 1974 everyone gathered around the kiln to listen to President Richard Nixon resign. A lot of veterans from the Vietnam War attended Earth, Air, Fire, Water, and they responded joyfully to the news.[72]

The major summer happening for jewelers was Summervail. In 1971 Jim Cotter and his studio assistant, Randy Milhoan, were discussing the possibility of putting together a workshop in Vail, Colorado, that would be a gathering for craftspeople and artists. After a night of drinking, they rang the sculptor Claus Oldenburg to see if he wanted to come out and teach. "We're handing the phone back and forth to each other and fortunately we didn't get through to him," recalls Cotter. "We wound up coming up with this idea, we could get our friends to come out here and teach and be pretty primitive."[73] After sobering up and agreeing it was still a good idea, they put out the word. Almost everyone that Cotter and Milhoan called said yes, and Summervail was born.

The Summervail Workshop, as it was officially known, began in July 1971 as a two-week session of craft and art courses for local adults and children held in Anholtz Ranch (now Ford Park and Betty Ford Gardens). From the beginning, it was closely connected to Colorado Mountain College, the local community college, and this arrangement allowed Summervail to use the institution's insurance and administrative organization and let any students who attended receive course credit. Because Anholtz Ranch had scant facilities, the

Fig. 2.8
Summervail clowns, Summervail Workshop for Art & Critical Studies, 1976 or 1977, showing metalsmith Stuart Bremner (red hat), ceramics sculptor Erick Abraham (sailor hat), metalsmith and sculptor Jim Cotter (plaid suit), and painter Randy Milhoan (striped shirt with shovel)

inaugural classes included activities that could be held outside: painting, drawing, watercolors, ceramics, silversmithing, macramé, photography, environmental design, magazine production, and theater. Tents were provided by the National Guard at Camp George West in Golden and served as classrooms. As Summervail grew in size and stature, its location moved twice: first to an A-frame building in Vail in 1973 (the site of the current library) and then in 1979 to Malloy Park, where Colorado Mountain College was based, in the neighboring town of Minturn. Facilities improved dramatically at each location.

More than just a summer camp for craftspeople, Summervail was a crucible for unfettered creativity. For some jewelers, it was the "anti-SNAG," a place where they could escape the organization's conservatism as well as the restrictions of academic employment. They were free to experiment and learn new techniques while seeing old friends, meeting new people, relaxing, and having fun. Lynda Watson, a longtime instructor and attendee, summarized its appeal: "There was something about being in the mountains and in that environment ... a lot of people came alive in that situation."[74] "It was like cultural democracy at its finest," remembers the metalsmith Jan Brooks, who regularly participated in jewelry conferences and events, and was an early Summervail attendee. "What you had was the opportunity to talk to people who were not in your discipline ... it was extremely level ... it was so liberating."[75] The jeweler Robert Ebendorf also acknowledges the special atmosphere of Summervail: "It was an opportunity where you could be anything, anybody, no matter what level of work you were at; you could come bring your bedroll, come put down the money and have your experience. If you wanted to sit and have long discussions about art it was available. If you wanted to sit with people and see a demonstration or be playful, so be it. It was a very important segue for non-academic, not organizational people. It was my tribe."[76]

Summervail was distinctive for fostering a sense of community. The program facilitated lifelong personal and professional relationships among the participants that often resulted in new opportunities, such as lecturing or demonstrating at each other's schools. In many ways, Summervail helped bring the field together, especially for makers who were not as excited by the more rigid structure of SNAG. Some came for a one-week or two-week session, whereas others stayed all summer, camping and working at Summervail or at Colorado Mountain College so that they could use its facilities after formal classes had ended. Often jewelers would incorporate Summervail into their vacations, coming to hang out, camp, hike, and possibly take a class.

In addition, everyone participated in all aspects of the community, from cooking and cleaning to teaching and organizing extracurricular activities. According to Jim Cotter, there was always a keg of beer to socialize around, and Sunday nights became a contest to see who could create the "coolest" dinner.[77] Mary Lee Hu's Chinese dinner and Jamie Bennett's Italian dinner are often cited as two of the most memorable for their cuisine and decorations. Other social events that demonstrated the program's spirit were after-hours themed cocktail parties by the lake. These events were both social and creative, with themes like "black ties and tails," "prom," and "blue suede shoes," complete with handmade costumes. (Fig. 2.8) Eleanor Moty recalls an impromptu "cellulose party": "You're thinking, cellulose, what am I supposed to do with that? I remember that Bruce Breckenridge came with bubble-wrap around his thighs. He said, cellulose? I thought you said cellulite! I came with rubber bands around my arms and legs with branches stuck into them, so I was a tree. The cleverness of people coming up with costumes was just remarkable."[78]

One year, "pyromania night" resulted in a huge bonfire with William Harper and some enamellists building a steel pole to lower enamel into the fire, some blacksmiths trying to get iron hot enough to forge, and some glassblowers melting beer bottles to blow glass. "There was a lot of alcohol and people were experimenting," remembers Jan Brooks. "How hot can we get this fire, what can we produce out of this fire, what can we discover trying to do this? It was not anything you would ever do unless you were in a group of people that invite some of this craziness, and it was so memorable and so much fun."[79] Then there were the plays and other performances that those taking part in Summervail staged in the streets of Vail, directly bringing the uninhibited creativity of the program into the community in the form of "happenings." At one point, the town of Vail became concerned about the "hippies of Summervail," but the relationship was generally cordial and strengthened by participation in the town's annual Fourth of July parade and hot-dog eating contests.

In the first years, Jim Cotter and Daniel Telleen took on the lion's share of the instruction responsibilities in jewelry and metals, with Cotter leading silver assemblage classes and Telleen teaching casting. After 1974 Cotter, Milhoan, Lane Coulter, and later Jane Gregorius, a California-based printmaker and educator, were responsible for inviting instructors to Summervail. It was a coveted invitation in the jewelry world, with many wishing to teach but ultimately not being invited. According to Coulter, "One of the things we agreed on right off the bat was if we get lobbied, that person doesn't get in, we're not playing that game."[80] The budget was a big concern for the organizers, as was the number of teaching slots, but another critical deciding factor was whether an individual was easygoing and would fit the community ethos of shared responsibilities and equal treatment.[81]

In Summervail's third year, Cotter had the idea of organizing a three-day symposium for metals that would feature demonstrations rather than lectures. The demonstrations made use of whatever materials were around, including using Drano for pickling the surface of the metal and casting with a vacuum cleaner. Contests such as "Saw/File/Solder" sprints, where a relay team of three makers raced to saw, file, and solder metal into a ring, were organized for fun. In 1975 the metals symposium was joined by symposia for ceramics, weaving, and photography. Painting and enamel symposia were later added to the catalogue. Some makers presented only at the symposia, whereas others taught classes as well as participated in the three-day events.

From its inception, Summervail brought in special guests to present on a variety of subjects ranging from architecture, film, and visual communication to nonprofit leadership, to vocational talks by auto mechanics and butchers. These topics always differed from those taught in the classes and workshops. By 1973 these presentations had become codified as "Critical Studies" and were led by assistant director Jane Gregorius; Milhoan had borrowed the idea from a California Institute of the Arts program with the same name.[82] The Summervail brochure for 1975 provided a list of what students could expect when they took Critical Studies: "In the past the program has given students access to such unlikely events as hot-dog eating contests ... amateur rodeos, entries into the annual 4th of July parade, raft trips down the Colorado River, camping trips, work on Christo's Valley Curtain, and hundreds of volleyball games."[83] Later, it became an increasingly vital part of the student and faculty experience, encompassing formal "wrap" sessions, lectures, heated arguments, slide-show presentations, movie screenings, and wine drinking.[84]

The time between classes, and during meals and the nightly campfires, was rich with conversation about light topics such as creativity, or heavier ones such as what was happening in the world. "There were a lot of political conversations," remembers Cotter. "I mean there'd be shouting matches, there'd be all kinds of things including laughter. It just went from one extreme to the other extreme. Once you were in the family, it was like a family reunion every summer."[85]

Summervail's last session was in 1984. The program closed due to the burden of administration that fell on people who had other full-time jobs, rather than a lack of enrollment. What began as a lark with a counterculture bent had turned into an established school, one with year-round responsibilities, even though it was only in session during the summer.

COUNTER CULTURE JEWELERS

Chapter Three

Counterculture Jewelers

The young bohemians in the counterculture were utopian pioneers of a new world. As Theodore Roszak wrote in 1968, "They seek to invent a cultural base for New Left politics, to discover new types of community, new family patterns, new sexual mores, new kinds of livelihood, new esthetic forms, new personal identities on the far side of power politics, the bourgeois home, and the consumer society."[86] Such experiments, based on the wholesale rejection of mainstream values, did not go over well with many authority figures. In 1967 Ronald Reagan, who was governor of California, said, "A hippie is someone who looks like Tarzan, walks like Jane, and smells like Cheetah." That same year, the TV journalist Harry Reasoner took to the airwaves during the CBS *News Hour* to criticize the hippies: "They, at their best, are trying for a kind of group sainthood, and saints running in groups are likely to be ludicrous." He told the audience that hippies traded on a corrupt ideal of innocence that properly belonged only to childhood: "People who can grow beards and make love are supposed to move from innocence to wisdom." While members of the counterculture did not see themselves as especially holy, they did believe that there was a better way to live than the officially sanctioned ladder of success that people who dismissed the hippies were busy peddling. Innocence and wisdom did not have to be mutually exclusive, no matter how strongly the authorities suggested otherwise.[87]

For a moment in the late 1960s, esoteric ideas and values that were previously restricted to fringe groups in American society popped up at the very center of mass culture, reaching millions of people. Stereo recordings and portable music players, along with FM radio, brought music into the homes and cars of Americans all around the country. Music spread the message of the counterculture more effectively than anything else, whether in the form of folk protest ballads with political messages or acid rock that seemed like the only sane response to the madness of the Vietnam War. The mimeograph machine (the precursor to the photocopier) enabled the proliferation of the "underground media," offering news and opinions that were vastly different from the mainstream media. Yet the sheer size of the baby boomer generation, and the hunger that advertisers had to reach this young demographic, meant that mainstream media was uniquely open to covering the counterculture. After all, it made great copy and got high ratings.[88]

The American jewelers who were part of the counterculture took part in the great experiment to invent new types of community that turned their back on mainstream America. In the late 1960s, Lynda Watson was a college student in Long Beach, California, with no money, who dressed like a hippie and was part of a co-op where she sold her jewelry. (Fig. 3.1) Watson had grown up in Orange County, which was known for its conservative leanings. Her father was a banker, a staunch Republican, and an acquaintance of Richard Nixon's. She was completely opposed to his political leanings and did not conform to his idea of what she should do and be. Her mother was a drama teacher and was sympathetic to her daughter's artistic leanings.[89]

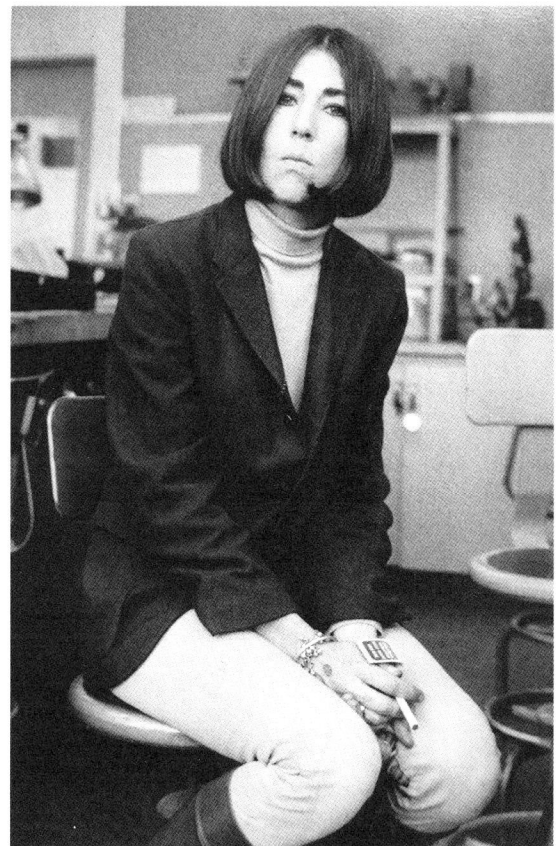

Fig. 3.1

Fig. 3.2

In 1958 Watson left home and attended community college at Orange Coast College in Costa Mesa, California, to get a degree in advertising design and illustration. She knew that her parents were not going to support her, and she wanted a creative way to make a living. After graduating in 1961, she applied to California State College at Long Beach but, being unable to take any art classes, instead completed a year at Chapman University in Orange, her hometown. By 1964 she had enrolled at California State College, Long Beach, for her BA in crafts, which she completed in 1966. Watson then began her MA at the same college in metals and craft. In 1967 she went to Rochester, New York, to take a class with Hans Christensen, who was famous for teaching traditional metalsmithing techniques at the Rochester Institute of Technology.

During the years that she pursued her master's degree, Watson was very poor. Some of the time, she lived in her van at the beach or in the school parking lot, and at other times she lived with two students from school in an apartment. Everyone was poor on the east side of Long Beach where they lived. Watson worked as a cocktail waitress and took any other part-time jobs she could find to support herself. Although her parents were well off, they refused to support her, and their wealth kept her from receiving scholarships from the school. Watson bought her clothes at a thrift store and typically wore boy's blazers, pants, and boots. As a hippie, she selected clothes that were both affordable and were an expression of her individuality. She tried drugs but did not use them much; she had too much work to do.[90]

Watson's *Landscape Neckpiece* (1968) has a dreamy quality in tune with the hippie culture with which she identified.[(Fig. 3.2)] It was selected to be part of the *Objects: USA* exhibition and illustrated in the catalogue. She made it during her last year at Long Beach, creating an imaginary landscape into which she could escape. Watson's work is filled with intricate details in silver — waves, mountains, birds, and flowers — that reflect her training as an illustrator and designer, as well as her craftsmanship and skill with the lost-wax technique. Escape, in the form of dropping out, was a prized ideal within the counterculture, whether it was achieved through drugs, sexual freedom, or moving to the countryside to live in harmony with nature.

Fig. 3.1
Lynda Watson in the jewelry lab at California State College, Long Beach, 1967 or 1968

Fig. 3.2
Lynda Watson
Landscape Neckpiece, 1968
Silver and enamel
11 × 9¼ inches
Museum of Arts and Design, New York, gift of the Johnson Wax Company, through the American Craft Council, 1977

Counterculture Jewelers

Although Watson did not actively take part in protests, she lived with a clear conviction about the importance of civil rights, the rights of women, environmental concerns, and the freedom to choose a different lifestyle. She read *The Whole Earth Catalog*, and as a student at Long Beach, she had been involved briefly with the Students for a Democratic Society (SDS), a national organization whose members took a leading role in protesting against the war in Vietnam.[91]

In 1970 Watson joined the staff at Cabrillo College in Aptos, California, where she was responsible for developing the Jewelry/Metals Department. Her Cabrillo lab assistant, Charlie, lived on a communal farm with several other "families" in the Santa Cruz mountains. They attempted to be self-sufficient by growing their own food and keeping animals. Watson spent time there unwinding from her job and visiting the sheep and goats—especially when there were babies. She observed them, drew them, and even featured them in her jewelry.

Sheep Bracelet (1973) was directly connected to the environmental issues that Watson cared about during this time.(Fig. 3.3) A patch of land called the Lighthouse Field, where sheep grazed and where she and her friends had memorable gatherings, was scheduled to be developed into a conference center. Watson and other locals protested and eventually got a measure passed by the city council to limit growth and development in the area.[92] This cast silver bracelet commemorates that fight. Watson lived her life in sympathy with the changing

Fig. 3.3
Lynda Watson
Sheep Bracelet, 1973
Silver
3 × 4 × ¾ inches

Fig. 3.4
William Clark
Police State Badge, 1969
Sterling silver and 14k gold
2 ⅞ × 3 × 4 inches
Museum of Arts and Design,
New York, 2012.20

times, but her jewelry most often did not contain references to specific events. Instead, it presents a type of escapist, dreamy response to the turmoil around her.

From 1964 to 1969, Watson was part of a co-op in Long Beach called the Mercury Head Workshop. The other members were a graphic designer, a jeweler who mostly did repairs, and another jeweler who was wealthy enough to pay the rent. The workshop was located in the Belmont Shores area of Long Beach, which was a predominantly gay part of town. Watson made wedding rings for gay couples and had two wealthy female clients who competed for the rings with the largest stones.[93] She also participated in the legendary Renaissance Pleasure Faire for a couple of years, selling her jewelry to the patrons who came to experience this reenactment of a

Fig. 3.3

Fig. 3.4

market town in Elizabethan England. However, Watson did not enjoy selling her work, and she decided to earn her living by teaching jewelry. This freed her to make jewelry purely as a creative outlet, free from market demands. As she said in 1979, "I don't try to sell anything. In fact, I don't even show much. My work is for myself and, often, it's just put away when I'm finished, except when I wear it."[94] Hippie culture frowned upon anyone or anything that was too commercial; to be accused of "selling out" was a bad trip that needed to be avoided.

Up the coast from the Southern California haunts of Watson, in the San Francisco Bay Area, William Clark was another jeweler whose life and work were shaped by the counterculture. The Bay Area in Northern California was a mecca for the counterculture in the 1960s. It includes the city of San Francisco, with its famous Haight-Ashbury district, which became ground zero for the hippies and the Summer of Love in 1967. It stretches across the Bay Bridge to Berkeley, where the local campus of the University of California became a hotbed of anti-war activism and political protest, and across the Golden Gate Bridge to Marin, and further inland to Napa and Sonoma, famous for their vineyards and stunning landscapes, and the destination of choice for hippie communes attempting to live in harmony with nature. It extends down the coast to what is now called Silicon Valley, where Stanford University computer scientists were experimenting with LSD and inventing the foundations of the Internet age. Many of these social and cultural developments found their way into Clark's jewelry. He made work that expressed his political stance against political repression, the war in Vietnam, overpopulation, and environmental collapse, but he also made wearable objects that celebrated the body and sexual freedom. Clark sometimes used found objects in his jewelry, and the narrative they conveyed was protest-oriented, with a strong sense of humor and satire.

Clark was born in St. Louis, Missouri, in 1942. His father worked as a chemist for Ralston Purina, then at Chevron Oil, so the family moved to Albany, California, then Berkeley, living there until William was twelve. His father transferred jobs and began working for what was then called Aramco, the Arabian-American Oil Company; the family eventually followed him to Saudi Arabia. There, Clark began to learn about jewelry, watching and learning from the artisan jewelers in the small villages near his home. When Clark was around the age of fifteen, his family returned to Berkeley. There, he took long hikes in the hills and collected geological specimens, which he cut and polished. Clark also made castings, cut semiprecious stones, and fabricated earrings, some of which he sold at small galleries in the Bay Area. After graduating from high school at age seventeen, he joined the U.S. Navy as an engineman, choosing service in the military over attending college because of his dyslexia. Luckily, he completed his service before the beginning of the active involvement of U.S. troops in the Vietnam War. He was honorably discharged and moved back to California. There, he began a diesel mechanics program at Laney College in Oakland in September 1963 and graduated in 1965.[95]

Fig. 3.5

Fig. 3.6

Around 1967, Clark enrolled at the California College of Arts and Crafts (CCAC) in Oakland to study jewelry and metalsmithing. He met a number of interesting jewelers and craftspeople who were students and teachers at the school, but could not quite manage the tuition fees. After winning school awards for some of his jewelry, he felt confident about his abilities as a self-taught jeweler and decided to drop out of school. Sometime between 1968 and 1970, he opened a small studio on Forty-First Street in Oakland, where he focused on making jewelry and began to exhibit his work in local shows and fairs.[96]

Clark's *Police State Badge* (1969) is an early work that reflects the widespread distrust of the police and the government's power.[(Fig. 3.4)] As Clark recalled in 2003, "The pin was made during the Vietnam War as a comment on the prosecution of a war based on the Gulf of Tonkin Resolution which was a false provocation! All of this led to persecution of war resisters and imprisonment of those who disagreed with [Presidents] Johnson and Nixon and in fact the Congress of the United States. The spying on those who avoided serving led me to think of the situation as a 'Police State.'"[97] The Gulf of Tonkin Resolution was put into effect in 1964 to give the American president (Lyndon Johnson at the time) unlimited powers to oppose "Communist aggression" in Southeast Asia. Congress passed the act after a U.S. Navy destroyer exchanged shots with North Vietnamese torpedo boats in the Gulf of Tonkin on two different occasions, and it marked the official entry of the United States into the Vietnam War. As it turned out, this event was a fabricated incident that gave Congress political cover to start the war. Once it was revealed as a hoax, it inflamed anti-war protests and the movement against the war.

The fear that America was becoming a police state was also a live issue in Berkeley, where Clark was living when he made this brooch. In April of that year, a piece of land owned by the University of California, Berkeley, was taken over by anti-war activists and named the People's Park. The activists' intention was to turn a rubble-strewn, muddy lot into a public park that could be used as a venue for gatherings and free speech. The California Highway Patrol and the Berkeley police were sent in to clear the occupiers, and in the clash between protestors and authorities a University of California student was killed, another man was permanently blinded, and 128 locals were admitted to the hospital with head trauma and shotgun wounds.[(Figs. 3.5, 3.6)] Anyone seeing Clark's brooch at the time would have felt that the message was both urgent and personal.

Curiously, the sterling silver and 14-karat-gold brooch is shaped like a sheriff's badge and not a police badge. It is the kind of badge worn by the archetypal handsome and honest sheriff of a one-horse town in the Wild West. In January 1969, Richard Nixon had been sworn in as American president, elected on a platform of law and order that he waged on behalf of his "silent majority"—those Americans who did not share in the revolutionary goals of the counterculture or take part in the marches and protests against the Vietnam War. Clark's brooch makes it clear that, by the late 1960s, he and many other Americans had serious doubts about the virtue and honor of those in authority.

In the early 1970s, Clark remained committed to tackling big issues in his jewelry. His *Survival Necklace* (1971) is a case in point, with its combination of silver letters spelling the word "survival" interspersed with small glass vials of food.[(Fig. 3.7)] "I often listened to KPFA (the radical Bay Area community-funded radio station) in the 1960s," Clark recalled much later. "This piece was an early prediction of the scarcity of food, water and other resources in the future (based on the escalating population)."[98] In 1968, three years before this work was made,

Fig. 3.5
View of a line of California National Guardsmen as they close off a street near People's Park, Berkeley, California, mid-1969

Fig. 3.6
National Guardsmen, who had been called by California Governor Ronald Reagan to quell demonstrations, surround a Vietnam War protester during the People's Park riot in Berkeley, California

 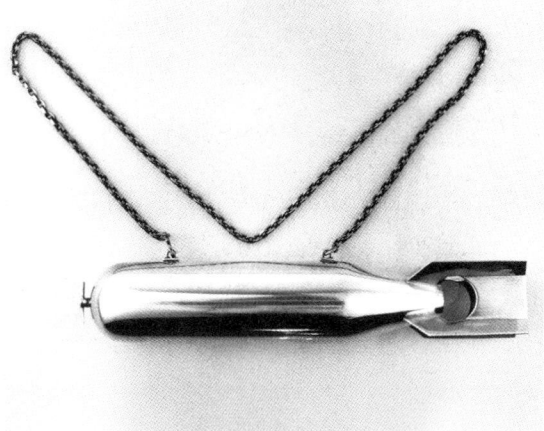

Fig. 3.7 Fig. 3.8

the Stanford University biologist Paul R. Ehrlich published his book *The Population Bomb*, in which he sensationally predicted that millions of people would starve to death in the 1970s and many of them would be Americans. With an alarmist tone he contended, "The battle to feed all of humanity is over. In the 1970s and 1980s hundreds of millions of people will starve to death in spite of any crash programs embarked upon now. At this late date nothing can prevent a substantial increase in the world death rate."[99] Selling millions of copies, the book added the fear of overpopulation to the fear of a nuclear war with the Soviets, which had led some Americans to build bomb shelters and stockpile food and other supplies. Clark's necklace was both witty and serious, mocking the possibility of sufficient preparations and serving as a kind of personal talisman that might protect and nourish the wearer.

Clark's *Necklace for the American Taxpayer* (1971) staged its political meanings through the mechanism of jewelry, as an object to be worn on the body. (Fig. 3.8) Although the American government was supposed to be deescalating the war in Vietnam in 1971, the fighting spread to Cambodia and Laos, and the publication of the leaked "Pentagon Papers" (an official report commissioned by the Department of Defense) not only revealed this undisclosed escalation but also provided evidence that successive administrations had been lying to the public about their true intentions in Southeast Asia. When the papers were released by the *New York Times* and other newspapers around the country, there was widespread outrage, with public protests against the war spiking dramatically. Clark's brass pendant was a pointed reminder that taxpayers and citizens were implicated in the decisions being made by the U.S. government on their behalf. It manifested this responsibility as a physical weight suspended from a silver chain around the neck. The critic Thomas Albright wrote favorably in the San Francisco *Chronicle* that works such as the *Survival Necklace* and *Necklace for the American Taxpayer* were "primarily sculptures that adapt the functional forms of traditional jewelry towards purely iconic ends."[100]

In 1971 Clark moved to Vancouver, British Colombia, Canada. He was worried that he might be called up to serve again with the navy due to his mechanical skills, but he also wanted to work with the German jeweler Karl Stittgen. There, Clark became involved in the local art scene and started constructing large sculptures. He met Evelyn Roth, a textile and performance artist who explored the intersections of sculpture and dance in her work, and the indigenous Canadian jeweler and sculptor Bill Reid, whose work dealt with Haida art and culture.[101] These two artists were important in developing the connections between jewelry and dance that became increasingly important in Clark's work in the early 1970s.

The move to Vancouver coincided with Clark starting to make a series of body adornments. Exhibited after he returned to the United States the following year, these were large objects shaped like spirals, trumpets, and antlers, rolled from brass sheets (a technique he had learned while living in the Middle East) and worn around the neck and over the shoulders. Like fairy wings or satyr horns, Clark's body adornments transformed those who wore them, elevating the wearer from the realm of the everyday to a space of fantasy. They offer a statement about playful escape and celebration of individuality.

Photographs survive that show these objects being worn in Muir Woods, a national park forest across the Golden Gate Bridge in Marin County. (Fig. 3.9) Against a backdrop of majestic redwood trees, semi-clothed wearers appear as part of a forest scene filled with mythical

Fig. 3.7
William Clark
Survival Necklace, 1971
Pyrex glass, fine silver, peanut butter, beef, green beans, eggs and bacon, dates, carrots, and tomato
17 ½ × 2 ¾ inches
Location unknown

Fig. 3.8
William Clark
Necklace for the American Taxpayer, 1971
Brass with silver chain
Chain: 17 inches;
pendant: 6 ¼ × 1 ¼ inches
Location unknown

Counterculture Jewelers

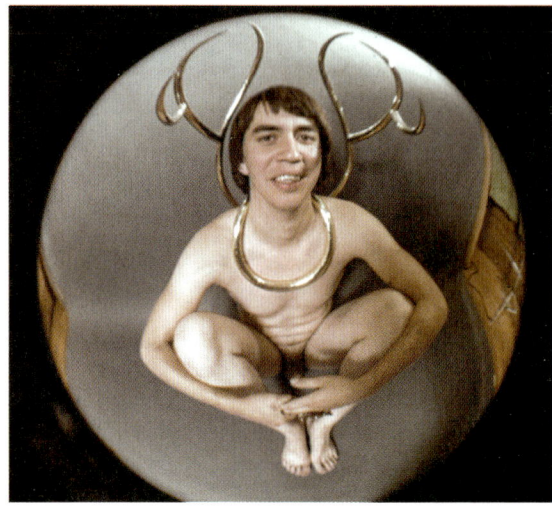

Fig. 3.9
Fig. 3.10

creatures sprouting horns, halos, and branches made of brass. These adornments could be seen as reflecting the mystical and socially liberated lifestyles that Clark and so many other Americans in the Bay Area were embracing.

Clark was active in the Bay Area craft scene before and after his time in Canada. He was a juror for the *Designer/Craftsman '71* exhibition at the Richmond Art Center and had a solo exhibition there; in addition, he showed his jewelry in the Concord Festival of the Arts at the Civic Arts Gallery and *The Metal Experience* at the Oakland Museum.[102] Clark used his large, brass, spiral body ornaments as social and political commentary, as seen in his solo shows at the Palo Alto Art Center in 1973 and the Legion of Honor in San Francisco in 1974.[103] In the latter, Clark arranged for the Bay Area dancer Margaret Fisher to perform while wearing his brass adornments on two occasions. The following year, he exhibited them at the University of California, Berkeley Art Museum, incorporating performances of the objects by David Wood, who had founded the school's dance program. A reviewer from *Artweek* witnessed such a performance at the Allrich Gallery in San Francisco and commented, "From a basic shape designed to rest on the shoulders, he forms a repertory of shapes, Fellini-esque spirals to brachiated antlers, capable of transforming the wearer into a celebrant of ancient mysteries or a performer of modern dance."[104]

By the second half of the 1970s, Clark's artistic endeavors had become more eclectic, and jewelry was not his only focus. He turned his attention to building custom-made houses, printmaking, painting, and producing other kinds of metalwork. Yet of this creative output, his jewelry best represents the fusion of politics and mysticism that was such an important part of the counterculture experiments of hippies and the other social tribes in the Bay Area. Novel ways of living and loving and being human were often grounded in a political view of the world. Clark was a true follower of the counterculture, more than willing to shed his clothes and put on one of his spiral body adornments, modeling his transformation by these brass horns and halos into someone carefree and innocent. (Fig. 3.10)

As much as studio craft and the counterculture seemed to fit together for some American jewelers, others found tension between the two. Born in Paterson, New Jersey, in 1943, Louis Mueller was an only child who became a troubled student and rebellious teenager. (Fig. 3.11) His father was a successful, conservative businessman who lectured him on how the government was being run by large corporations, echoing some of the concerns of the counterculture.

As a young man, Mueller was unhappy and lacked direction in his life. He found his way to the School for American Crafts at the Rochester Institute of Technology (RIT). He initially studied graphic arts, since the school's program had a good reputation. Yet when a couple of his friends and fellow students told him that he had the temperament of a metalsmith, he went to the metalsmithing department to meet with professor Hans Christensen and transfer into his class. Christensen was Danish and taught class in a strict European way, imparting to his students the Scandinavian style of jewelry with its bold, organic metal forms and semiprecious stones. The high expectations that Christensen had of his students got Mueller to buckle down and apply himself, but Christensen did not like the Pop Art images or the architectural structures that Mueller was including in his jewelry. Christensen made no secret of the fact that he thought Mueller's enameled badges, cigar-band rings, and belt buckles were vulgar. Mueller rented a little studio away from the classroom and continued to produce jewelry with these unacceptable images on his own time.[105] He made jewelry during the weekdays at RIT, and at night and on the weekends he would get high on drugs and study what he had made.

Mueller's jewelry of the later 1960s was fed by American pop culture and Pop Art, the drug culture that he was part of, and his anger about America's involvement in the Vietnam War. Seeing the use of corporate logos in the work of Andy Warhol and Roy Lichtenstein, and loving their graphic references, he produced a series of rings and a necklace that featured corporate logos, reproduced in champlevé enamel with opaque colors

Fig. 3.9
Dancers in Muir Woods in
California wearing body ornaments
by William Clark, early 1970s

Fig. 3.10
William Clark in a bubble, 1971

Fig. 3.11
Louis Mueller in Morocco
in a rented Volkswagen van, 1971

Fig. 3.12
Louis Mueller
Texaco, 1967
Ring
Silver, copper, and enamel
Overall: ⅞ × ⅞ × ½ inches
The Museum of Fine Arts, Boston,
The Daphne Farago Collection,
gift of Daphne Farago, 2006.386

Fig. 3.11

Fig. 3.12

Counterculture Jewelers

that connected graphically to the flat, bright colors preferred during this period.(Fig. 3.12) He felt, as he describes it now, a kind of "lazy freedom" to borrow commercial logos, including those of the drug company Bayer, the petroleum company Texaco, and the tobacco company Camel. Mueller was not alone in his interest in this kind of subject matter. Other American jewelers like J. Fred Woell were also rummaging through the landscape of American consumerism and including pop-culture references in their work. Mueller had seen Woell's *Come Alive, You're in the Pepsi Generation* (1966), but he thought it was too messy and busy. He preferred his logos taken straight, elegantly represented in enamel, and he was a singular voice in his decision to faithfully adopt the graphics of these corporations without additional commentary.[106]

Sometimes, though, Mueller got political. In 1968 he made a bracelet called *Colonial America*, a commentary about the American government's eagerness to get involved in conflicts in other parts of the world.(Fig. 3.13) Vietnam was on everyone's mind, but Mueller decided to make his point through the Korean War of the 1950s, where China and the Soviet Union backed North Korea against the United States and the United Nations, who backed South Korea. It was a disturbing echo of the deadly struggle then being waged in another region of Asia a decade later. The sterling-silver bracelet has three enameled flags: the South Korean flag, the North Korean flag, and the colonial American flag with thirteen stars in a circle on a blue field. America's thirteen colonies had originally rebelled against the tyranny of England, but by the late 1960s America was the one playing the role of tyrant and colonizer.

Despite what the *Colonial America* bracelet seems to suggest, Mueller had an ambivalent relationship to politics and political protest. Like all young American men during the Vietnam War, he faced the threat of being drafted into the army and serving in Vietnam. He had heard that one way to avoid that fate was to be under a doctor's care, so he got braces from an orthodontist, who wrote him a letter saying that Mueller was his patient. Mueller flashed this letter before the draft board on each of the three times he was called up, until finally he turned twenty-six and was no longer eligible for the draft.[107] Since he had a deferral, he did not feel the need to protest or be part of anti-war demonstrations, and he had started to hate politics. Although he knew that other jewelers used politics as a theme and a motivation, he did not reference it much himself: the explicit subject matter of *Colonial America* is an exception in his work.

Fig. 3.13
Louis Mueller
Colonial America, 1968
Bracelet
Sterling silver and enamel
3 ¾ × 1 ¾ inches
Collection of the artist

Fig. 3.13

Fig. 3.14

Like a number of other American jewelers, Mueller was intrigued by cartoon characters, and some made their way into his jewelry. A belt buckle from 1967 featured the pristine large S from Superman's costume, rendered in blue and silver rather than the red and yellow that Americans knew from the comic strip and the television series of the 1950s. More interestingly, Wonder Woman showed up in a sterling-silver bracelet from 1968, decorated with a pattern of three large stars interspersed with two small ones, all in brass.(Fig. 3.14) Since her creation in 1941, Wonder Woman had gone through several transformations. Now in the age of the birth-control pill and the growing clamor for equal rights for women, she lost her Amazonian superpowers and took on the human role of Diana Prince, modeled on Emma Peel from the BBC's *Avengers* series. She ran a boutique, fought crime with her detective allies, and worked in military intelligence. The name Diana Prince became synonymous with secret identities and ulterior motives and activities. Mueller's bracelet, made for a class assignment, was a refined version of the indestructible gauntlets made by Aphrodite that the original Wonder Woman wore, capable of deflecting any of humanity's destructive weapons.

After graduating from RIT and then the Rhode Island School of Design in Providence, Mueller went to Oakland in 1971 to teach at the California College of Arts and Crafts (CCAC). It was an eye-opening experience. The metal-arts studio was poorly equipped compared to what he was used to back East, with hardly more than a spool of eighteen-gauge brass wire, a couple of jeweler's benches, and an annealing station. Driving around, he encountered plenty of evidence of the counterculture in the form of head shops, peace signs, ethnic beads, and students wearing patchouli oil. These were just some of the cultural markers of an important social difference. Oakland was open and loose compared to the uptightness he remembered from his time in Rochester.[108]

Fig. 3.14
Louis Mueller
Wonder Woman, 1968
Bracelet
Sterling silver and brass
1 ¼ × 2 ½ inches
Collection of the artist

The ethnic beads proudly worn by hippies were perhaps the most visible sign of the counterculture's fascination with what were sometimes called, during the period, "primitive" cultures. The hippie movement celebrated the pre-modern and the pre-industrial. Young Americans flocked to rural communes and happily took up an agrarian way of life. They dressed in fashions evocative of the Wild West purchased from the vintage stores of San Francisco. They idolized Native Americans, who represented authenticity and a connection with the spiritual realm and the natural world. The counterculture was deeply skeptical about modernity's technological progress as manifested in postwar American society, and alternatives were eagerly embraced.[109]

As hippies looked for examples of how to live a full and authentic life, they naturally drew on the artistic traditions of alternative cultural systems and beliefs. "Many of us have hungered for a cultural identity strong enough to produce our own versions of the native costumes of Afghanistan or Guatemala, for a community life rich enough for us to need our own totems comparable to African or Native American masks and ritual objects," wrote Alexandra Jacopetti in her book *Native Funk and Flash: An Emerging Folk Art* from 1974. A potpourri of different cultures and religions satisfied that hunger. As Jacopetti explained, "My sixties mind was blown by all the teachings made available. Secret doctrines from all cultures, now easily at hand — 'Tibet's Great Yogi Milarepa,' 'The Book of the Hopi,' 'The Teachings of Don Juan,' the 'I Ching' — arcane secrets of Tantra, Yantra, Mantra, Mudra and Asana, at popular prices."[110]

Hippies also painted, stitched, and assembled objects to wear, use, and display in their homes, making a new kind of popular art that expressed these mysteries in a vivid mixture of artistic styles, symbols, materials, and forms that were as eclectic as the world's art traditions, belief systems, and religions. As Allen Ginsberg said in 1967, "The reason the hippies have taken on these beads, appurtenances, music, of shamanistic groups, of ecstatic trance-state types, is because they are beginning to explore, for the first time, the universe of consciousness of other cultures besides their own."[111]

At the same time, some American jewelers were transforming the scale, materials, and techniques of their own work through a fascination with similar sources. Arline Fisch's *Peacock and Dragonfly*, a pectoral from 1969, is a studio-jewelry version of the flamboyant adornments and costumes that countercultural tribes would gleefully wear to establish their refusal to submit to mainstream codes of dress and behavior.(Fig. 3.15) It incorporates a found antique-ivory carving of a dragonfly, framed by a dramatic fan of oxidized and shiny silver teardrop shapes that evoke the lavish display of a peacock's tail. Although this neckpiece was more likely to be worn to the opera or theater than a be-in or protest march, it reflects the spirit of fantasy and exotic clothing that was prevalent at the time.

Fisch, who was born in Brooklyn in 1931, completed a BS in art at Skidmore College in Saratoga Springs, New York, in 1952, followed by an MA in art from the University of Illinois in Urbana in 1954. Seeking to improve her technical skills, she moved to Denmark in 1956, funded by a Fulbright grant, where she attended the Kunsthaandvaerkerskolen (School of Arts and Crafts) in Copenhagen for one year, while also working in the workshop of the goldsmith Bernhard Hertz. Fisch had decided on Denmark because of the high reputation of contemporary Scandinavian metalwork; it was, along with Sweden, the place where silver was happening in the 1950s.[112]

The Danish example of skilled workmanship and bold, simple forms was underpinned by a philosophy of "truth to materials" that demanded an aesthetic effect that could be interpreted as honesty when it came to materials and techniques. Yet this focus did not leave much room for artistic experimentation, and Fisch was not keen to end up as a designer for the jewelry industry. A decade later, during a study trip to South America in 1963, Fisch visited museums in Peru, where she encountered fragments of pre-Columbian garments that combined textile and metalwork in the form of panels of gold stitched to a woven fabric. These archaeological specimens blurred the boundaries between clothing and adornment and inspired Fisch to experiment with large wearable objects.[113] She began sewing pierced silver plates onto velvet and weaving them into a warp of purple silk and lavender linen yarns.

Another Fulbright grant in 1966–67 allowed Fisch to spend time looking at the Mongolian collection at the National Museum in Copenhagen, as well as exhibitions of folk clothing at the Benaki Museum in Athens, Greece. She traveled to Peru once again in 1968 as part of the American delegation attending the World Crafts Council General Assembly, an event that included the opportunity to view woven gold objects at the Gallo Gold Museum in Lima. Previous to these travels, Fisch's jewelry had been direct and informal, retaining a hint of the technical rigor she had learned from her time in Denmark, but imbued with a greater sense of irregularity that came from her exposure to weaving and other textile techniques. After her travels, she began making large-scale wearable adornments such as *Halter and Skirt* (1968), and her jewelry responded to the same forces that saw metallic elements appear in the clothes and accessories of fashion designers such as Paco Rabanne and the widespread embrace of ethnic and tribal costume.[114](Fig. 3.16) It also responded to the trend of going topless; in *Halter and Skirt,* silver forms discretely hide the wearer's breasts but also reveal plenty of skin, in contrast to the flowing printed velvet skirt made by textile designer Jack Lenor Larsen. The outfit includes chains that move with the wearer's body, and a polished metal surface that appears and disappears depending on the reflections and light of the environment in which the garment is being worn. It is an outfit that would not have been out of place during the halcyon days of the Summer of Love in the previous year, although it was much fancier than what most people were wearing.

Fig. 3.15
Arline Fisch
Peacock and Dragonfly, 1969
Neckpiece
Sterling silver and antique ivory
4 ½ × 11 inches
Collection of the artist

Fig. 3.15

Counterculture Jewelers

Fig. 3.16

Fig. 3.17

Although Fisch's designs were in line with the fashion statements of the counterculture, they were not overtly political. Likewise, the jeweler Ramona Solberg always denied there was any activist or political content in her jewelry; she would say, If I want to send a message, I'll go to the Western Union and send a telegram.[115] But in all three of the exhibitions of ethnic jewelry that she curated for museums in Bellingham, Bellevue, and Seattle (drawing on her own collection as well as pieces owned by other jewelers and collectors), she directly challenged the cultural hierarchy that valued "primitive" or "tribal" objects and the perception that they were different from those produced by Western makers—a gesture very much in tune with the spirit of the 1960s and 1970s. Collecting examples of adornment from around the world became popular, especially in and around Seattle and Washington State. Contemporary jewelers were among a number of individuals who systematically amassed large collections that reflected the widespread taste for ethnic adornment that defined the style of the counterculture.

Although Solberg did not make hippie jewelry—her work is stylistically a world away from the beads and other adornments available at markets and fairs around the country at the time—she prominently incorporated found objects from ancient and contemporary non-Western cultures.(Fig. 3.17) Solberg, who was born in 1921, enrolled in the Women's Army Corps in 1943, completing her service in 1950. Making the most of the G.I. Bill that funded study for those returning from military service, she went to Mexico in 1950, where she studied weaving and jewelry making at Bellas Artes in San Miguel de Allende and at the Universidad de Michoacán in Morelia. On her return to the United States, she attended the University of Washington in Seattle, where she studied with the legendary jeweler Ruth Penington, who taught legions of Northwest jewelers, including Don Tompkins. Solberg's jewelry generally followed the modernism of her teacher; Penington often incorporated natural materials such as beach pebbles and fur, nonprecious materials like ebony and ivory, and enamel into her silver and gold jewelry, and she had an appreciation for the styles and materials of archaic and non-Western adornment.[116] In the early 1950s, Solberg had started to incorporate found objects from non-Western cultures and visual nods to ethnic art in her jewelry, but she was also committed to a "truth to materials" approach in her work. "I am now anxious to go further into the realm of unusual combinations," she wrote in 1956, "as long as the end result is an honest treatment of the material and not just spectacular sensationalism."[117]

Fig. 3.16
Arline Fisch
Halter and Skirt, 1968
Sterling silver and printed velvet
Halter: 22 × 11 inches;
skirt: 46 × 24 inches
Museum of Arts and Design, New York, gift of Bettianne Welch, 1991

Fig. 3.17
Ramona Solberg
Mitla, c. 1951
Brooch
Silver and pre-Columbian clay artifact
3½ × 2¼ inches

Counterculture Jewelers

At Central Washington State University, in Ellensburg, Solberg taught in both the industrial arts and the art departments and instructed students in metals, leather, printmaking, and art history. Ed Hawes, a colleague at the school, and his wife, Juanita Hawes, a jeweler, had an extensive collection of ethnic jewelry from Africa, India, and South America, with which Solberg became familiar. At this time, Solberg also met Gloria Huntington, a professor in Seattle who was doing research on Native American beaded bags. Huntington commissioned Solberg to make a necklace using rolled copper and trade beads, and paying for it with beads as well. Both of these relationships opened up a wider category of "world adornment" to Solberg and to her students.[118]

In 1967 Solberg made her first pendant using found ivory dominos purchased from a Seattle thrift store, and this motif became an artistic signature in her jewelry. Her interest in these objects was formal and practical: dominos were small, cheap, geometric, boldly patterned, and made of different materials, including ivory or Bakelite. There is no evidence that Solberg prized them for their cultural meanings as game pieces and the associated ideas of play or winning and losing.[119] Although Solberg's intention was to highlight the dominos' abstract shapes and particular materials, the game pieces remain identifiable as found objects with a specific cultural history.

In the following year, Solberg made *Shaman's Necklace* (1968), featured in the exhibition and publication *Objects: USA*.(Fig. 3.18) It includes an eclectic combination of objects, including a penny, a Brazilian figa, Guatemalan milagros, and Alaskan artifacts, which are lined up on a silver armature. "Long a collector of curios, I found some of my 'treasures' too small for satisfactory display," wrote Solberg in the exhibition catalogue. "I assembled favorite objects into jewelry and, recalling the magic necklaces of the Northwest Indians, called this piece SHAMAN'S NECKLACE."[120] Although the neckpiece is radical for incorporating found objects, it is also conservative in its reliance on the genres of Scandinavian modernism. Forged silver torques were a specialty of Scandinavian modernism during this time, and Solberg's use of this archetype serves as a foil to the found objects in *Shaman's Necklace*.

Ethnic adornment was a prominent feature of Solberg's book *Inventive Jewelry-Making*, published in 1972. A manual for making jewelry without elaborate technical skills, and using materials available in everyday life, the book straddles various dynamics: do-it-yourself hippie jewelry, experimentation with found objects, interest in ethnic jewelry, and the value of craft as education. Solberg included plenty of examples of adornment from Africa, Mexico, and the Pacific Islands, mixing studio craft jewelry with folk and traditional objects. While recognizing that these jewelry traditions were distinct, she also believed in their commonalities; one might learn as much from an anonymous maker in Pakistan or in the Admiralty Islands as from the work of Solberg or that of her jewelry colleagues and students.

In the late 1960s and early 1970s, a number of American jewelers made work that proved they had been paying attention to adornment from other parts of the world. In most cases, it is not possible to pinpoint connections to any particular culture; rather, it was more a generalized feeling of "primitiveness," the same kind of casual fascination with otherness that characterized the counterculture's love of ethnic adornment and furnishings. These objects were enjoyed without any real need or desire to understand what they meant to the people who made and used them. They had a stagey, theatrical quality and had as much to do with fantasy as anthropology.

Sometimes, though, American jewelers were quite specific in their references to other cultures, and the appropriation of forms was used to make a point. This is the case with Ken Cory's *Squash Blossom Necklace* (1974).(Fig. 3.19) Based on the traditional Hopi squash-blossom necklace, Cory's version is constructed from empty .22 rifle shells, light bulbs, and a pendant made from a curved, cast-bronze pencil in the shape of a crescent moon. In 1972, while teaching jewelry at Central Washington State College in Ellensburg, Cory was actively collecting Native American jewelry and beadwork, especially the Columbia Plateau beaded bags and clothes made by the Yakama people who live in the region around Ellensburg. Native American adornment was an important issue for some contemporary jewelers living on the West Coast and in the Southwest of the United States, partly because it was so ubiquitous, being sold in every truck stop in the region, and partly because it raised serious questions about authenticity and the clash of cultures.[121]

Addressing Native American jewelry in the United States during this period involved tackling what it meant culturally. Cory did this by entangling indigenous forms and aesthetics with consumer culture. This encounter can be read in different ways: as critique, as capitulation, as affirmation, as amusement. But it was not about indifference, nor invisibility, which opens up the possibility that his jewelry offered social or political critique. Leslie LePere, who collaborated with Cory as one of the Pencil Brothers, described him as being passionate about Native American adornment and beadwork and said that there was definitely a purpose behind his explicit references. "I think in large part as a result of his aesthetic love for it, he also was in love with the fact they were in the minority," LePere recalls. "I think he was showing respect for their individualism and their aesthetic not only because he liked it visually but because there were a whole bunch of people that didn't."[122]

Fig. 3.18
Ramona Solberg
Shaman's Necklace, 1968
Silver, Alaskan ivory, and found objects
10 ³⁄₈ × 5 ³⁄₈ × ¾ inches
Museum of Arts and Design,
New York, gift of the Johnson Wax
Company, through the American
Craft Council, 1977

Fig. 3.19

The attention that some American jewelers paid to ethnic adornment had an organized face in the activities of the World Craft Council (WCC), an institution driven by the vision, energy, and financial resources of Aileen Osborn Webb. Osborn Webb had already been instrumental in founding the American Craftsmen's Cooperative Council (1939), the retail outlet America House in New York City (1940), the journal *Craft Horizons* (1942), the School for American Craftsmen (1946), and the Museum of Contemporary Crafts (1956).

The idea of an international organization was first proposed by Osborn Webb in 1962, and during a world tour she recruited many of the 250 delegates from 20 countries to attend the "First World Congress of Craftsmen," held in New York City in 1964. At this conference, Osborn Webb articulated her vision of all the world's craftspeople united across race, class, gender, and geographic lines, based on the idea that the respect for individuality so central in American studio craft could elevate craft in every country from joyless labor lacking aesthetic direction to vibrant art craft that would find a ready market in the capitalist West. Osborn Webb felt strongly that national craft communities could be blended to create an international craft community.[123] People embraced the idea, and by the time of the 1966 meeting in Geneva, the WCC had 252 members.

The WCC congresses, held every two years in a different country around the world, were an opportunity for artist and governmental delegates to interact with local craftspeople and see the craft practices and communities that the efforts of the WCC would protect and elevate. For the third biennial assembly, held in Peru in 1968, more than 800 delegates from 45 countries descended on the country. For two weeks, they met, talked, debated, and roamed the local craft markets, acquiring contemporary Peruvian handcrafts as well as archaeological objects extracted from the burial grounds at Chancay and purchased from gravediggers or antique dealers in Lima. Interactions with living craftspeople were accompanied by study visits to see the extraordinary wealth of pre-Inca pottery and textiles in public museums and private mansions. The finely worked gold objects in the newly finished Museo del Oro (Museum of Gold) stunned everyone, including Arline Fisch. These activities were the backdrop to the group's formal discussions, which centered on the economic and aesthetic problems and dilemmas of folk craftspeople, and the challenge of squaring the differences between the "internationalized artist-craftsman reaching for individual expression" and the "folk and tribal craftsman extending and refining his national and local traditions."[124]

When the WCC congress was held in Toronto, Canada, in 1974, the event attracted more than a thousand delegates. "Whatever their differences of race, tradition, geography, or social order, the world's craftsmen have one thing—one great gift—in common," wrote James S. Plaut, the secretary-general of the WCC, in the book *In Praise of Hands*, published to accompany an ambitious exhibition of the same name that coincided with the Canadian meeting. "They work, create, and achieve *with their hands*."[125]

Fig. 3.19
Ken Cory
Squash Blossom Necklace, 1974
Shells, light bulbs, cast bronze, leather, sterling silver, copper, and found objects
15 ¾ × 4 × ⅝ inches
Helen Williams Drutt Family Collection

Plaut argued that a generation of young people living in America had been struggling against craft's traditional enemies of technology, automation, and dehumanization. Initially their protest had been anti-establishment and nihilistic, involving "dropping out" as a rebellion against the complacency of social institutions and the values of their parents. But their attitude had slowly evolved into a new and positive notion of how life should be lived. As Plaut wrote:

> Escape from the establishment led naturally to the rediscovery of life as it was lived "before technology," life *without* labor-saving devices, life *with* independence and *within* nature, life to be made more precious by one's own discoveries and the capacity to shape one's own environment. Young people have left the cities to rejoin and husband the land, to build their own dwellings, grow and raise their own food, make their own clothing, form their own utensils. Craftsmanship in all endeavors has been reasserted, newly esteemed and made vital. The industrial society's dismissal of the craftsman as a nonconformist, irrelevant eccentric has been laid to rest.[126]

As young Americans transformed their own values, they started to look differently at other parts of the world, where craftspeople were an integral and effective part of society and central to the local economy because they made objects with their hands for themselves, their families, and their communities to use in daily life. Non-Western craftspeople were an authentic and powerful example of the holistic lifestyle that switched-on Americans were seeking to achieve in their rural communes. "In our dangerously dehumanized time," wrote Plaut, "the hands of man, producing the artifacts of many societies to meet an infinite number of human needs, offer some hope that man may remain the master of his world."[127] It was an encouraging message of hope, and a clear demonstration that, for some, studio craft was deeply sympathetic to the values and agendas of the counterculture.

While the WCC was trying to develop economic opportunities for craftspeople around the world, the market for craft in America was evolving in a tangled and multidirectional way, full of contradictions in attitudes toward selling and professionalization. American craftspeople shared the counterculture's disdainful attitude toward commercial activities—being accused of

Fig. 3.20

"selling out" was an insult—but they also wanted to live off the work they made with their own hands. Being creative and finding a way to be self-sufficient were counterculture ambitions too. Yet how could they avoid being sucked into the American economic engine? The answer to that question took many forms, and new models were created to sustain craftspeople, all of which depended to some degree on the robust economy of the times.

During the 1960s, the United States experienced its longest period of economic expansion. The attainment of the American Dream—the opportunity to work and have a nice home in the suburbs with the latest-model car in the driveway and state-of-the-art appliances in the kitchen—began to seem a reality. President John F. Kennedy accelerated economic growth by increasing government spending, cutting taxes, increasing the minimum wage and unemployment compensation, establishing the Peace Corps, and pushing the space race to surpass the Soviet Union. Kennedy's successor, President Lyndon Johnson, built on Kennedy's visions and launched the "Great Society," which spread the benefits of America's successful economy to more citizens through Medicare, food stamps, and educational initiatives.

During this time, big corporations were developing new ways to promote products and expand consumer demand. A marketing concept developed in the 1950s promoted focusing on consumer needs, wants, and behaviors, with extensive marketing research to help in the development of new products. The idea of focusing on the consumer rather than production was a radical change that led to a whole new industry of marketing and branding. Yet there was a dark side to all this innovation, as not everything that the corporations produced was beneficial. For example, the Dow Chemical Company produced the insecticide DDT; the public loved it, until Rachael Carson exposed its dangers in her book *Silent Spring* in 1962, which documented the environmental devastation caused by pesticides. Drugs like thalidomide, a new sleeping pill that was tested in a clinical trial involving twenty thousand patients in the United States, turned out to cause birth defects in babies. False promises and hollow ideas promoted by corporate America were sniffed out by a new skeptical generation and condemned.

Against the backdrop of these contradictory social and economic forces, studio craftspeople chose to target the increasingly wealthy American consumer while emphasizing the difference between what they made and mass-produced consumer products. Craft was anti-corporate—comprising unique objects made by hand by a creative individual rather than a machine, and not the product of market research. The obviously handmade object became a symbol of the consumer's own originality and uniqueness. The act of purchasing studio ceramics, textiles, or jewelry was a modest way to take part in the social revolution.

The countercultural symbolism of studio craft was reinforced by the craft fair, which was based on the model of the country fair selling livestock, preserves, and basketry, as well as fresh-baked foods and other locally produced goods. In the late 1960s, the Northeastern Regional Assembly branch of the ACC held the first craft fair in Stowe, Vermont; soon after, it moved to the larger town of Bennington in the same state. The event was called "Confrontation," in a nod to the protests, marches, and assassinations that were convulsing American society at the time. The fair was sprawling, with individual craftspeople setting up booths of their own design, constructed from makeshift materials like wood, bricks, metal, cardboard, and plastic, covered with blankets. Some were housed in tents and tepees. Some vendors just laid out a blanket on the ground to display their goods or sold work from their vans. Lounge chairs provided customers with a place to sit between sales, and banners of tie-dyed material were hung around the booths, making it a colorful and wildly inventive bazaar. Exhibitors played guitars, drank beer or wine, exchanged techniques, explained processes, and nursed their babies.[128]

The best demonstration of the countercultural credibility of craft fairs was that there was even one at the famous Woodstock Festival in 1969. While Jimi Hendrix played the *Star-Spangled Banner* national anthem on his guitar as a protest against the Vietnam War, the Bindy Bazaar was taking place in the nearby woods.(Fig. 3.20) The organization of the fair was spontaneous. People had created booths by hanging blankets from ropes tied between the trees, and small tables displayed their wares—mostly hippie gear, such as beaded necklaces, headbands, and fringed jackets. Much of the craft for sale had a back-to-the-land vibe, heavily influenced by Native American design. No contemporary jewelry was on display, and not much that could be considered studio craft.[129] It was a meeting place, where transactions of trading, bartering, and selling could take place.

Fig. 3.20
Bindy Bazaar, Woodstock Festival, 1969

Fig. 3.21
Outdoor craft displays at the *Northeast Craft Fair 12*, held by the American Crafts Council on June 23–25, 1977, in Rhinebeck, New York. Courtesy American Craft Council Library & Archives

After the success of the Vermont fair, the ACC established an offshoot organization called American Craft Enterprises, led by Carol Sedestrom Ross. In 1973 she held the first fair on country fairgrounds at Rhinebeck, in upstate New York. It would thereafter take place annually. (Fig. 3.21) In the first year, 570 artists showed their work inside the big red agricultural barns and outside in tents on the lawns. Demonstration spaces were set up for glass blowing, pot throwing, blacksmithing, weaving, and other techniques. Walking through the fair allowed customers to purchase art but also to be educated about craft practices.

Bennett Bean, a ceramist who participated in the early fairs at Rhinebeck, recalls,

Those fairs were the hot new cultural event. Before the fair opened, they had a rope about 50 feet wide at the gate and behind the rope there were 300 women and at 10 o'clock they dropped the rope

Fig. 3.21

Fig. 3.22

and they literally ran to buy. It was just unbelievable. By 10:30 people were sold out for the next year. They would literally put a sign up saying Sold Out Until Next Year. That was the kind of level of excitement. When you first got into Rhinebeck you were given a tent and if you were any good or came back you worked your way into a building. The buildings were basically large red livestock sheds used for country fairs with high ceilings and no windows. It was really a gathering of the clan. You didn't see most of these people who were up in the woods making work all year. Everyone would get their very best stuff and they would show up and it was like show and tell. It was extremely honest because you could see what someone had done for the year. It was all there and then you could see if anyone liked it because they either had holes in their booth or it was all still there and they had really bad body language.[130]

In Rhinebeck's first years, almost 90 percent of the craftspeople held another job to support themselves economically. A decade later, this figure had reversed, with 90 percent of the exhibitors making their living from selling their crafts.[131] In 1979 Bean remembers a woodworker arriving at the fair with a credit-card machine, carried by an assistant in the air like a votive offering. It was a sign that money had arrived.

The jeweler Carolyn Kriegman was at Rhinebeck. (Fig. 3.22) Her booth was more thoughtfully constructed than most, with beautifully made deep display cases with tongue-and-groove corners. A large fiber sculpture stood above the cases, and another hung on the back wall. Both seem to relate to the large plastic neckpieces that made her reputation in the late 1960s, but the jewelry she had for sale at the time was probably much more conservative; silver and stones would be more to the taste of the American public than experimental objects in new materials that stretched the definition of wearability.

The craftspeople at Rhinebeck wanted to impress the audience as well as each other with their skills and their imagination. Fantastic and fanciful vases, perfume bottles, bowls, rings and earrings, desks and chairs, woven wall hangings, macramé, and raku pots were for sale. Yet many of the makers felt conflicted. On the one hand, they needed to make a living; on the other hand, making work that the public liked and bought was dangerously close to "selling out." In the end, making a living won out, and craft fairs became ubiquitous in the late 1960s and 1970s.

Many craftspeople traveled across the country from fair to fair, returning to the studio to supplement their supply of products. While on the road, they camped in their vans at night and sold and bartered their works during the day. It was a hard but liberating way to live. Craftspeople at the fairs and on the road formed a type of tribe, which included those who also taught at universities. It was the exact opposite of the corporate model.

As craft fairs boomed in the 1970s, so did craft galleries and shops. Galleries often took work on consignment, organized one-person or themed shows, advertised and promoted the select makers they represented, and, through the objects on display in the gallery, expressed the taste of the owner. Shops were typical retail outlets, purchasing work from artists outright, sometimes advertising, but not holding exhibitions. In many ways, the people who decided to open shops and galleries held the same values as the craftspeople whose work they showed. They were passionate about studio craft and admired those who made their living with their hands. Quite a few of the best-known galleries and most of the shops displayed a number of crafts, including jewelry.

One of the earliest craft retail outlets was Shop One, established by the jeweler Ron Pearson, the woodworker Tage Frid, the potter Frans Wildenhain, and the metalsmith Jack Prip in 1953 in Rochester, New York. They knew each other through the School for American Crafts at RIT. Alongside their teaching obligations, they produced their own work and opened Shop One to sell it. Their standards were high, and they were determined to make the shop work financially without support from a wealthy donor. They wanted to promote craft and directly connect the maker to the customer, allowing them to produce special commissions.[132] The shop also represented a number of other craftspeople from the region until its closure in 1976.

On the West Coast, one of the earliest shops to feature exclusively jewelry was called Nanny's Design in Jewelry. It opened in 1955 on Grant Street in San Francisco and showed the work of Merry Renk, Irena Brynner, Robert Winston, and Claire Falkenstein. The jewelry on display seemed to teeter between the modernist aesthetics of the 1950s and the contemporary jewelry of the next decade, at the end of which Nanny closed her gallery. Nanny Benderson had come to San Francisco in 1934 from Germany to escape the growing menace of Hitler, and she had an intimate approach to showing the jewelry that she loved. Her jewelers, like Claire Falkenstein, had a personal relationship with her and valued her opinion.[133]

In 1965 Ruth Snyderman opened one of the earliest craft galleries called the Works in Philadelphia on Locust Street. Rick Snyderman, Ruth's husband, joined her in 1972. In the early days, they showed North African, Peruvian, Polish, and then Inuit work, which had

Fig. 3.22
Jewelry maker Carolyn Kriegman at the *Northeast Craft Fair 9,* held by the American Craft Council on June 28 – 30, 1974, in Rhinebeck, New York

Fig. 3.23
The Works gallery, 1960s

been introduced to them by friends. They then traveled to Appalachia to meet with craftspeople from Tennessee, Kentucky, and North Carolina. The Snydermans brought back brooms, chairs, and baskets from the Cherokee Nation. At some point in the late 1960s, they took a trip to Maine, where they chanced upon a map called "Handcraft Trails" and visited all of the artists on the trail. About that time or shortly thereafter, they bought a house in Maine and went there regularly. Some of the jewelers they showed included Colette, Bob Natalini, Thomas Mann, Linda Penzur, who made whole-body jewelry, and Jonathan Stember.

Their first location was a basement space; a room in the back displayed jewelry in cases with old-fashion breakfronts. In 1970 they moved to a new and much larger location on South Street, with a long counter and built-in cases along the wall. (Fig. 3.23) This area of Philadelphia was run down and had been mostly abandoned; in a community-minded effort, they helped to bring it back to life with a group that they started called the South Street Renaissance. They also founded an open-air craft market on the weekends, which was part of their creative and enterprising promotion of craft to the community.

Philadelphia was a center for crafts in America during the 1960s, with important artists such as the ceramicists William Daley and Rudolf Staffel, the fiber artist Ted Hallman, and the furniture maker Daniel Jackson, as well as numerous jewelers teaching in the city's art schools as well as maintaining their own

Fig. 3.23

Counterculture Jewelers

studio practices. This rich environment, complete with exhibitions at the Philadelphia Museum of Art and the Philadelphia Civic Center, and coupled with a strong advocacy group, the Philadelphia Council of Professional Craftsmen, stimulated awareness of American craft as well as a base of collectors in the city.

A year after the Works gallery opened on the East Coast, Betty and Stanley K. Sheinbaum established a craft gallery in Santa Barbara, California, called Galeria del Sol. They were excited by the cultural explosion that was happening all around them, and selling craft was a way to get involved. As Betty Sheinbaum recalled in 1976,

> In California in the 1960s, there was a tremendous cultural revolution, in the arts particularly. I know it dealt a lot with clothing and fashion, and so on, but it went much deeper than that. It was a way of life and a value system that was showing itself in the artist who was turning toward the contemporary crafts. A lot of the kids that I knew, who were not going into their father's business, were becoming extremely skilled and exciting artists with new concepts. They were shaking up not only the value system but the art world as well. I hoped that this would change things, not only our fashions, but our environment — the way we lived, how we lived. I felt it was all tied into one movement.[134]

Five years later, in 1971, they established the nonprofit Fairtree Fine Crafts Institute and opened the Fairtree Gallery on Madison Avenue in New York City. They were interested in educating the public about what was going on in American studio craft and wanted to encourage consumers to fill their homes with handcrafted objects and furniture.[135] Robert Ebendorf was among the jewelers they promoted. Stan Reifel, the executive director of the institute, wanted to alter the lifestyles of Americans by celebrating their heritage of making. "We're trying to revitalize that aspect of our culture," he said, "which seems to be pure and so necessary. In the task of survival, utility has never been enough. Objects are made unique through the skills and creativity of the artist and the craftsman."[136]

Lee Nordness is perhaps best known for organizing the *Objects: USA* exhibition and catalogue in 1969. He also owned a gallery on Madison Avenue in New York City that opened in 1958 initially showing fine art, but by the mid-1960s he was adding craftspeople to his stable. Although much of his focus was on fiber, glass, and ceramics, Nordness did show jewelry in his gallery, including work by Lynda Watson, Arline Fisch, J. Fred Woell, and other jewelers included in the *Objects: USA* exhibition, as well as organized gallery exhibitions dedicated solely to jewelry. Nordness's representation of craftspeople gave the field further credibility. No doubt many of his post–*Objects: USA* clients came to the gallery because of his association with the exhibition and the Museum of Contemporary Crafts. Although the commercial success of his craft activities is unknown, they were a great benefit to the field at large, up until his gallery closed in the mid-1980s.

Another important West Coast gallery was Obiko in San Francisco, which showed wearable works by artists and some jewelry. Sandra Sakata opened the gallery in 1972. At the time, she was living with two roommates, Alex Mate and Lee Brooks, who worked together making jewelry.(Fig. 3.24) They were hippies and part of the gay community, creating wearable objects that drew

Fig. 3.24

Fig. 3.25

upon the themes and aesthetics of the counterculture subcultures of the Bay Area. Obiko was less concerned with studio craft than with makers who channeled the spirit of the counterculture—a counterculture that had continued to flourish in the aftermath of the Summer of Love and that had briefly turned Haight–Ashbury into the epicenter of the hippie movement in the late 1960s. Along with works by Alex and Lee (as they were known), Sakata stocked the work of Leslie Correll, who made jewelry with feathers, buttons, and beads in a style that echoed the forms and materials of ethnic adornment.

After seeing Obiko in San Francisco, Julie Schafler Dale was inspired to provide her own showcase for the revolution. Her gallery, Julie: Artisan Gallery, on Madison Avenue in New York City, was principally known for its outrageous clothes, but it also showed jewelry, including work by Marci Zelmanoff, Cara Croninger, Judith Brown, and Laurie Hall. As she recalls,

> The generation which came of age in the 1960s had sparked social upheaval with the inherent breaking of traditions, search for identity, return to basics and fundamental thrust towards self-expression. It was in the air we breathed, vividly reflected in career choices, political advocacy issues, new art forms, music, drama, performance .... and of course, in the way we dressed. Imbedded in this atmosphere of revaluation and reinvention was the impulse to travel. Journeys to Third World countries revealed a wealth of visual stimulation in cultures where art, lifestyle and traditional artisanal skills merged seamlessly. Out of this rich environment emerged a new chapter in the history of American Craft.[137]

Obiko and Julie: Artisan Gallery might have been a little outside the usual haunts of the studio craft movement, but the energies that they represented were also finding a home in more official venues. In the 1960s and 1970s, the curator Paul Smith was opening up the galleries of the Museum of Contemporary Crafts in New York City to exhibitions like *Fur and Feathers* (1971), which not only brought the outrageous clothing of the period before new audiences but created important links between the counterculture and studio craft. In the catalogue, Smith said that the exhibition was concerned with environmental issues, but he also included Native American and ethnic adornment, reflecting the counterculture's fascination with other cultures.[138] The process had started earlier, with *The Art of Personal Adornment* exhibition held at the Museum of Contemporary Crafts in 1965. As Smith wrote in the accompanying catalogue, "We have chosen to minimize the magnificent and lavish court jewels of the Renaissance, Baroque and Rococo eras in favor of other ethnic cultures which are, in beauty of design and craftsmanship, especially pertinent to the mood of our contemporary life and its artistic expression."[139]

Perhaps the jewelry gallery with the most significant name recognition from that time was the Helen Drutt Gallery in Philadelphia. It was established by Drutt, the former executive director of the Philadelphia Council of Professional Craftsmen (PCPC), in October 1973 and located in a nineteenth-century brownstone near the Philadelphia College of Art. Drutt says, "It was Daniel Jackson and Olaf Skoogfors who initially encouraged me to open a gallery and find a permanent place where we could *constantly* exhibit—it would not be a shop, but a crafts gallery that would address the artistic community in the same way that any fine-arts gallery addressed its stable of artists."[140] Drutt rarely published exhibition catalogues in the 1970s and 1980s, mostly due to their expense, but she sent out press releases, invitations, images, and maker biographies to a wide mailing list.

Fig. 3.24
Alex Mate and Lee Brooks

Fig. 3.25
Helen Drutt in the Helen Drutt Gallery, Philadelphia, c. 1979

Counterculture Jewelers

At the time that she opened her gallery, Drutt was steeped in American craft, having organized mixed-media exhibitions in the Philadelphia area, teaching the first course in contemporary craft history at the Philadelphia College of Art, and working with local professional artists at the PCPC. She had also seen *Objects: USA*, which had a big impact on her knowledge of American craft artists across the country. Through all of these activities, she became committed to showing craft in her gallery at the highest level, specifically making the decision not to show anything less than museum-quality work.

The Helen Drutt Gallery's inaugural exhibition, held in February 1974, featured objects in fiber, ceramics, and metal, including jewelry by Gary Griffin, Stanley Lechtzin, Eleanor Moty, Albert Paley, Olaf Skoogfors, J. Fred Woell, and the Pencil Brothers. As intended, Drutt conceived the exhibition in the same manner as shows in fine-art galleries, creating and mailing invitation cards with a specially designed gallery logo, soliciting press coverage, and arranging the jewelry in one long, internally lit, stainless-steel case, which was quite different than a typical craft-gallery display.(Fig. 3.25) Drutt's gallery occupied the front two parlor rooms of a nineteenth-century row house. When she leased the space, she discovered a vintage purple rug in the back room, which she kept, and she painted the walls of the back room a deep purple (her favorite color). She referred to this room as the "jewelry den," and it also contained her desk, while the front room featured ceramics in wall cases and on pedestals, along with the building's original marble fireplace. Fiber works hung on the walls of both rooms, alongside the furniture that was also sometimes exhibited. The jewelry inventory was kept in a safe in the back room; it was displayed in the large jewelry case between exhibitions. On rare occasions, additional wall-hung cases were installed like paintings to display more jewelry for special exhibitions.[141]

Throughout the gallery's thirty-year history, Drutt was committed to showing jewelry and small sculptural metalwork by the artists she represented. She specifically did not want to show holloware, as it was available from other venues in Philadelphia.[142] Drutt was the sole curator for her gallery, working directly with the artists to choose and display their work. Her exhibitions ranged from solo shows to thematic ones, and each was presented with the same seriousness of intent. Aesthetically, Drutt was drawn to jewelry that highlighted technical advancement; incorporated both metal, alternative materials, and a wide range of scale; and narrative as well as nonpictorial jewelry, primarily made by East Coast and Midwestern jewelers. She generally steered away from the more politically minded assemblage work made on the West Coast, though as the gallery progressed in years, some of this type of jewelry, like that made by Don and Merrily Tompkins, Ramona Solberg, and J. Fred Woell, were shown. In addition, beginning in 1975, Drutt also held a biannual exhibition of the Tyler School of Art MFA graduates in metal so that collectors could see work by the next generation of artists.

By the late 1970s and early 1980s, Drutt was also working with jewelers from Great Britain, the Netherlands, and Spain, such as Marta Breis, Ramon Puig Cuyàs, Paul Derrez, Emmy van Leersum, Joke van Ommen, Wendy Ramshaw, David Watkins, and Lam de Wolf, thereby expanding what was shown in the United States through her curatorial choices and also facilitating connections between American and European jewelers whom she had met on her travels or through lecture tours. Drutt primarily became aware of international jewelers through exhibition catalogues and European travel. For example, she attended the 1973 World Crafts Council conference in Dublin, where she met Graham Hughes, the legendary curator of London's Goldsmith's Hall. This connection led her to find out about British jewelers in Goldsmith's collection; it also led her to Electrum Gallery, also in London, which introduced her to other British as well as Dutch jewelers, among other international jewelers. At the 1980 WCC conference in Vienna, Drutt met the Italian jeweler Bruno Martinazzi, which led to her showing his jewelry in her gallery. Lecture tours by European jewelers were also organized by the WCC and other entities at this time, bringing artists such as Gijs Bakker, Claus Bury, and Emmy van Leersum to Philadelphia during the mid-1970s. Drutt's gallery, as well as the art schools and museums, became a key stop on the artists' visits, and she regularly organized opportunities for local artists and collectors to meet visiting artists. In addition, on her travels in America or abroad in the 1970s, Drutt always wore American jewelry. As such, she was, in her own words, a "walking billboard," introducing jewelry by Skoogfors or Lechtzin, among others, to curators, artists, collectors, and laypeople as she attended lectures, dinners, and other events.

Other galleries on the East Coast were also dedicated solely to jewelry, especially in New York City. Sculpture to Wear opened in 1973 in the Plaza Hotel by Joan Sonnabend, whose husband, Roger Sonnabend, owned the hotel. Joan thought it was important to display art in the lobby of the hotel.[143] She was familiar with the art world, so it came naturally to her to present work by well-known artists such as Hans Arp, Alexander Calder, Max Ernst, and Pablo Picasso, alongside work by jewelers like Robert Lee Morris and Miye Matsukata.[144]

In 1977, the year that Sculpture to Wear closed, Robert Lee Morris, a jeweler and former employee, opened Artwear Gallery in New York. He intended for this venue, eventually located in Soho, to change the public's attitude toward jewelry by staging group shows with trendy themes. He said that he started the gallery to showcase his own work, which did not fit into any other setting—it was neither fine jewelry nor fashion, nor art, but a combination of them all. His interest in anthropology, and in tribal and ethnic jewelry, and his eventual connection to the fashion world led him to design jewelry with bold, simple shapes. For displaying jewelry, he used large glass vitrines rather than small cases, and often full-scale, elegant mannequins. Some of them had dark skin, African features, capes, and elaborate headdresses, indicating the origin of his inspiration. These dramatic exhibitions displayed Morris's own jewelry alongside work by Cara Croninger, Ted Muehling, and Thomas Gentille, as well as European jewelry by makers such as Bruno Martinazzi. Though Artwear Gallery eventually closed in 1994,[145] it had been a favorite gallery of collectors as well as those in the fashion business, introducing them to both studio jewelry and more fashion-oriented wares.

Aaron Faber Gallery was another New York City gallery devoted exclusively to jewelry. Founded in 1974 by Edward and Patricia Kiley Faber, its first location was a tiny space in the heart of the jewelry district.[146] Within three years, they had moved it to Fifty-Third Street, across from the Museum of Modern Art and down the street from the American Craft Museum. Early on, they showed American jewelers like Glenda Arentzen, Earl Pardon, Marci Zelmanoff, Richard Kimball, the Finnish artist Björn Weckström, enamelist Jamie Bennett, and others while also including collectible vintage timepieces and classic jewelry.

It is impossible to list all of the studio craft galleries and shops that opened in the 1960s and 1970s, but it was a vibrant and exciting time in the craft marketplace. The owners of these galleries and shops were passionate advocates for the work they sold and very knowledgeable about the craftspeople who made it and how it was made. Many of the relationships between dealers and makers developed into long-lasting friendships. Dealers were also the ones who found those who made exceptional work and helped to promote them and enabled them to make a living. They performed not only a commercial but also an educational function. Clients learned about the quality of the craftsmanship and the story being conveyed from the dealer. This educated group of clients then provided support for the field at the highest level. This support was extremely important for the craftspeople who wanted to push their work to aesthetic and technical extremes. Throughout the United States, as a new gallery or shop emerged, it spurred a whole new set of enthusiasts in that area. Shops, galleries, and craft fairs formed the structure of the craft marketplace, and their rapid expansion in the 1970s underpinned the success of American studio craft in that decade.

FUNK JEWELRY

Chapter Four

Funk Jewelry

In the 1940s and 1950s, a group of writers, poets, artists, filmmakers, and musicians began to look for new values that would replace the commonly held ideas promoted by mainstream America. They worked in the aftermath of the horrors of World War II and the brutal destruction of the Holocaust and lived with the threat of nuclear annihilation that loomed over the Cold War standoff between the United States and the Soviet Union. They saw authorized political beliefs enforced by the chilling activities of the House Committee on Un-American Activities, and the witch hunt for any Communist sympathizers who threatened the American way of life. They resisted the standardization and commercialism of the American Dream with its suburban tract housing, TV dinners, and enticing offer of prosperity and the good life if only individuals were prepared to sacrifice their freedom and individuality in favor of bland conformity. "Should we be surprised that in the age of 'the lonely crowd,' 'the organization man,' and the 'hidden persuaders' we would get a generation, or at least a segment, that is sickened on the inside and rebellious on the outside at having seen human existence being squeezed into organized molds of conformity?" wrote the Reverend Howard Moody, who ministered to the citizens of Greenwich Village, New York City, in 1959. "I wonder if it is as incongruous as we like to think—this generation we have spawned, whose primary interests seem to be fast cars, long trips, jive, junk, jazz and all other related kicks."[147]

What is now known as the Beat movement or the Beat generation began in 1944, when the writers Jack Kerouac (who published the novel *On the Road* in 1955), Allen Ginsberg (the poet of "Howl," first performed in public in 1955), and William Burroughs (who published

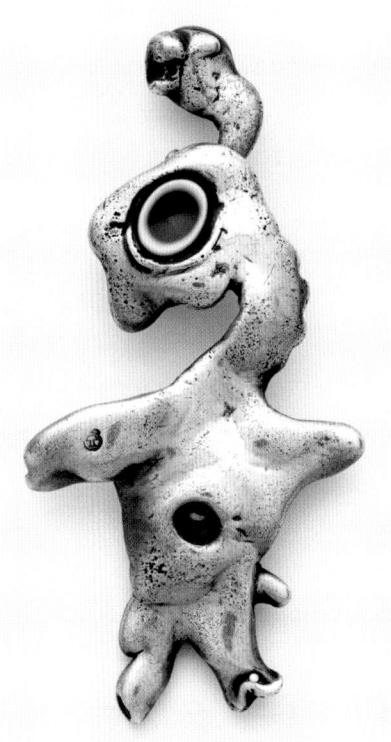 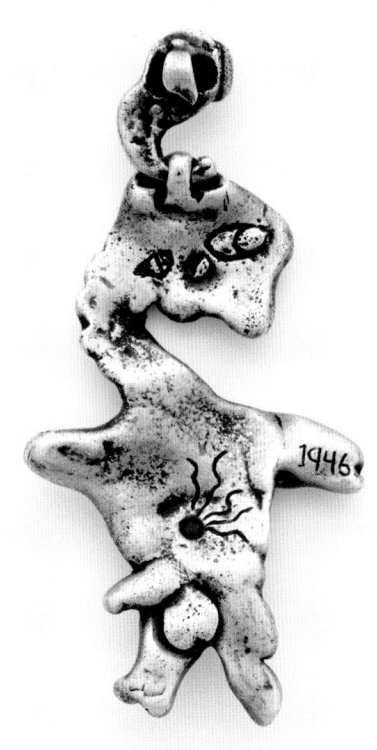

Fig. 4.1

the novel *Naked Lunch* in 1959) met at Columbia University in New York City. They saw themselves as the founders of a new school of American literature, bound together by their desire to resist the status quo and to show their audience a new vision of America that acknowledged the gap between America's promise and its reality. They celebrated the outsider, the outcast, the outlaw, the junkie, and anyone who rebelled against mainstream values.

The term "beat" came from hip language of the 1940s. Frequently used by the denizens who lurked around Times Square in New York City, "beat" meant exhausted, at the bottom of the social heap, or rejected by society, but it also implied being emptied out and therefore wide open and receptive to seeing things in a new way. Kerouac promoted the term as being related to "beatitude" and "beatific," as a way to counteract its negative associations and to emphasize that the Beat movement was seeking the light and the transformation of religious illumination.

By the end of the 1950s, a small underground movement of "Beats" had become widely known. As *Life* magazine suggested in 1959, the Beats were "some of the hairiest, scrawniest and most discontented specimens of all time," who "refuse to sample the seeping juices of American plenty and American social advance." Then there were the clichés, perhaps the most enduring one being the cool hipster in a grungy basement club, dressed in black, playing the bongo drums and reciting poetry against a jazz soundtrack.

Although writers accepted the name "Beat" more readily than artists, they had a shared sensibility: an acceptance of alienation, the absurd, the importance of the individual, the preference for madness over sanity or logic, and the necessity of visionary experiences, whether achieved through drugs, jazz, exotic religion, or relentless travel from place to place. The Beat movement collapsed the ecstatic and the horrific, the beatific and the beaten, mystical wonder and squalid realism. They had no desire to respect the boundaries of different media or art practices, and freely mixed literature, art, and performance. As a result, art moved beyond the academy, museum, and concert hall and appeared in streets, coffeehouses, and nightclubs. Immediacy, spontaneity, and improvisation were celebrated by the Beat movement, along with anything marginal, impure, and debased.[148]

Some American jewelers working in the 1940s and 1950s picked up on these countercultural energies. Like the writers, musicians, and fine artists of the Beat movement, these jewelers were frustrated by convention and made their work as a way to express their desire for social change.[149] Many could be found in New York City, which was a hotspot for postwar art, with its large number of galleries, museums, and venues for performing arts such as jazz, theater, and dance. The city's art scene was enhanced further by the presence and output of European artists who had moved there to escape the turmoil of World War II. All this activity attracted committed, intellectual audiences who were willing to support experimental culture.

In particular, jewelers gravitated toward Greenwich Village, home to the Whitney Museum of American Art, dealer galleries, and places where Abstract Expressionists and other artists of the time gathered, drank,

Fig. 4.1
Sam Kramer
Cyclops, 1946
(front and back)
Brooch
Sterling silver and glass
4 ½ inches high
Collection of Deedie Potter Rose, promised gift to the Dallas Museum of Art

fought, and painted. Paul Lobel, Frank Rebajes, Art Smith, and Bill Tendler had shops and studios on West Fourth Street, while Sam Kramer was not far away on West Eight Street. Another enclave of jewelers was midtown Manhattan. This district housed the Museum of Modern Art, the Museum of Non-Objective Painting (now the Guggenheim), and the Museum of Contemporary Crafts, and jewelers such as Ed Weiner, Irena Brynner, and Henry Steig set up shop there.

In the summer months, some jewelers, along with other prominent artists and New Yorkers, would flee the stifling heat of the city for the longtime artist colony of Provincetown, Massachusetts. This bohemian beach community was where the painter Hans Hofmann had his famous painting school. Weiner, Lobel, Steig, and Jules Brenner maintained summer studios there, as well as temporary shops where they sold their own jewelry alongside the work of local artists. Their stores became informal salons, filled with artistic chatter as the guests drank liquor from glass jam jars.[150] Weiner recalled that well-known artists including Hofmann and Adolph Gottlieb were among the customers willing to "suspend a certain amount of taste to help a struggling young artist."[151]

Of the New York City jewelers, Sam Kramer was the most extravagant example of the Beat generation's anarchism and rebellious flouting of social conventions.[(Fig. 4.1)] He presented himself as a true eccentric, with a bushy black beard and droopy Habsburg mustache, often greeting customers in his pajamas and claiming that they would have to wake him from his slumbers in the collapsible cot that he kept in his studio.[152] The door to his shop on West Eighth Street had a bronze doorknob in the shape of a hand, so that customers entering would shake hands with it; in winter, it was covered with a pigskin glove. The shop window featured a plastic sculpture of a biomorphic cell-like figure reclining on a half-shell, along with blinking lights and a giant red eye that stared back at customers. To promote his shop, Kramer hired young female dancers to dress in black tights and green makeup and walk the city streets as "Sam's Space Girls," distributing handbills advertising his jewelry. He half-hoped that they would get arrested for disturbing the peace and thus bring his jewelry notoriety. He billed himself as a maker of "Fantastic Jewelry for People Who Are Slightly Mad" and advertised his work with a card that read "We have things to titillate the damnedest ego—utter weirdities conceived in moment of semi-madness."[153] A 1955 profile of Kramer in the *Saturday Evening Post* reported that "a timid lady once ventured into Sam's shop, glimpsed a brooch, uttered a little cry and fled … . 'She was really disturbed,' Sam recalled with satisfaction. 'Wow!'"[154]

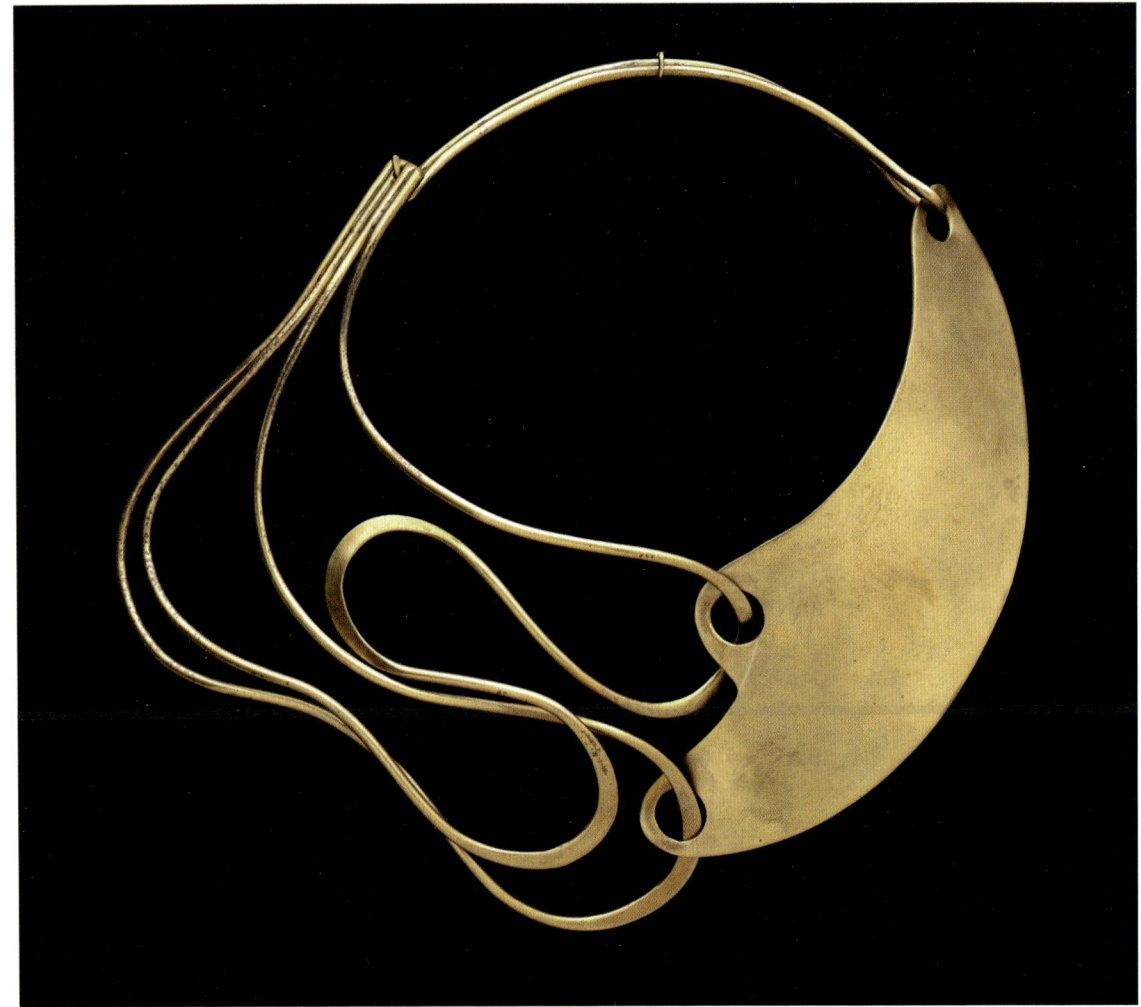

Fig. 4.2

Art Smith, whose studio was on West Fourth Street in Greenwich Village, was one of the few African Americans involved in the studio craft movement, and he knew many of the leading Black artists and writers working in New York City. He was friends with the dancer and choreographer Talley Beatty, and through him he became part of a group of musicians, dancers, writers, and artists known informally as the "Neal Salon," after the dancer Frank Neal. Smith designed body ornaments for Beatty's dance troupe, which left a trace on his jewelry, not just in terms of its scale and theatricality but also in the way it responded to and interacted with the wearer's body.(Fig. 4.2) "A good piece of jewelry literally caresses the body and fondles it," he said in 1971, "plays with it." He was a founder of the Duke Ellington Society and made cuff links for the famous composer and bandleader that incorporated the first five notes of Ellington's famous song "Mood Indigo," as well as jewelry for the musician's family.[155]

The Beat movement also flourished on the West Coast, particularly in San Francisco. There, Allen Ginsberg read his poem "Howl" in public for the first time in October 1955 at the Six Gallery, a converted car-repair shop downtown on Fillmore Street. Five other poets performed that night, and their poems represented ideas that would later define the counterculture of the 1960s and 1970s: Zen, a growing concern for the environment, and a fascination with indigenous peoples. Ginsberg brought Jack Kerouac with him; the then-unknown writer sat on the floor, slugging Burgundy wine, repeating Ginsberg's lines, and scat singing in between, creating a kind of chanted, religious-revival-meeting rhythm.[156]

San Francisco was a sanctuary in the 1950s, tolerant toward differences (a character inherited from its Gold Rush origins). It had charming Victorian architecture, great cafés, and art and craft schools, where

Fig. 4.2
Arthur "Art" Smith
Neckpiece (Positive/Negative), 1948
Wire and sheet brass
6 ¾ × 8 × 1 ½ inches
The Museum of Fine Arts, Houston, museum purchase funded by the African American Art Advisory Association, 2000.246

students could be trained and artists could teach and make a living.[157] North Beach was the bohemian enclave, with its low rents and ample studio space, cheap Italian food, and informal bars. The famous City Lights Bookstore was there, and it attracted students and teachers from the nearby California School of Fine Arts. "It was as if North Beach had a kind of dome over it," wrote the poet Michael McClure in 1972. "There you could mix with the old bohemians and the old anarchists and the young kids wearing sandals and growing beards for the first time. There would be little bars where you could sip wine and see people writing poems and playing chess and talking mysteriously about peyote."[158]

Jewelers were part of this scene, too. Peter Macchiarini's shop at 1529 Grant Avenue was a gathering place for artists and jewelers, who would stop by to intellectualize about art and mingle with customers before heading over to the New Tivoli Bar for their regular, early evening rendezvous.[159] There was even a West Coast version of Sam Kramer: Bob Winston, heavily bedecked in jewelry and with a belt holding various metalsmithing tools. He was famous for outrageous customer interactions, like the time two elderly ladies approached him at a San Francisco art festival and asked if his rings could be altered to fit; Winston, grabbing a mallet from his tool belt, ordered them to put their knuckles on the table so he could solve the problem.[160]

For the most part, jewelers in California did not establish shops like their peers in New York City but sold their work through craft galleries, outdoor art festivals, and anywhere else that modern art was accepted and supported. One of the most important initiatives in the Bay Area was a collaborative effort on the part of jewelers including Irena Brynner, Margaret De Patta, Peter Macchiarini, Merry Renk, Francis Sperisen, and Bob Winston to establish the San Francisco Metal Arts

Fig. 4.3
American poets Allen Ginsberg (left, with beard) and Gregory Corso (center) read poetry at the Five Spot Cafe, New York City, February 22, 1964

Guild in 1951, as a way to educate and provide business support for modern jewelers and metalsmiths working in Northern California.[161]

On both coasts, experimental American jewelry in the 1940s and 1950s appealed to a clientele that was interested in avant-garde jazz, dance, and art.(Fig. 4.3) It was a kind of identification badge that showed you were a cultural pioneer, seeking an alternative to mainstream American society. About 1947, the art historian Blanche Brown visited Ed Weiner's shop in midtown Manhattan and purchased a square silver brooch "because it looked great, I could afford it and it identified me with the group of my choice—aesthetically aware, intellectually inclined and politically progressive. It celebrated the hand of the artist rather than the market value of the materials. Diamonds were the badge of the philistine."[162]

Yet the work that these American jewelers made during those decades was not connected to the aesthetic experiments of the Beat movement. Rather, they generally drew upon artistic movements, incorporating geometric forms, the rigorous lines and spatial games of Constructivism, the weird organic shapes of biomorphism, a touch of Cubism, and a fair bit of borrowing from African art. Only a few, like Sam Kramer, found their inspiration in the strange juxtapositions, sexually charged scenarios, and found objects of Surrealism and Dada.

Fig. 4.3

The values of the Beat movement led to a new freedom to include everything and anything in art and literature. As poets started using slang and swear words and mixing high and low culture (Walt Whitman next to Hollywood movies), so too did artists begin raiding the detritus of everyday life, making assemblages from objects that were both absurd and sublime. Familiar objects, no matter how strangely used, and figurative images, rather than abstract ones, offered a vernacular visual language that would appeal to viewers, breaking down the idea that art should occupy an exalted plane removed from life. This approach embraced humor and craft, although without the perfection and technical skill of studio craft.

In the Bay Area, the Beat movement gave birth to an attitude sometimes described as "funky." Artists like Wally Hedrick incorporated words into their artwork, long sequences that included puns and rhymes, bringing together the acceptable and respected with the unacceptable and vulgar—the artist Botticelli might be linked to Bottom Jelly, or the philosopher Schopenhauer to the phrase Shopping Hour.[163] Bruce Conner made assemblages that were crude bundles of objects, including nylon stockings that were stretched across surfaces or stuffed with detritus and knotted shut, window shades, fur, old jewelry, and photographs, all liberally coated with wax and dirt. The results were spooky, morbidly erotic, anguished. In a characteristically funky gesture, Conner founded the Rat Bastard Protective Association in 1958, a membership organization that included artists, poets, and even a publisher. The name came from the slang phrase "rat bastard," which the poet Michael McClure had overheard at a gym, and from the Scavengers Protective Society (representing San Francisco garbage collectors). By refusing to segregate high and popular culture, and finding spirituality in the street, funky art was a visual-art parallel to the poetry and novels of Ginsberg and Kerouac.[164]

Unlike the East Coast, which had an established network of galleries, collectors, and audiences to support artists and provide them with an income and the trappings of success, the Bay Area did not have a real art economy in the same way. For artists, taking the discarded items of an increasingly affluent American society and reconfiguring them into deviant objects was an excellent way to make sense of being outsiders. Assemblage and found objects made the most of the make-do skills of the home handyman that had emerged from the austerity of the Great Depression in the 1930s and the restrictions of the World War II years; it also tapped into the customization that was central to the culture of the California hot-rod and motorbike scenes.[165]

One American jeweler whose history intriguingly intersects with the legacy of the Beat movement in the Bay Area is Ken Cory, who was born in Kirkland, Washington, in 1943. Cory's father, Robert, worked as a radio electrician in the Lake Washington shipyards during World War II. When the war ended, the family moved to Pullman, where Robert got a job at Washington State College (now University), first teaching chemistry and then studying the effects of radiation on plants in the botany department. He constantly tinkered with the family home, changing and enlarging it, proud of his skills as a handyman; Robert never threw anything away, keeping piles of stuff that might become useful in the yard and in a shed out back. Cory's mother, Susan, sewed curtains and clothes for herself and her family, cooked and cleaned, and canned the produce from the large garden that her husband tended. The family maintained a level of care and artistry in the domestic environment while also following the motto "do it cheap and do it right." Cory was obsessed with cars, building plastic models and spending hours sketching fins, fenders, grills, hood ornaments, and custom paint designs. When he graduated from high school and got his first car, a secondhand 1957 Plymouth, he sewed the "tuck-and-roll" seat upholstery himself.[166]

Cory's DIY tendencies were encouraged by Victor Moore, his art teacher at Pullman High School. Moore was a colorful, flamboyant character; when the school insisted that male teachers should wear neckties, he grew his neck hair long and braided it into a "hair tie." Moore was also a collector of random objects, a habit that Cory embraced. Later, when he was a student at the California College of Arts and Crafts (CCAC) in Oakland, Cory built a wall in his dorm room, constructed from old wooden boxes and large tin containers scavenged from Chinatown in San Francisco. He filled it with found objects, books, rocks, and bottles — anything he thought was special, quirky, beautiful, common, or unusual.[167]

At the urging of his father, Cory applied to Stanford University when he graduated from Pullman High, but he was not accepted. After a year at Washington State University, Cory convinced his father to let him go to art school. In 1963 he enrolled at CCAC to pursue a BFA. There, he signed up for a jewelry workshop taught by George Laisner, an émigré from Czechoslovakia who had studied in Chicago and had joined the university teaching staff in 1937. Laisner was a modernist, and Cory's first jewelry experiments were classic examples of what he later mockingly called "Mo Derne": bold,

Fig. 4.4
Ken Cory
Fish, c. 1963
Pendant
Silver and agate
2 ¼ × 1 ⅛ × ½ inches
Estate of Ken Cory

Fig. 4.5
Poster for the *Hairy Who* exhibition at the San Francisco Art Institute in 1968, offset lithograph
21 ¼ × 16 ⅝ inches

Fig. 4.6
Ken Cory
(Untitled) Drain, 1968
Brooch
Bronze, Plexiglas, and plastic wire
1 ⅞ × 1 ½ × 1 inches
Tacoma Museum of Art, gift of the Estate of Ken Cory, 198.29.5

Fig. 4.4

Fig. 4.6

Fig. 4.5

highly stylized, and abstract forms heavily indebted to Scandinavian jewelry.[168] (Fig. 4.4) This was the type of jewelry being taught and made in the metalworking studios of CCAC, and the kind being made by most modern jewelers on the East Coast and West Coast of America in the 1940s and 1950s.

While he was studying at CCAC, Cory absorbed a great deal from the rich stew of art and culture available to him in the Bay Area. He was very interested in the work of the Hairy Who,(Fig. 4.5) a group of six Chicago artists that included James Falconer, Art Green, Gladys Nilsson, Jim Nutt, Suellen Rocca, and Karl Wirsum, who had met as students at the School of the Art Institute of Chicago in the early 1960s. From 1966 to 1969, they organized five exhibitions, including one in 1968 that Cory attended at the gallery of the San Francisco Art Institute. Members of the Hairy Who embraced kitsch, comic-book-style images, verbal puns, and folk and outsider art. Like Pop artists, the Hairy Who were interested in objects and images from everyday life, but they did not embrace commercial processes. Instead, they tended to use fine-art techniques, creating tightly drawn and immaculately painted works in which the refinement contrasted with the crude nature of their subject matter and distorted forms.[169] Cory appreciated their aesthetic and rebelliousness, and he adopted some of their artistic strategies for his jewelry. Their impact can be seen, for instance, in the sinuous, coiling, twisting, and meandering forms in plexiglass emerging from bronze geometric shapes that he began making in 1967.(Fig. 4.6)

More than anything else, the Funk movement, which was ascendant when Cory was at CCAC, proved to be decisive. Emanating particularly from Oakland, the San Francisco Art Institute, and the University of California, Davis, the term "Funk" was related to the "funky" art of the Beat movement. The movement gained national recognition through the 1967 Berkeley Art Museum exhibition *Funk*, which largely featured sculptors and ceramicists, though the term could describe a much wider spectrum of art and craft. The curator, Peter Selz, described Funk as,

> hot rather than cool; it is committed rather than disengaged; it is bizarre rather than formal; it is sensuous; and frequently it is quite ugly and ungainly. Although usually three-dimensional, it is non-sculptural in any traditional way, and irreverent in attitude. It is symbolic in content and evocative in feeling. Like many contemporary novels, films, and plays, Funk art looks at things which traditionally were not meant to be looked at. Although never precise or illustrative, its subliminal post-Freudian imagery often suggests erotic and scatological forms or relationships; but often when these images are examined more closely, they do not read in a traditional or recognizable manner and are open to a multiplicity of interpretations ... . Funk is visual double-talk, it makes fun of itself, although often (though by no means all the time) it is dead serious. Making allusions, the artist is able, once more, to deprecate himself with a true sense of the ironic.[170]

Fig. 4.7
Robert Arneson
His and Hers, 1964
Stoneware with overglaze
34 × 24 × 28 inches
Cantor Arts Center Collection, museum purchase from the Modern and Contemporary Art Fund and funds realized through the deaccession and sale of gifts from several generous donors, 2007.35.a–d

According to Selz, Funk was about satire and free association. With a nod to artistic antecedents, Funk did not care about public morality and sought to overthrow it (like Dada) or replace it (like Surrealism). "If these artists express anything at all, it is senselessness, absurdity, and fun," wrote Selz. "They find delight in nonsense, they abandon all the strait jackets of rationality, and with an intuitive sense of humor they present their own elemental feelings and visceral processes. If there is any moral, 'it's for you to find out.'"[171] It was a perfect movement for the counterculture to embrace. It was fun; it was sexy; and it was frowned upon by the mainstream establishment and by the East Coast art scene. It was fundamentally alternative.

When it came to studio craft, ceramics led the way when it came to Funk, thanks to Robert Arneson at the University of California, Davis. The environment that Arneson entered at Davis in 1962 was untouched

Fig. 4.7

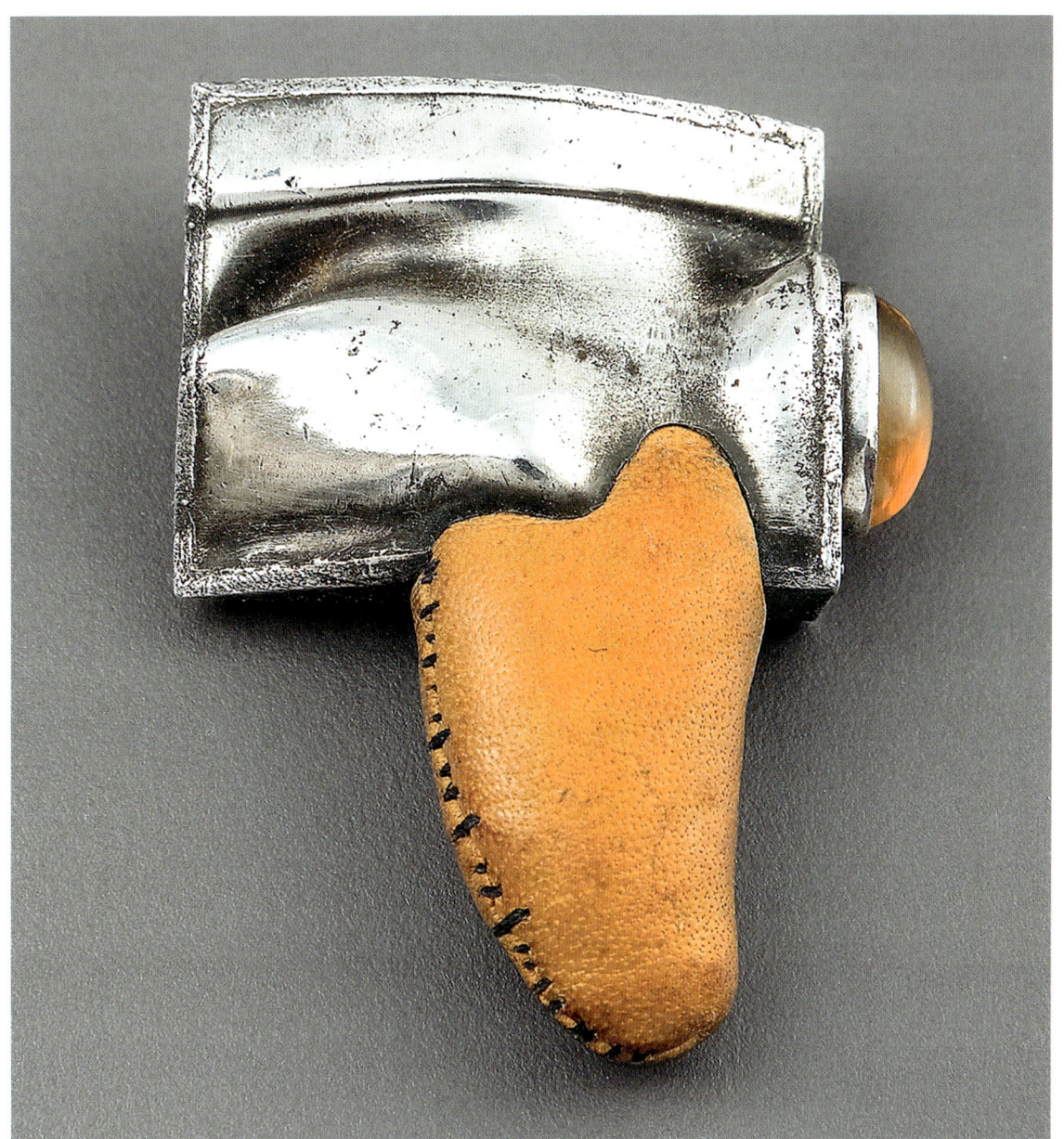

Fig. 4.8

by the hierarchies that plagued many other art schools. As he recalled later, "There was no academic infighting. Above all, there was no one to say this is the right way, that is the wrong way, and everybody could work as they saw fit."[172] This freedom, combined with the geographic isolation of the art school in Davis from the wider art scene, allowed an extraordinary intimacy to develop among Arneson, his students, visiting ceramists, and other art department faculty members, resulting in an environment that enhanced creativity and experimentation.[173] The subject matter that turned up in the work of Arneson and his students ranged from daily life experiences to larger themes of American society and global politics. Scatological matters abound in Arneson's *Toilets*, *Urinals*, and *Trophies*; politics is the subject of his *Busts*; and Americana and corporate branding appear in works such as *Oreo* and *Crisco*.[Fig. 4.7] His students, such as David Gilhooly, tackled issues concerning the environment and food consumption. Regardless of subject matter, their figurative and narrative forms were imbued with satire, humor, subversion, or irony.

Fig. 4.8
Ken Cory
Tongue, 1967
Brooch
Sterling silver, amber, and leather
2 × 1½ × ½ inches
Tacoma Art Museum, gift of the
Estate of Ken Cory, 1998.29.4

Funk Jewelry

Arneson focused on what he called "neglected images," which he re-created in clay with gloopy surfaces and shrill, screeching glazes. What separated his work from Pop Art was the idiosyncratic and intense investment of personal, autobiographical meaning in these banal, everyday objects. In the early 1960s, the intersection of painting and sculpture was of intense interest to the art world, and Arneson's clay objects showed powerfully how this could be achieved. His so-called neglected images were "hotter" than Pop Art examples such as Claus Oldenburg's soft sculptures of hamburgers or cigarettes, and "cooler" than Peter Voulkos's Abstract Expressionist ceramics. They perfectly mirrored the rebellious iconoclasm and hip humor of the counterculture in the mid-1960s.[174]

After leaving CCAC in mid-1967 with his BFA, Cory returned to Washington State University (WSU) to begin work on his MFA. There, he produced his first Funk jewelry, including *Tongue* (1967), a brooch made of cast silver, leather, and a piece of cabochon-cut amber. (Fig. 4.8) This provocative, sensual, and irreverent work juxtaposes high and low, hard and soft, permanent and perishable, and precious and common materials. The brooch shows a tongue sticking out, begging the question: What is the intended target of this gesture? Is it rude or playful, a rejection or an invitation?

Fig. 4.9
Don Tompkins
Janis Joplin, 1970
Pendant
Sterling silver, brass, and cultured pearl
9 ¾ × 4 ¼ × ¾ inches
The Museum of Fine Arts, Houston, Helen Williams Drutt Collection, gift of Helen Williams Drutt English, 2006.657

In the second half of the 1960s, and into the 1970s, the small town of Ellensburg in central Washington State became an unlikely center for counterculture jewelry, and an important outpost of the Funk movement. If the university town of Davis, California, were the Athens of Funk, then those of Seattle and Ellensburg (ninety miles from Seattle across the Cascade Mountains) were Funk's Alexandria, a provincial outpost where Funk was adapted and transformed. As an attitude and approach to making, Funk was useful and attractive: the irreverence appealed to young artists,

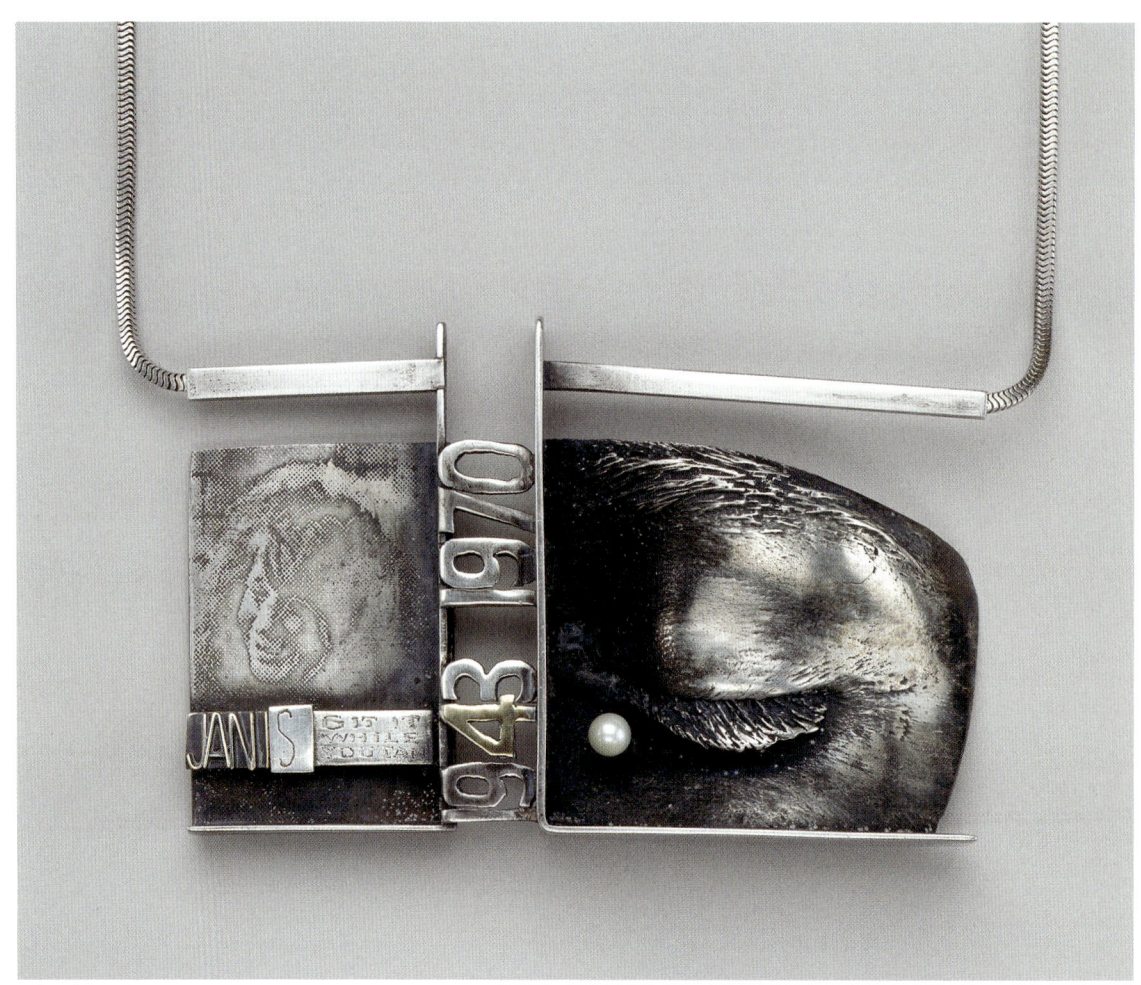

Fig. 4.9

Fig. 4.10

Fig. 4.11

while its adaptability and promiscuous attitude toward materials meant that there were no barriers for craftspeople to overcome. Ultimately, it provided a way for regional artists to free themselves from the dominant art style of modernist abstraction.[175]

In 1956 the jeweler Ramona Solberg got a job teaching at Central Washington State College (later Central Washington University [CWU]) in Ellensburg. Soon after, she invited Don Tompkins to join the jewelry department. At Central Washington State College, Tompkins began working on the *Commemorative Medals* series, which has certain Funk qualities. He mixed traditional and nontraditional materials, including found objects, and he plundered consumer and popular culture for subjects and images, populating his jewelry with high and low sources from the world of literature, the visual arts, TV, and comics. He frequently incorporated text into his work, being one of the first studio jewelers to do so.

His *Commemorative Medal* for Janis Joplin is a memorial to the singer, one of his favorite musicians, who died of an accidental heroin overdose in a Hollywood hotel in October 1970, the same year the work was made. (Fig. 4.9) On the left is a photo-etched image of the singer smiling in happier times; on the right is a silver cast of a woman's closed eye, with a pearl like a tear sitting on the cheek. Between them are Joplin's birth and death dates. *Pearl* is the name of Joplin's posthumous album that was released in 1971 and became a massive hit.

Tompkins's jewelry shared many aesthetic qualities with the work of his successor at Central Washington State College, Ken Cory. However, Tompkins was a bit more Beat, cool, ordered, and introspective. Cory was much more Funk, hot, spontaneous, and extroverted, behaving badly in the provinces. He was also hippie. In a photograph taken around 1968 or 1969 and published in the *Objects: USA* catalogue, he sits behind the wheel of a convertible, with his long hair, beard, and fringed leather jacket. (Fig. 4.10) Another, taken in 1973, shows him straddling the horizontal spout of a fountain in Seattle's Pioneer Square, with one hand holding the gushing spout and the other resting on his hip—appearing like a man at ease pissing in public. (Fig. 4.11)

When Cory arrived in Ellensburg in 1972, he had already gained recognition as a jeweler, both through his own practice and through his collaboration with Leslie LePere, called the Pencil Brothers. Cory and LePere met at a summer ceramics class at Washington State University (WSU) in Pullman in 1966. LePere had grown up on a wheat farm in Harrington, Washington, and aspired to be an architect, but a wonky technical drawing triangle and a lack of aptitude led him to transfer to the fine arts program at WSU. As LePere recalls, Cory had long, straight hair down to his shoulders, which was a novelty

Fig. 4.10
Ken Cory, from the
Objects: USA catalogue, 1968,
Courtesy to Estate of Ken Cory

Fig. 4.11
Ken Cory in Pioneer Square,
Seattle, 1973

Funk Jewelry

85

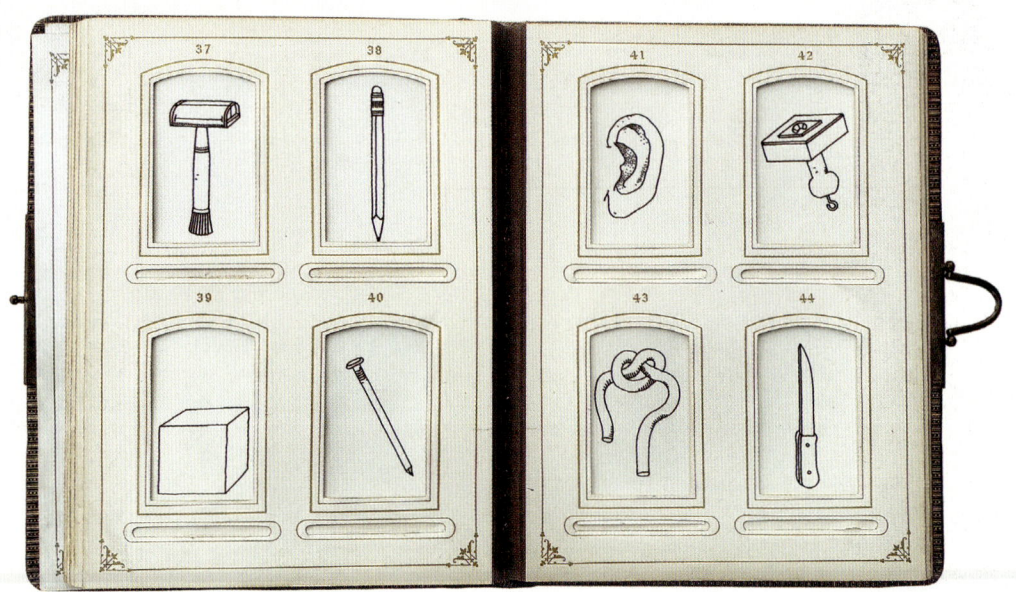

Fig. 4.12

in central Washington at the time.¹⁷⁶ LePere was driving his father's 1949 yellow Ford pickup, a car that Cory instantly loved. After class, Cory got a ride home, and on the way, they scavenged toy soldiers and reflectors from some trash cans in an alley in downtown Pullman. It was the start of an important friendship and working relationship. They tried, in LePere's words, "to make something unusual, to use common everyday happenings as the research method for formulating handmade art, and to use the art as the direction for research. Reflections from one's everyday observations. We were naughty along the way."¹⁷⁷

Cory and LePere were together at WSU from 1966 to 1970, during which time Cory completed his MFA in sculpture, and LePere finished his BFA and then embarked on an MFA in painting. They first collaborated on a piece of jewelry in 1969, naming themselves the Art Team. They were keen to overthrow the idea of the artist as a solitary genius in favor of art as a shared activity. As Cory wrote in a notebook from that year, "If one man conceives an idea and another man manipulates this idea into a finished work both men are of equal importance for the work could not have been finished without the talents of either man."¹⁷⁸ They looked to jazz for a model of shared creativity that could represent how they wanted to collaborate with each other.¹⁷⁹

By 1972, they had become the Pencil Brothers. LePere had been drawing cartoons under the pen name Pencil. One weekend, Cory showed him an enamel emblem from a Dodge truck radiator that said, "Dodge Brothers, Detroit U.S.A." LePere suggested that they could be the Pencil Brothers, and Cory added that LePere could be "Lead" and he could be "Red"; "better Red than Lead," he thought.¹⁸⁰ Throughout the 1970s, they made enameled copper belt buckles, switch plates, ashtrays, and wall pieces, as well as brooches. LePere, who had by then moved to Seattle, would head up to Ellensburg on the weekends with ten dollars in his pocket, which was enough for the train fare and a feast of beer and hamburgers. Together, they would go for long walks in the woods, where they would make strange constructions from sticks and stones using string and Swiss Army knives.

LePere had a fascination with "standard objects," things like matchsticks, bologna sandwiches, or pencils—common, everyday items.⁽ᶠⁱᵍ· ⁴·¹²⁾ LePere monumentalized such objects in a series of graphic ink drawings, creating images that look like they belong in a product

Fig. 4.12
Leslie LePere
Page from *Standard Objects as the Subject*, 1971
Ink on paper
11 × 18 × 2 inches
Collection of Leslie LePere

Fig. 4.13

catalogue or a visual encyclopedia of quotidian forms. By taking them out of context and depicting them in a deadpan manner, he made these objects appear strange and dynamic. LePere wrote in his master's thesis, "There are objects that hover, objects that are physically close, objects that are performing their natural function and ones that become friends."[181]

Although LePere received his master's degree in painting, he produced objects, many of them wearable, in his partnership with Cory. For his part, Cory remained a jeweler, but his work changed in response to LePere's visual imagery. He began to make narrative jewelry in the sense that each work featured figurative images, composed in a way that presented a moment from a larger story. Cory's favorite technique of champlevé enamel copper — an old, technically skilled process that appealed to him precisely because it was not fashionable — was a perfect way to render the whole family of "standard objects" in a bold, graphic, and vividly colored style.

The Pencil Brothers' subject matter was diverse: the number 5 appears frequently, sometimes signifying earth, air, fire, water, and void (or self), and sometimes the colors red, yellow, blue, white, and black. Many of the works are four-cornered compositions with a void in the center, which is another manifestation of five, but also a sexual reference to what they saw as the unknown, the mystery of the yoni as it is known in Hindu art, the vagina. LePere recalls, "One of the keys to all of the P. Boys [Pencil Brothers'] work ... was the goal of achieving a balance, the result of combining opposites: male–female, frame–picture, yang–yin, black–white, soft–hard, man-made/natural, geometric–organic, hot–cold, static–directional."[182] Cory made reference to this duality, too, when he described the pencil as "the American yin-yang symbol—creative on one end, destructive on the other."[183] The Pencil Brothers celebrated the things that they loved from American consumer culture and the everyday world around them; it was boys' imagery, with dirty puns and rebellious attitudes, but it was also provocative, trenchant, and funny.

An early wall piece, *Camel* (1971), represents some of the themes that emerged from their collaboration: sex, mysticism, and irreverence.(Fig. 4.13) Cory sent LePere

Fig. 4.13
Pencil Brothers
Camel, 1971
Wall piece
Enamel on copper, glass, and colored pencil
4 1/8 × 4 1/4 × 3/8 inches
Tacoma Art Museum, gift of Leslie LePere

Funk Jewelry

the enamel on copper frame, a square with four small circles at each corner, featuring a star, a heart, a hippie-style crescent moon with a face, and a blue-and-white target. A cutout of a camel, shaped like the one on the popular cigarette label, is superimposed over the composition. LePere responded by drawing a frankfurter on a skewer, roasting over flames. The image was related to a series of colored pencil and ink drawings of flying frankfurters visiting important historical locations that LePere had completed as part of his graduate work at WSU. In the United States, frankfurters are sometimes called wieners, which is also a slang term for penis, so the message of this image is put your wiener in a fire and get it warmed up — in other words, have sex.[184] LePere and Cory thought of the finished object as "camelflage."

A later brass and enamel on copper belt buckle by Cory called *How to Fix Your Snake* (1976) has similar sexual innuendo.(Fig. 4.14) It shows a nude woman from the waist down standing in water and brandishing a stick at a snake (a metaphor for the penis). As a buckle, it is designed to be worn on a belt (another kind of snake), a flagrant and funny nod to the sexual act that is located directly above the wearer's genitals.

The Pencil Brothers did not favor explicit references to political figures or events in their work. Certainly, they were aware of politics; in the late 1960s, it was almost impossible not to be personally touched by the wider controversies that were shaking up the status

Fig. 4.14
Ken Cory
How to Fix Your Snake, 1976
Belt buckle
Brass, enamel on copper
2 ¾ inches diameter,
½ inches deep
Los Angeles County Museum of Art, gift of Lois and Bob Boardman, M2014.198.55

Fig. 4.14

Fig. 4.15

quo. Instead, what they provided was satirical social commentary, provocation, and a celebration of individuality that was in line with the values of the counterculture. LePere recalls, "That was the political statement. No matter which philosophy or religion or political party or aesthetic party you believe in, we have the right to make fun of it. Our attempt there was drop dead serious. Serious as a damn heart attack. We have the right as individuals to explore that territory, to have that as our message, as our doctrine."[185]

However, the Pencil Brothers did produce one overtly political work: a wall piece titled *Egypt* (1974).[Fig. 4.15] It includes an enamel on copper frame featuring a yellow smiley face, a peace sign, a Richard Nixon political button, and a purple flower, all of which were loaded symbols in the 1960s and 1970s, politicized either by their purpose or society's reaction to the groups who used the symbols. Yet *Egypt* brings them together in a single work; in combination, they become a generalized and therefore ambivalent or ambiguous representation of a moment or period. LePere's drawing inside the frame is of a strange denuded landscape in which pencils grow from the earth, presided over by a large parrot perched on a tree stump. The work is grounded in the time and place in which it was made, alert to the political and social significance of the year 1974, but it also resists any easy identification with the currents animating this moment. What group could claim this object as a rallying cry for its cause? The politics of *Egypt* were based on irritation and disruption: Cory and LePere wanted to make a work that would have something in it that would piss everyone off, no matter what faction they belonged to.[186]

In 1973, a year after Cory had moved to Ellensburg, Funk was on his mind. Maybe his job teaching jewelry at Central Washington State College encouraged him

Fig. 4.15
The Pencil Brothers
Egypt, 1974
Wall piece
Enamel on copper, glass, graphite, and wood
4 × 4 × ½ inches
Collection of Leslie LePere

Funk Jewelry

89

to articulate his personal artistic philosophy. Whatever the reason, he began writing definitions of Funk in his notebooks.

> Funk art = tribal art.
> 1966 – a new tribe emerges from underground. Tribe members develop communal, spiritual art. Funk artists use tribal rather than personal themes. Funk art is decorative and illustrative.
> Those who aren't part of the tribe are considered foreign.
> The tribe uses hide.
> Imitators are usually detected.
> Funk art stumps intellectuals.
> Funk artists are intellectuals. (True or false?)
> Tribal secrets are hidden from foreigners.
> Tribal artists study art of other tribes.
> Eclecticism isn't avoided.
> Electricity is.
> What good is a new car if you have no gasoline? A skilled mechanic can make useful objects. Tribal art and religion are polytheistic.
> Tree stump.
> Stump routes.[187]

In this list, Cory notes that Funk emerged in 1966; at that time, he had witnessed its coverage in the press while living in the Bay Area. He had been an aspiring member of the tribe, close to the Funk breakthrough in his own work. He also recognized early on that Funk art was tribal art. Later, in the 1970s, Cory would study and collect Native American beadwork and jewelry, and by the middle of that decade he made jewelry that appropriated Native styles, sometimes signing them Ellen X. Redheart or with a heart-shaped stamp, a joking way to suggest that they were not authorized or proper Cory works.[188] What is most amusing about this list is the way Cory embodies a Funk attitude: he does not explain Funk but demonstrates it in action, serving up a text full of puns and zigzagging logic.

If Funk was tribal art, then it was made for a specific community, an audience who shared the cultural references and the beliefs about what art should be and do. "Work is being designed for display in galleries rather than for interaction between the artist and his friends and/or his acquaintances," Cory wrote in a notebook dated 1969 – 71. "The artist is directing his spiritual observations towards an inarticulate thing incapable of responding appropriately." It did not seem right to Cory to make work that might be shown to just anyone, rather than to other members of the tribe. "An artist should be selective about his audience," he concluded, "expressing himself to those who understand him and who he understands."[189]

He wrote another list about Funk in 1973:

> 1. East coast is sophisticated.
> 2. West coast is proud of its lack of sophistication.
> 3. Funk is West coast pop.
> 4. Good Funk is always out of date.
> 5. Next time infinity won't end.
> 6. Funk is good clean fun.
> 7. There is always an exception to the rule.
> 8. Funk is the love of imperfection.
> 9. The Funk artist is proud of his mistakes.
> 10. The Funk artist is very tolerant but he won't put up with any shit he doesn't agree with.
> 11. Funk artists are smart.
> 12. Contemporary art is a thing of the past.[190]

The tension between the "sophisticated" East Coast art scene and the provincial West Coast one had been established in the Beat movement in the 1950s. Funk artists turned what might have been a deficiency into a strength, positioning themselves against the modernism — especially Abstract Expressionism — that was championed by powerful East Coast institutions. Instead, they reveled in those elements that set their art apart: figurative depictions, crude sexual innuendoes, and the imagery and freedom of the Wild West.

Don Tompkins's sister, the jeweler Merrily Tompkins, was also connected to Cory in Ellensburg and shared the Funk spirit. She was born in 1947 in Everett, Washington, twenty-five miles north of Seattle on the Puget Sound. Her mother and father were schoolteachers, first in the North Dakota prairies and then in Snohomish and Skagit Counties in Washington State. "Oh, my funny, difficult, oddball, collector father," she recalls.

Fig. 4.16
Merrily Tompkins, no date
Courtesy Merrily Tompkins Estate, Ellensburg

Fig. 4.17
Merrily Tompkins
Dad's Payday, 1968
Pendant
Sterling silver, photograph, fabric, and found object
4 ½ × 4 × ¼ inches
Collection of the Merrily Tompkins Estate, Ellensburg

Fig. 4.17

"He was a real salvage operator, dumpster-diving before they even had a name for it. He'd bring crazy shit home ... sorting it all into some mysterious organizational scheme that made sense only to him. There were pocket-knives, tiny perfume bottles, all kinds of costume jewelry and bangles, matchbooks, key chains, watch fobs, hair combs, pretty buttons. As a kid I used to sneak in to where he kept the boxes of stuff and go through them for hours and just drool over everything."[191] Tompkins also took up the habit, making her own extraordinary and chaotic collection of old shoes, nails, toys, frames, tools, skeletons and skulls, rocks, shells, deer heads, sticks, boxes, baskets, folk art, cigar boxes, dolls, American flags, posters, comics, magazines, and books that populated her studio and house.

Despite having teachers as parents, Tompkins did not attend school with much enthusiasm. In 1966 she enrolled at the University of Washington in Seattle, but when her brother Don started teaching metalsmithing at Central Washington State College in Ellensburg, she transferred there and studied with him from 1967 to 1969. She never completed her degree, which did not worry her; she was more of a free spirit, or as she says, a hippie. (Fig. 4.16)

Although Merrily Tompkins moved to Seattle in 1972 and lived there for a couple of years, she always related best to people in the country. Accordingly, she responded to the aesthetics and values of folk art: "The tenderly rendered and worked-over, soulful and divinely-driven kind, made ingeniously, out of whatever stuff those folks have at hand, much the way my father and my farmer/rancher uncles operated, much the way things were built in those great old 'Popular Mechanics' magazines of the 40s and early 50s, which I grew up loving and studying."[192] This statement captures Tompkins's attitude towards making. She loved the unpretentious

Funk Jewelry

Fig. 4.18

Fig. 4.19

and funny quality of folk art and the way things got put together with the kinds of scraps her father found in the dumpster. Like Funk, her attitude was unconventional and oppositional to acceptable forms.

In 1968, while still in Ellensburg, Merrily Tompkins made a pendant called *Dad's Payday*, which reflects this idea of assemblage.[Fig. 4.17] The work is similar to her brother's series of *Commemorative Medals*, which he was making at the same time. Her pendant uses a loose grid to organize the parts: the title, punched out in silver, a Roosevelt political pin, a small photo of her father, a button from her father's favorite denim coveralls, and a metal "Payday" suspender buckle.

By the 1970s, Tompkins was producing some very funny and unapologetically sexually frank jewelry. Her *Snatch Purse* (1975) has a top section in copper with champlevé enamel showing a train entering a tunnel.[Fig. 4.18] When the purse is opened, the engine enters the dark hole drilled through the landscape; the meaning is obvious. The leather purse features a merkin made of beaver fur and is designed to hang at the wearer's crotch, its triangle of fur suggestively placed between the wearer's legs. Beaver, like snatch, is a colloquial name for a woman's vagina, and *Snatch Purse* conveys the freedom that women were beginning to claim in the 1970s: the freedom to be sexually powerful and in control of their own bodies and desires, and the freedom to express those feelings in public. There is a strong connection here to feminism and the movement to assert women's rights, but Tompkins is too playful and eccentric to address these issues directly.

Merrily Tompkins met Ken Cory in 1972 upon moving to Seattle. She was introduced by Leslie LePere, whom she knew through the Manolides Gallery in Seattle, where they both showed their work. The gallery was run by Jim Manolides, a man of many talents and with many irons in the fire. He worked as an art dealer and a bartender, he owned a cigar store and a racehorse named Savannah Blue Jeans, he was a musician who played with a rock group called the Frantics, and later with a band called Junior Cadillac, and he had been married four times. The jeweler Ramona Solberg, who had been Manolides's art teacher in middle school, had told him, "You are either going to prison or you will be famous."[193] He avoided jail and became a key player in the Seattle art scene. Manolides was a fan of the Funk movement, and his gallery became the center of a community of like-minded jewelers, artists (such as Roy De Forest and William T. Wiley), and ceramists (including Robert Arneson, Clayton Bailey, Michael T. Gardiner, and David Gilhooly).

Fig. 4.20

Fig. 4.18
Merrily Tompkins
Snatch Purse, 1975
Copper, enamel, leather, beaver fur, ermine tails, and coin purse
4 ½ × 4 × ⅜ inches
Collection of the Merrily Tompkins Estate, Ellensburg

Fig. 4.19
Merrily Tompkins
Thank You Hide, 1976
Pendant
Copper, brass, sterling silver, enamels, wood, leather, and found objects
15 ½ × 5 ¼ × ¾ inches
The Museum of Fine Arts, Houston, Helen Williams Drutt Collection, museum purchase funded by the Caroline Wiess Law Foundation, 2002.4130

Fig. 4.20
William T. Wiley
Thank You Hide, 1970–71
Wood, leather, ink, charcoal on cowhide, pickaxe, found objects, and watercolors
74 × 160 ½ inches
Des Moines Art Center, purchased with funds from the Coffin Fine Arts Trust; Nathan Emory Coffin Collection of the Des Moines Art Center, 1977.9

Manolides is the subject of Tompkins's pendant *Thank You Hide* (1976).^(Fig. 4.19) The title is borrowed from a William T. Wiley assemblage of the same name made in 1970–71, which Tompkins may have seen at the Manolides Gallery.^(Fig. 4.20) Wiley's work is an animal hide in the vague shape of America stretched between a shelf and the floor with the words "Thank You" stamped across it, and a collection of disparate items including a rusted spike, broken bottle, an arrowhead, the skin of an iguana, a piece of petrified wood with the words "Nomad is an island," and a shelf above the hide featuring bottles, branches, a jar labeled "Fresh Bait," a copy of the philosopher Friedrich Nietzsche's book *Beyond Good and Evil*, and a stick with fishing line attached to a pickaxe. The story is that Wiley was given Nietzsche's book, read an excerpt, and was grateful, hence the message on the hide, while the other objects relate to Wiley's childhood pastimes of fishing and searching for arrowheads.

Wiley sported a drooping mustache, faded denim clothes, and a black felt cowboy hat, and he had a wryly laconic and nonjudgmental attitude. With his homespun materials and processes, he seemed like an easygoing Zen frontiersman. He became a model for many West Coast artists who emulated his laid-back and life-is-art rusticity. In 1971 the New York art critic Hilton Kramer described his work as "Dude Ranch Dada."[194]

Merrily Tompkins also stamped "Thank You" on a stretched piece of leather in her necklace. Next to it is a likeness of Jim Manolides in metal, complete with mustache and cowboy hat, standing with a horse and holding a trophy—perhaps the one he received when his racehorse won the filly of the year. The object on the left is a token from a San Francisco trolley, and on the right is a New York City subway token. By pulling on one and then the other, the piece is primed, and then a final pull on the miniature record hanging below throws the pie in Manolides's face. It is a funny but serious piece—a comment on what Tompkins did not like about the dealer and her romantic relationship with him. As she recalled, "Jim was just kind of controlling and bossy and I didn't want to do that anymore. I didn't want to work with him anymore in that way."[195] She left the relationship, and then the gallery, and then the city of Seattle, all in 1973.

Tompkins and Cory were faithful friends and sometime lovers until Cory's death in 1994. "He taught me to trust my instincts and my own vision, as an artist and a person," remembers Tompkins.[196] When they were together, they cruised junk stores and flea markets, camped, rafted on local rivers, and took road trips.

Funk Jewelry 93

Fig. 4.21

At one point, she got a surprising letter from Cory proposing marriage, an offer she did not accept. Ultimately, their relationship lasted a long time but never involved a wedding ring. They just enjoyed working side by side, and were both carefree, a bit reckless, and had little regard for social expectations or rules.

Slow Boat (1976) is about Tompkins's relationship with Ken Cory.[Fig. 4.21] The pencil hanging at the base of the pendant is a nod to the Pencil Brothers, and Cory, the figure in the canoe, paddles upstream along a river under a full moon with a winged red Pegasus jumping on the shore. Additional symbols, including a barber's pole, a bowling pin, and a woman's shoe, complete the scene, along with the word "Ok" and a question mark. Like much of Tompkins's work, *Slow Boat* is filled with personal narratives and inside jokes. Given that Cory sometimes worked on Tompkins's jewelry, and enamel was his specialty, this piece might represent a portrait of him as a craftsperson and as Tompkins's friend and lover.

Funk offered a rich, deep vein for artists to mine in pursuing their individual inquiries into sex, everyday objects, nature, yin and yang, and anything else they might imagine. It granted them the freedom to do as they pleased but still feel part of a community of like-minded artists. This freedom was what the youth of America craved, and a Funk attitude was the path to achieving it for these Ellensburg jewelers.

Fig. 4.21
Merrily Tompkins
Slow Boat, 1976
Pendant
Enamel, sterling silver, wood, copper, brass, painted stone, pencil, ballpoint-pen spring, waxed lacing, Tiger Balm tin, and domino
16 ¾ × 4 ⅛ × 1 inches
Helen Williams Drutt Family Collection

THE POLITICS OF AMERICAN JEWELRY

Chapter Five

The Politics of American Jewelry

In 1967 and 1968, the jeweler Robert Ebendorf made a series of twelve assemblages designed to be hung on the wall rather than worn on the body. Incorporating found objects and weathered, beat-up materials, these square-format works were like a poetic tour of an America unsettled by the political and social battles being waged between the mainstream and the counterculture. Ebendorf mostly steered clear of directly citing contemporary politics, choosing instead to use old photographs from the nineteenth century and amusing if somewhat unsettling titles. In a panel named *Canned Heat*, a formal tintype portrait of three people posed in a photographer's studio is framed by the circular base of an old tin can rimmed with glass beads, and a border cut from weathered sheet metal held in place by copper nails that forms a crosshair pattern, as if the viewer were looking at the sitters through the scope of a rifle.

However, a sprinkling of politics did appear amid the deliberately awkward nostalgia and sentimentality. One of the twelve panels, *Population Explosion* (1967), would have been charged by the contemporary debate about the coming apocalypse caused by unchecked growth in the number of human beings occupying a finite planet.[Fig. 5.1] A child's face cast from a doll, mouth open, is set in the worn lid of a tin can, and surrounded by a border of glass beads, which is then framed by aluminum foil and sections of rusted metal. It is an unstable icon, possibly a warning, a hungry child of the future, mouth open in protest, or perhaps a memorial, a child from the last generation to enjoy a birthright that included a future unburdened by suffering and extinction.

Ebendorf was born in Topeka, Kansas, in 1938. At a young age, he discovered his interest in making things through watching his grandfather work at his tailor shop. Ebendorf's mother encouraged his interest and creativity as well as instilled in him the ability to observe the details of daily life closely. He received his BFA in metal and jewelry design in 1960 and his MFA in three-dimensional design in 1962 from the University of Kansas. One year later, he was awarded a Fulbright grant to study for a year in Norway. When he returned to the United States, he was thrust into the turmoil that convulsed American society in the mid-1960s. Teaching at Stetson University in Deland, Florida, he observed America's increasing involvement in the Vietnam War and followed the media coverage of the three civil rights marches from Selma to Montgomery in Alabama in 1965. Later, when Ebendorf was working at the University of Georgia in Athens in 1968, he encountered several disturbing signs of racism — whites-only signs on toilets, and African Americans who would step off the sidewalk into the gutter to allow white Americans to pass. In the summer months, he attended Black churches in the Georgia countryside, where he would sing, pray, and eat with the ministers and parishioners, sensing, as much as an outsider could, the pain of being Black in a society that did not grant equal rights to all citizens.[197]

Ebendorf was in Athens when Martin Luther King, Jr., was assassinated in Memphis, Tennessee, in April 1968. Like many Americans, he watched the funeral procession on television, but the assassination affected him personally. At the University of Georgia, he attended sit-ins and spoke about the events in his studio and classroom; however, he did not travel, as some did, to Washington, D.C., or Memphis to take part in protests and marches.

"Some people had their voice going to Washington and marching, some people took their voice to the pulpit, and some did it emotionally over coffee," he recalls.[198] Ebendorf did not engage in overt gestures of protest, but the series of twelve assemblages that he made in 1967 and 1968 registered his reaction to current events. One work, now lost, was called *Dig It Bigot*, and its combination of old photographs, war images, and military badges was his personal challenge to racist America in a time of angry protest against the Vietnam War.

Like J. Fred Woell and Don Tompkins, who had started exploring the potential of assemblage in their jewelry in the mid- to late 1960s, Ebendorf began incorporating a wide range of materials and objects into his work, including old tintype and daguerreotype photographs, tin cans, iron wire, and even eggshells. For him and his colleagues, this challenge to the precious materials and conventional techniques of jewelry also opened up their work to the contemporary issues of the time. In the late 1960s, Ebendorf assumed that he was the only one in the United States working with assemblage and found objects in his jewelry. He happily discovered this was not true when he met J. Fred Woell at the first conference and exhibition of the Society of North American Goldsmiths (SNAG) in 1970. Ebendorf recalls sensing that Woell was someone who heard the same music

Fig. 5.1
Robert Ebendorf
Population Explosion, 1967
Wall piece
Perforated steel, aluminum foil, lid to a can, glass beads, cast metal, nails, and brads, mounted on wood
Frame: 12 ⅝ × 12 ⅝ × 1 ¼ inches
Georgia Museum of Art, University of Georgia, gift of Ron Porter and Joe Price, GMOA 2019.291

Fig. 5.1

as he did.[199] One year later, he left the University of Georgia to teach at the State University of New York in New Paltz. Whereas Woell continued to make political references in his jewelry, the same was not true for Ebendorf. He worked with alternative materials and mixed media to explore their potential for aesthetic juxtapositions rather than their ability to present specific narratives about political and social issues. With their specific political intentions, *Population Explosion* and *Dig It Bigot* remain rare examples of this kind of engagement in his jewelry.

In October 1967, a protest march against the Vietnam War took place in Washington, D.C. Among the fifty thousand demonstrators were activist academics and students, housewives, doctors, and the famous author Norman Mailer, as well as a group of witches, warlocks, holy men, seers, prophets, mystics, saints, sorcerers, shamans, troubadours, minstrels, bards, roadmen, and madmen (in the words of the *East Village Other* underground newspaper). While there were plenty of people picketing, having sit-downs, giving speeches, and marching, the mystics and magicians cast spells against what they perceived as the demon-controlled Pentagon, the distinctively shaped headquarters of the Department of Defense, trying to levitate the building off the ground.[200] The military police protecting the Pentagon had not been given instructions on how to deal with these hippies dressed as witches, wizards, and jesters, dancing ecstatically to the psychedelic music of The Fugs, who were themselves performing in the costumes of Hindu gurus.[201]

The jeweler Thomas Mann, who participated in this march, remembers,

> For the first time in my young life I witnessed, heard and then participated in an otherworldly highly charged emotional spiritual chanting, that apparently was the psychic energy that would affect the levitation. Smoke was in the air everywhere, joints were being passed…. Besides the pot, psychedelics were being passed around as well, so the vibe in the crowd was an ecstatic one. At some point in the day I sat in on a political planning session where it was obvious that this event wasn't a one-off thing but the beginning of a movement. I signed up then and there, in my mind and heart, vowed to participate, facilitate and activate whatever I could in opposition to the Vietnam War…. While the physical levitation of the Pentagon failed, it levitated the movement and me in a dramatic way.[202]

Mann was a conscientious objector, attending school at East Stroudsburg University in Pennsylvania, about four-and-a-half hours outside of Washington, D.C. He was involved with a student group that had previously organized marches in the country's capital, where they and other protesters had been arrested two or three times, taken to football stadiums, and detained for a few hours.

More than anything else, the Vietnam War cast a terrible shadow over American society in the late 1960s and early 1970s. The history of American military involvement in Southeast Asia went back to the mid-twentieth century, when Vietnamese nationalist movements began demanding self-government and the overthrow of French colonialism. The most prominent and successful of these groups was the Viet Minh organization, led by the Communist Ho Chi Minh. In 1945 he led his forces in a victorious campaign to take control of the capital, Hanoi, and declared Vietnam independent of French control. The French did not agree, and after the disruption of World War II, they drove the Communists into North Vietnam. Ho Chi Minh appealed to the United States for help, but the Americans, concerned about the threat of Communism, sided with the French. Eventually, in 1954, the Vietnamese resistance movement defeated its French enemies, and a peace settlement divided the country into North Vietnam, controlled by Ho Chi Minh, and South Vietnam, controlled by a French-backed head of state.

This division was supposed to be temporary, with free elections to reunite Vietnam planned for 1956. However, the Cold War policy of the United States led it to support the anti-Communist politician Ngo Dinh Diem, and the elections were canceled. The resistance was led by Ho Chi Minh and the National Liberation Front, which became known as the Vietcong. President John F. Kennedy sent American military advisors to Vietnam in 1962 to train the South Vietnamese army. By the end of 1966, more than four hundred thousand American troops were in Vietnam, due to President Lyndon Johnson's escalation of the war.

In the Tet Offensive in 1968, the Vietcong attacked nearly thirty American targets in South Vietnam, in what was widely viewed as a defeat for the United States. In the same year, the My Lai massacre occurred, in which American soldiers killed hundreds of unarmed Vietnamese civilians. Support for the war in the United States plummeted. President Richard Nixon, who had replaced Johnson in 1969, argued that a "silent majority" of Americans supported the war, and while he withdrew some troops, he also illegally bombed Vietcong bases in Cambodia and Laos. Diplomatic maneuvering with China and the Soviet Union in 1972 led to a cease-fire in January 1973, with the last American combat personnel leaving Vietnam in March of that year. The South Vietnamese capital of Saigon fell to the North Vietnamese in April 1975, and the country was reunited as the Socialist Republic of Vietnam.

For many American jewelers like Thomas Mann, the Vietnam War was a personal issue. Young men were at risk of being drafted to serve in a war with a high casualty rate. Many were skeptical of the U.S. government, feeling that they were not receiving truthful information about the extent of the war and the country's involvement. Like other Americans, jewelers found ways to express their feelings—and opposition—sometimes in explicit and public ways. In February 1966, Barry Merritt helped fund and added his signature to an advertisement in Rochester's *Democrat and Chronicle* newspaper that protested the U.S. involvement in the Vietnam War. "While we hold differing opinions about America's role in Vietnam, we abhor the tragic loss of American and Vietnamese lives," the text read. "We fear the conflict will result in a massive ground war in Asia or to a worldwide nuclear holocaust. Therefore, we urge our government, acting in cooperation with the United Nations, to persevere

Fig. 5.2

in seeking a cease-fire and negotiations leading toward a just and equitable settlement acceptable to the people of Viet Nam."[203] Merritt's feelings about the war did not necessarily find their way into his jewelry practice, but he did feel the need to register his opposition as part of a growing and increasingly angry movement.

In 1968 or 1969, the artist Leslie LePere, who went on to collaborate with the jeweler Ken Cory as part of the Pencil Brothers, was asked by an anti-war group to paint a protest billboard that was erected on the highway between Pullman, Washington, where LePere was attending art school at Washington State University, and Moscow, Idaho, home of the University of Idaho. Created in sections and put up by the sign company, the billboard had the message "Bullets and junk kill—work for peace."[204] (Fig. 5.2)

The jeweler David LaPlantz was also caught up in events surrounding the Vietnam War. On April 30, 1970, the night that President Nixon gave a speech about the United States' involvement in Cambodia, LaPlantz was at Southern Illinois University in Carbondale, attending a blacksmithing conference organized by L. Brent Kington. Afraid that the campus would erupt with riots and protests, Kington urged the conference members to leave town. Instead, they hunkered down in the wooded area where the blacksmithing conference was being held to wait things out. The next day, while on campus, they saw students being chased and questioned by what LaPlantz describes as "official looking people." Upon his return to Colorado State University in Fort Collins, where he taught in the metals department, one of the oldest buildings on campus was set on fire, and the students organized a boycott of their classes. "It really was painful for me," recalls LaPlantz, "so I said, okay folks don't come to class if you don't want to, I get it, but I have to be here for those people that are not going to join you. I would like to join you but I'm split. I have a responsibility for the studio."[205]

For some American jewelers, personal beliefs led to personal action, but the scale of opposition to the war meant that almost all jewelers felt its effects in their own lives, whether or not they were themselves active protesters. A much smaller number of American jewelers took up the theme of the Vietnam War in their jewelry, producing their own material protests about the war and the social and political dynamics that fed the military-industrial complex.

Fig. 5.2
Leslie LePere
Billboard along the highway between Pullman, Washington, and Moscow, Idaho, 1970, sponsored by The Peace and Justice Organization of the Palouse

Fig. 5.3

Fig. 5.3
Richard Mawdsley
The Tank, 1970
Pendant
Sterling silver and enamel
3 ¾ × 2 ½ inches
Location unknown

Fig. 5.4
Irving Petlin, Jon Hendricks, and Frazer Dougherty
Q. And babies? A. And babies., 1970
Offset lithography on paper
Photograph by Ronald L. Haeberle
Published by the Artists' Poster Committee of the Art Workers Coalition, New York City.
Courtesy Smithsonian American Art Museum, gift of Jon Hendricks

In 1970 the jeweler Richard Mawdsley completed a sterling silver and enamel pendant called *The Tank*. (Fig. 5.3) The head of President Richard Nixon pokes out of the hatch on top of a whimsical and elaborately decorated tank, festooned with guns and machine parts. Nixon had narrowly beaten the democratic candidate Hubert Humphrey in the November 1968 elections, and although he had campaigned on a promise of bringing "peace with honor" in Vietnam by ending the draft and reducing the number of American troops in Southeast Asia, he in fact presided over an increase in military forces and authorized the bombing of North Vietnamese sanctuaries in Cambodia. His notorious public address in November 1969 appealed to the "silent majority" of Americans who were not out marching in the streets to support America's actions in Vietnam, claiming, "North Vietnam cannot defeat or humiliate the United States. Only Americans can do that."

The same month, news broke of the My Lai massacre from the year before, in which American soldiers had invaded two small settlements in the village of Son My in South Vietnam, killing hundreds of unarmed Vietnamese civilians, mostly women, children, and old men, raping some of the women before they were killed and mutilating some of the bodies. Many Americans were outraged by the atrocity, and it contributed to the growing opposition to the war. The Art Workers' Coalition turned a photograph of some of the bodies into a poster, overprinting it in red with the words "Q. And babies? A. And babies." (Fig. 5.4) These words came from a televised interview by Mike Wallace with an American soldier, Paul Meadlo, who had been part of the killing and who had acknowledged that they had slaughtered infants. Horrified Americans watched as a visibly stunned Wallace asked, "And babies?" "And babies," confirmed Meadlo. Under massive public pressure as opposition to the war grew stronger, President Nixon announced in May 1970 that American troops would be withdrawn from Cambodia, and the gradual withdrawal of soldiers from South Vietnam got underway. In Mawdsley's pendant, Nixon faces the viewer head on, but the tank points off to the left, still on track to the war despite the President's attention being elsewhere.

Born in 1945, Mawdsley grew up in Wichita, Kansas, but also spent a lot of time at his grandparents' farm in the rural part of that state. He first earned a teaching degree from Kansas State Teaching College (now Emporia State University) in 1967 before studying metalsmithing with Carlyle Smith at the University of Kansas in Lawrence (KU). While at KU, Mawdsley's strongest influences were the jewelers L. Brent Kington, whom he had met at an American Craft Council (ACC) conference, John Paul Miller, who juried the annual Kansas Designer Craftsman show in Mawdsley's first year, and J. Fred Woell, whose narrative jewelry he had seen in the pages of *Craft Horizons*. For Mawdsley, each brought something useful: Kington legitimized a Baroque attitude to contemporary expression, Miller showed how the classical techniques of ornament could find a home in contemporary jewelry, and Woell demonstrated the exciting potential of narrative jewelry.[206] From these three sources—an unlikely combination—Mawdsley fashioned a distinctive approach to contemporary jewelry, which could, when required, address political issues.

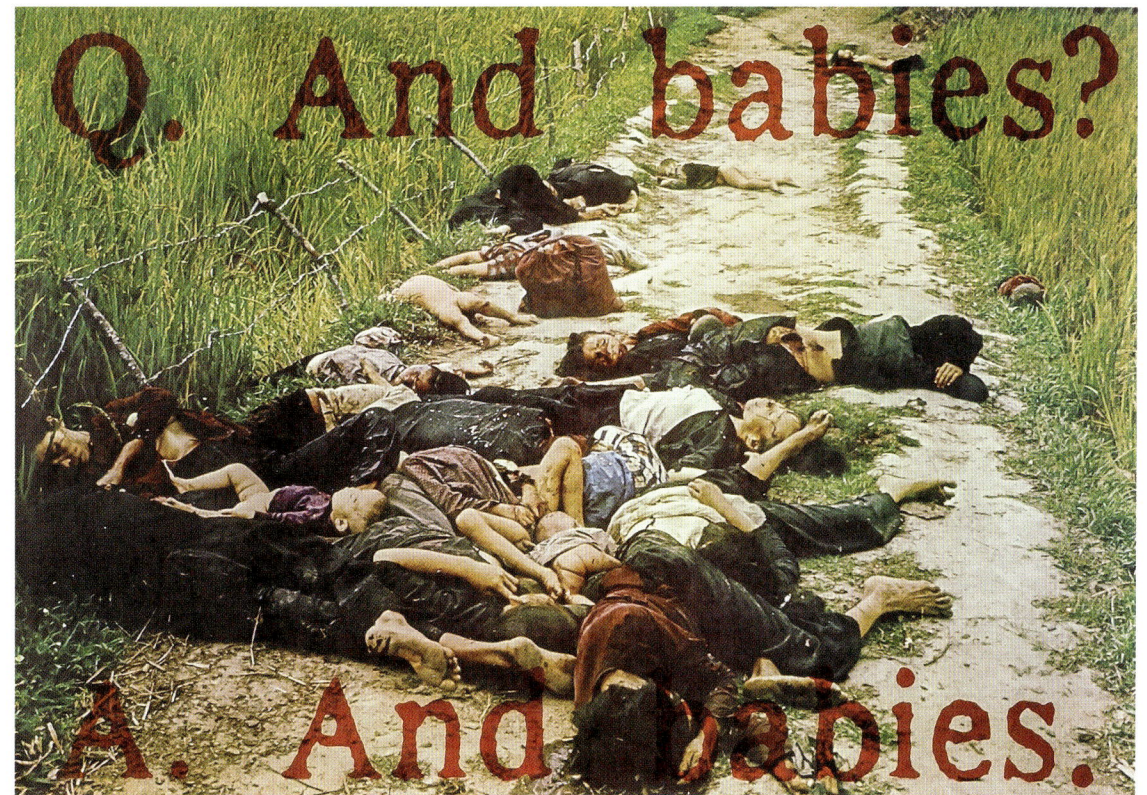

Fig. 5.4

While living in Emporia, and then Lawrence, Mawdsley was not personally involved in the protests and other social movements of the late 1960s. He recalls that, as a graduate student on the sprawling KU campus, "I was up in my little cubbyhole with my nose to the grindstone, I wasn't very involved. I don't remember any campus demonstrations, anything at all. Every evening I went down to the campus student center, ate supper for 50 cents, and watched Walter Cronkite, and that was my exposure to the outside world."[207] Yet even for a busy student, it was impossible not to be affected by some of the events of the time, like the assassinations of Martin Luther King, Jr., and Robert Kennedy, and the increasing intensity of protests against the American involvement in the Vietnam War. The latter was personal, since Mawdsley was young enough to be eligible for the draft, but he was never at great risk of being called up. At KU, he taught jewelry classes to occupational therapy students so that they could, in turn, teach these skills to returning soldiers. Letters from professors at KU to the draft board emphasizing his important contribution to the war effort helped him avoid conscription. In 1969 he took a job teaching at Illinois State University in Normal. Two years later, he received a draft number beginning with 150, and was told that it was highly unlikely to get drafted with a number above 120. Yet for all the promises of safety, it was still a worry.[208]

Mawdsley taught at Illinois State University until 1978, and the years that he spent there were important in developing his professional practice as a jeweler. He became involved with SNAG, attending its first conference in St. Paul, Minnesota, in 1970 and showing four works in the *Goldsmith '70* exhibition. The conference and exhibition were pivotal moments for him, exposing his jewelry to a wider audience of peers and introducing him to leading American jewelers, academics, curators, and tastemakers such as curator Paul Smith, and jewelers Olaf Skoogfors and Stanley Lechtzin.

Mawdsley was exploring the use of hand-cut metal tubing, which he assembled into recognizable forms and embellished. As a child, he had grown up on a farm, surrounded by machines of different kinds and the technology associated with agriculture. Mawdsley reimagined these machines as an adult and remade them in sterling silver, conjuring a memory of an American golden age, grounded in a fanciful version of the Midwest's regional past. Surprisingly, this approach proved to be adaptable to contemporary issues. In 1968 Mawdsley began work on the *War Protest* series, which was his artistic response to the Vietnam War. This series, which he continued into the mid-1970s, was very loosely defined, with some pieces being retroactively assigned to it. Its antecedents can be traced to an undergraduate work that he made called *Bottling Machine* from 1966, a pendant featuring a flying machine. Mawdsley identifies it as the start of an "anti-establishment, anti-industrial-military complex" mood in his jewelry.[209] The idea of the "industrial-military complex" first emerged in 1961 when the outgoing President, Dwight D. Eisenhower, warned the American people in a televised address that they needed to be aware of the growing power of a huge military establishment and a large arms industry. Although the alliance between military and industrial leaders was necessary to protect the United States against the Cold

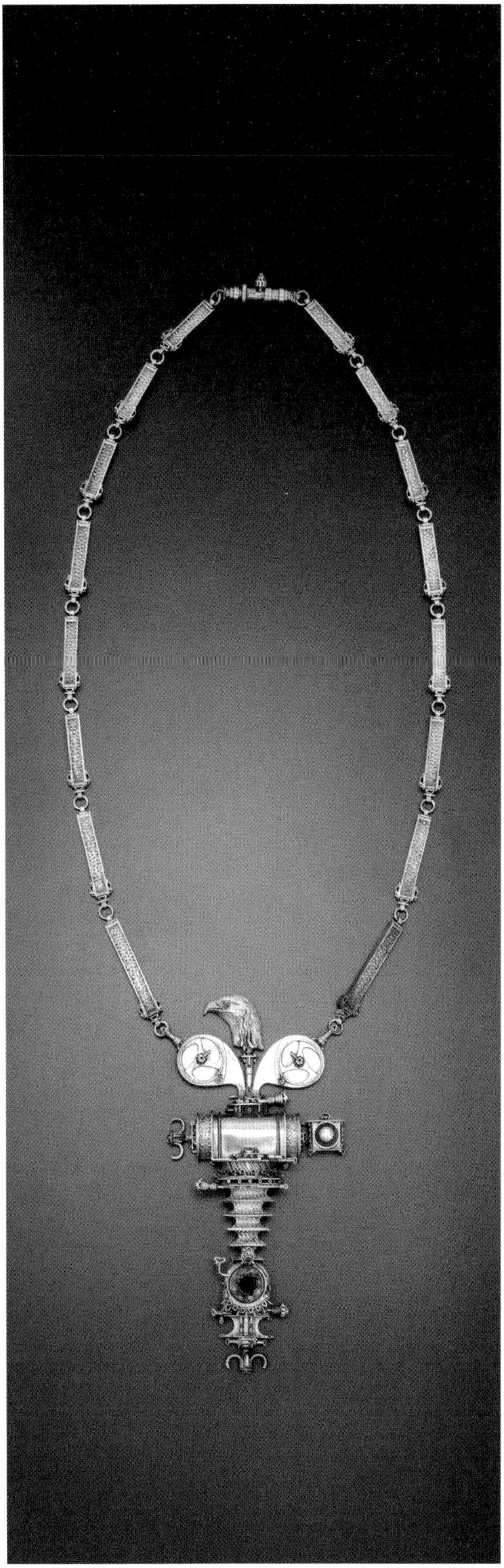

Fig. 5.5

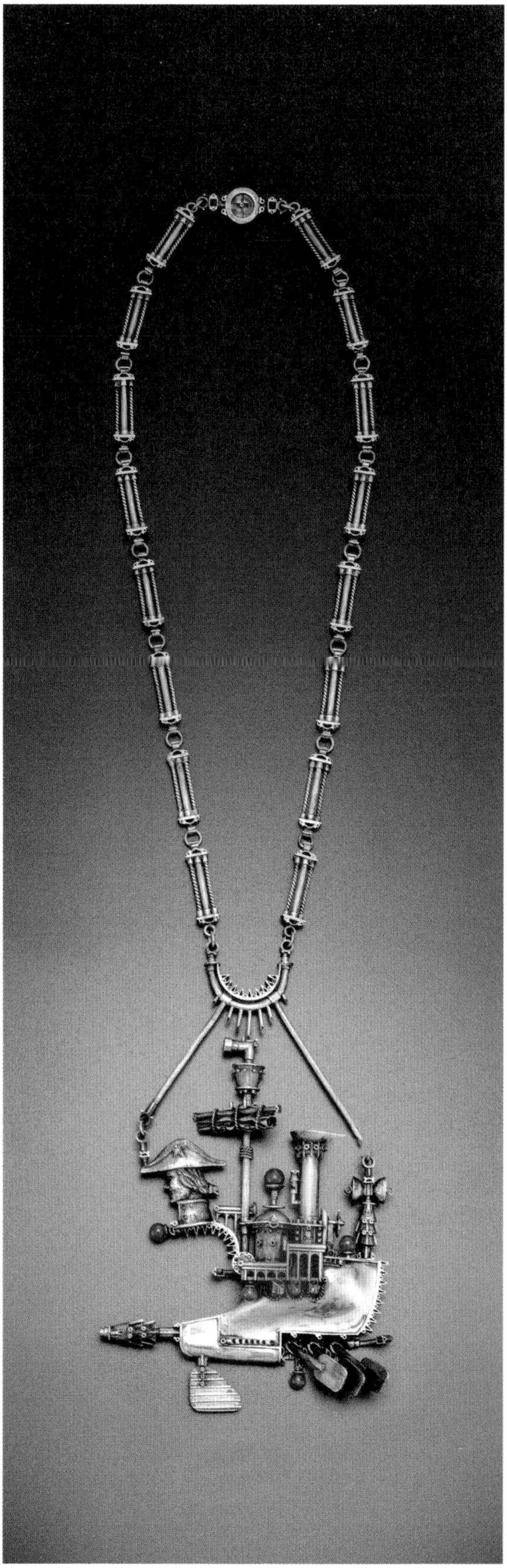

Fig. 5.6

104

War threats, it was vulnerable to abuse. As the President said in his farewell speech to the American people, "Only an alert and knowledgeable citizenry can compel the proper meshing of the huge industrial and military machinery of defense with our peaceful methods and goals, so that security and liberty may prosper together."

Mawdsley added to his *War Protest* series in 1971 with a pendant called *Camera*.(Fig. 5.5) The elaborate movie camera in this work is based on an old camera in his grandparents' possession, and it represents the important role that journalists, photographers, and filmmakers played in disseminating the realities of the Vietnam War. Like the best of Mawdsley's jewelry, *Camera* is intensely detailed with intricately crafted elements created from sterling silver tubing, including two film reels, a 35mm film canister, the head of a shutter release, a framing window, bellows, and a large lens, all crowned by the head of a bald eagle, a symbol of American freedom, strength, and independence.

The year that Mawdsley made this pendant, the organization Vietnam Veterans Against the War, which had been founded in 1967, sponsored a media event in Detroit called the Winter Soldier Investigation. In late January and early February, more than a hundred members of the American military publicly testified to war crimes they had committed or witnessed in Vietnam between 1963 and 1970. In March, Lieutenant William Calley was convicted and sentenced to life in prison for his role in the My Lai massacre; many Americans were appalled by the severity of the sentence, while others were appalled that only one member of the American military was held accountable for the atrocity. In April, Vietnam Veterans Against the War staged a protest in Washington, D.C., which concluded with more than eight hundred veterans throwing their medals over the barricades that had been erected to keep protesters off the steps of the U.S. Capitol. In June, the *New York Times* and other newspapers began publishing the so-called Pentagon Papers, a study prepared by the American government about its decisions in Vietnam that revealed that American presidents had been manipulating the public and the U.S. Congress through misrepresentation and secrecy.

Another pendant that Mawdsley made in 1971, *The Pequod*, draws on Herman Melville's 1851 novel *Moby-Dick* (as experienced through the 1956 Gregory Peck film) to comment on America's equally quixotic and ultimately destructive pursuit of the specter of Communism.(Fig. 5.6) Captain Ahab, master of the whaling vessel Pequod, is consumed by an obsession to kill the giant white sperm whale known as Moby Dick; he risks and loses everything in the chase. That subject must have seemed suggestive to Americans who questioned the growing loss of life in the Vietnam War.

In 1970 there was a notable surge in anti-war activity in the United States, and in the violence of the government's response. The jeweler Mary Ann Scherr was at Kent State University on May 4, 1970, when the Ohio State National Guard opened fire on unarmed students who were protesting the Vietnam War's escalation to include the invasion of Cambodia, a neutral country. Four students were killed and nine were wounded. During the unrest, the university's metals studio, which was about 150 yards away from the hill where the National Guard troops shot the students, had been closed because of the threat of violence. "The students revolting had threatened to bomb the metals studio because each bench in the studio was equipped with live gas jets that could torch the school as a bomb," she recalled in 2001. "The faculty was sympathetic, ambivalent, frightened—along with the students. Those days were very unique: students were strong, independent, power-filled with a different mind-set for personal expression. They responded to the violence of the war through a single voice, which penetrated their ability to possess a personal opinion about their art and their lives."[210]

The Kent State massacre, as it became known in some circles, received national coverage and had an impact on public opinion about the rightness of America's involvement in the Vietnam War. The folk-rock group Crosby, Stills, Nash and Young released a song called "Ohio" just a few weeks later, using lyrics that Neil Young had written after seeing photos of the shootings in *Life* magazine: "Gotta get down to it / Soldiers are cutting us down / What if you knew her / And found her dead on the ground / How can you run when you know?"[211]

The Kent State massacre is the subject of Bruce Metcalf's *Worms from Mars Invade an Authentic New England Village & Are Attacked by the National Guard*, which he made the following year in 1971.(Fig. 5.7) It is not a piece of jewelry that can be worn but something more akin to the world of children's toys or miniatures and model making. The members of the National Guard in Metcalf's work are in fact hand-painted lead figures, a contemporary version of miniature soldiers. Red-painted lead worms represent their enemy.

Fig. 5.5
Richard Mawdsley
Camera, 1971
Pendant
Sterling silver, amethyst, and pearl
14 ½ × 2 ½ × ½ inches
The Museum of Fine Arts, Houston,
Helen Williams Drutt Collection,
museum purchase funded by
the Morgan Foundation in honor
of Catherine Asher Morgan,
2002.3950

Fig. 5.6
Richard Mawdsley
The Pequod, 1971
Pendant
Sterling silver, green onyx, and
carnelian
18 × 3 × ¾ inches
The Museum of Fine Arts, Houston,
Helen Williams Drutt Collection,
museum purchase funded by the
estate of Jack T. McCann,
2002.3951

Fig. 5.7

Metcalf's work is an anti-war statement, and it can be interpreted quite directly in terms of current events: the worms stand for the Vietnam protesters against whom the National Guard is being deployed, and the figures can be arranged so they rush to engage one another. However, the satire is what makes this work so compelling. The National Guard soldiers are caricatures, with gaping mouths and helmets slipping over their eyes. The invaders are worms with impressive teeth. The conflict takes place in a sentimental, nostalgic representation of an American town. Metcalf wittily undercuts this cliché's power with his inclusion of, among other buildings, an outhouse constructed from cardboard with lithograph-printed decoration.

All of the visual and conceptual elements that Metcalf deploys in *Worms from Mars* are carefully selected for their satirical sharpness. Worms are a sign that something is rotten at the core, and conservative rhetoric at the time worked hard to evoke the sense of crisis in civic life and patriotism, important values being eaten away by the destabilizing ideas of peaceniks and protesters insinuating themselves into the national conversation. "Worm" is an abusive term for a weak or despicable person, and worms invading an "authentic" New England village show the rot in the body politic, which both protesters and the forces controlling the National Guard believed to be true; what was rotting, and who was responsible, was where the crucial differences lay.

Metcalf was born in Amherst, Massachusetts, in 1949, and grew up there. This rural, New England town was filled with historical buildings and the sophisticated buzz of ideas and culture generated by professors and students at its three universities: the University of Massachusetts at Amherst, Amherst College, and Hampshire College. Metcalf's father, who had an MBA from Harvard University, worked in the insurance industry, and his mother was a homemaker; both were Republicans, and they supported the American War in Vietnam. Metcalf enrolled at Syracuse University in upstate New York in 1967, just a few years after Don Tompkins had studied there. He started out as a liberal arts major, but switched to architecture in 1968, and then to jewelry in 1970.

Metcalf arrived at Syracuse just as the counterculture was taking off, and he quickly became a hippie, joining a vocal and visible minority of students, growing his hair long, wearing vibrantly colored pants and a beaded necklace.[(Fig. 5.8)] He smoked dope for the first time at the end of his freshman year, and then experimented with LSD and mushrooms. In 1968, the year that Metcalf should have been attending his architecture classes, he was taking part in an idealistic movement that saw drugs as a way to expand one's consciousness. Metcalf listened to the Beatles' trippy album *Sgt. Pepper's Lonely Hearts Club Band* and to the psychedelic guru Timothy Leary, who preached the gospel of LSD. Drugs were a way to achieve what Mario Savio, an activist and member of the Berkeley Free Speech Movement, called a dedication to the life of the imagination.[212]

In 1971, the year he made *Worms from Mars*, Metcalf was drawing cartoons for the student newspaper in his spare time.(Fig. 5.9) Unlike most ambitious jewelers in the late 1960s and early 1970s, who looked to fine art and made small sculptures as a way to stretch the borders of contemporary jewelry, Metcalf was busy mining the possibilities of model making, Edwardian toys, and cartooning. His work did not conform to the expectations of art school: it was too whimsical and humorous, too narrative and symbolic, too small, and made from non-precious materials. He was a populist, keen to make work that would communicate with people. Cartoons were all about communication, lubricated by humor, and they provided a vehicle for grappling with compelling issues in the wider culture.[213]

As Metcalf recalls, it was a heated moment in the United States, especially when it came to the question of the Vietnam War. Society was polarized into pro- and anti-war camps, and the militarization of domestic politics saw the establishment seeking to demonize anti-war protestors as unpatriotic. President Richard Nixon consolidated power through the adroit use of paranoia; a "red-baiter" from his early days as a politician, he tried to undermine resistance to the Vietnam War by associating those who opposed it with the threat of Communism and Socialism. Metcalf's *Worms from Mars* was an attempt to say something about this confusing and bruising combination of paranoia, war, and militarization.[214]

Fig. 5.9

Fig. 5.8

Fig. 5.7
Bruce Metcalf
Worms from Mars Invade an Authentic New England Village & Are Attacked by the National Guard, 1971
Painted lead and galvanized steel, lithograph on cardboard
Height of figures: 1½ inches
Collection of the artist

Fig. 5.8
Bruce Metcalf, c. 1975
Collection of the artist

Fig. 5.9
Bruce Metcalf
Waldo the Paranoid Parakeet, 1971
Ink on paper
Approx. 4 × 8 inches
Collection of the artist

The Politics of American Jewelry

Metcalf also made a wearable version of *Worms from Mars*, in the form of epaulets, ornamental elements worn on the shoulders of formal military dress.(Fig. 5.10) In each, three members of the National Guard stride into battle, proudly holding aloft the Stars and Stripes. The military's ludicrous love of pomp and circumstance is heightened in this work, just as Metcalf intended.

Military medals figure prominently in the jewelry of Barry Merritt. He made *Buffalo Bill Badge* (1970) during a particularly violent time in anti-war protest and government response.(Fig. 5.11) Merritt placed a photograph of William Frederick "Buffalo Bill" Cody (1846–1917) in a forged, silver buffalo's head followed by the text "Pistol-D," the American flag, and a cast "Medal of Honor" with a target with bullet holes at its center. Buffalo Bill was still considered an American legend at the time that Merritt created this brooch. He was celebrated as a scout for the army during the American Civil War as well as for his marksmanship and showmanship, both of which were on display in his theatrical extravaganza Buffalo Bill's Wild West, which toured the United States and Europe in the 1880s. Precisely why Merritt chose Buffalo Bill to highlight as a symbol of American heroism at the time of the Vietnam War is unknown, but given that he had a strong anti-war position, he likely wanted to highlight the growing contrast between America's past greatness and its less heroic present. Merritt was among a number of American jewelers who created "medals" in the 1960s and early 1970s, taking the military honor as a starting point for commentary on the seriousness or satirical nature of war, depending on an artist's stance on Vietnam.

Fig. 5.10

Fig. 5.10
Bruce Metcalf
Epaulets, 1971
Painted lead and galvanized steel, leather
Approx. 2¼ × 3¼ inches
Collection of the artist

Fig. 5.11
Barry Merritt
Buffalo Bill Badge, 1970
Silver, bronze, and ivory
Location unknown

Fig. 5.11

Many Americans loved to hate President Nixon, and J. Fred Woell, Don Tompkins, and Jim Cotter all took him on in their jewelry in the early 1970s. The idea for Woell's sculpture of Nixon, made in 1970,(Fig. 5.12) was born one rainy day in Michigan when Woell spotted a bumper sticker for Nixon upside down in the gutter. Noxin, it read. "Good title!" he exclaimed.²¹⁵ The sculpture took the form of a giant mask with peephole eyes; the viewer would be able to see right through "Tricky Dicky," the derogatory nickname for Nixon. Woell first modeled the mask in plasticine and then cast it in epoxy. He included various newsprint photographs of Nixon's activities in the epoxy, among them his escalation of the Vietnam War and his tepid response to the problem of desegregation in the American South. The obscured images create the creepy five-o'clock shadow on the President's chin, jaw, and cheeks. His broad grin is augmented by star-spangled teeth, as if Nixon had been chewing on the American flag and forgot to floss.

In 1972 Joan Mondale included Woell's *Noxin* in her book *Politics in Art*. Mondale was affectionately known as "Joan of Art" because of her vigorous and enthusiastic promotion of art and craft; she was also married to the Democratic politician Walter Mondale, who, at the time she wrote her book, was a U.S. Senator and became Vice President of the United States in 1977. Considering her political affiliations, Mondale was no doubt sympathetic to the satire in Woell's portrait of Nixon, yet she managed to adroitly present the sculpture in terms that might even have proved acceptable to a Republican. Beginning with a quote by Woell that describes everyone as a politician, masking our true selves to protect those around us, and striving to be something bigger and better than our private selves, Mondale proclaimed, "The job of being President of the United States is bigger than any one man." Acknowledging that Woell has made his own comments about President Nixon in the work, she suggests that the photographs under the surface of the figure's skin "depict important moments in Nixon's political career," while the map of America with a question mark imprinted on his forehead suggests "the problems he faces as President." Mondale ends on a high note: "The artist tries to point out in this portrait that the mask of the politician is not the politician's alone. The demands of his office alter and color his whole being."²¹⁶ Mondale's eliding of the political commentary, in a book published while Nixon was seeking a second term, was similar to the inventive ways that the owner of the Birmingham Gallery, where the sculpture was first exhibited, dealt with the potentially offensive details. Explaining the American flag and question mark prominently displayed on Nixon's forehead, the dealer jauntily asked his very Republican audience, "Who else would have more on his mind about the United States than the President?"²¹⁷

Don Tompkins's *Nixon (Bring Us Together)*, made in the early 1970s as part of his *Commemorative Medals* series, conflates the President with Mickey Mouse, standing with a grin on his face and his arms wide open, ready to receive the love of everyone who visits the

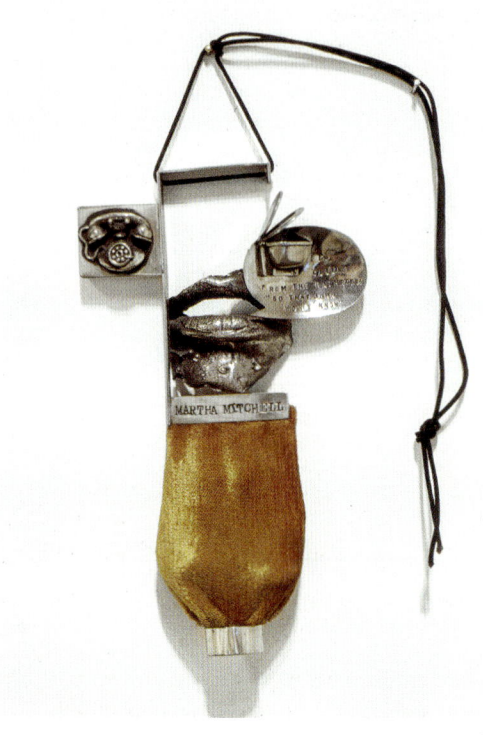

Fig. 5.12

Fig. 5.12
J. Fred Woell
Noxin, 1970
Epoxy
21 × 11 × 13 inches
Honolulu Museum of Art

Fig. 5.15
Don Tompkins
Martha Mitchell, 1972
Pendant
Sterling silver, brass, velvet, and toy noisemaker
Collection of the Tompkins family

Fig. 5.15

Fig. 5.13

Fig. 5.14

Magic Kingdom.(Fig. 5.13) The Disney character often appeared on blotter acid (LSD tabs), which were a sure route to a chemically induced magical kingdom. His open-armed gesture resembles the one shown in a famous photograph of Mary Ann Vecchio kneeling near the dead body of Jeffrey Miller, a student at Kent State, with a terrified expression on her face.(Fig. 5.14) In this manner, Tompkins suggests that grief will accompany Nixon's work of national unity. Whereas Mickey, originally a loveable rogue, eventually became a nice guy, for many Americans Nixon was no nice guy, neither honest nor a hero. Through this medal, Tompkins implies that Nixon's presidency is a "Mickey Mouse" operation. For anyone living in the early 1970s, the idea that Nixon was the man to bring Americans together would have seemed laughable, especially since he thrived on the divide-and-conquer tactics that helped him get reelected to the presidency in 1972. The musician Frank Zappa conveyed this aspect of the President directly in his 1974 song "Son of Orange County": "And in your dreams/You can see yourself/As a prophet/Saving the world/The words from your lips /(I AM NOT A CROOK)/I just can't believe you are such/A fool."[218]

Tompkins again addressed the theme of Nixon in his pendant *Martha Mitchell* (1972).(Fig. 5.15) The subject was the wife of Attorney General John Mitchell, who was also the head of the Committee to Re-elect the President, also known by the acronym CREEP. Martha Mitchell was an outspoken socialite who was known as "Martha the Mouth" and the "Mouth of the South" because of her frank, uncensored, and highly public comments in favor of Republican causes.

When her husband became caught up in the growing Watergate scandal, Martha took on a starring role. The scandal erupted in June 1972 when five Republican burglars broke into the Democratic National Committee headquarters in the Watergate office complex in Washington, D.C. As the story broke in the media, Martha's husband left her with a security detail that was intended to keep her away from the television and the phone. He did not want her to figure out that one of the burglars was James McCord, Jr., a man she knew, and start investigating the situation. What followed was a tawdry drama. On one occasion, Martha was speaking on the phone with a reporter when her security detail pulled the cord out of the wall. On another occasion, she was kidnapped by her security detail in a California hotel room and sedated against her will. Later, in 1977, Nixon blamed Martha for distracting her husband during the events of Watergate, to the point where he was unable to concentrate on the problem and contain the situation. As he told the journalist David Frost, "If it hadn't been for Martha Mitchell, there'd have been no Watergate."

In Tompkins's pendant, a pair of lips and chin with "Martha Mitchell" stamped underneath it are accompanied by a cast toy telephone, a speech bubble with an open toilet attached to it, stamped words, and a noisemaker. Tompkins makes clear what he thought about his subject and the nature of what came out of her mouth. Critics appreciated his topicality. One review published in *Craft Horizons* in 1973 commented, "Most amusing was the satiric comment on Martha Mitchell, clearly stating the case with castings in silver, from telephone, gabbing mouth to toilet bowl."[219]

Fig. 5.13
Don Tompkins
Nixon (Bring Us Together), c. 1970
Pendant
Sterling silver, brass, synthetic stone, and found photograph
⅝ × 4¾ × ⅝ inches
Collection of the Tompkins family

Fig. 5.14
John Filo
Mary Ann Vecchio (kneeling) with the body of Jeffrey Miller, May 4, 1970
Black-and-white photograph

Another jeweler who regularly invoked Nixon during the period was Jim Cotter. In 1973 Cotter was invited to have a solo exhibition at a gallery in Oklahoma City featuring his jewelry and mixed-media objects. Some of the works addressed his concerns about the economic impact of the changing nature of farming and the plight of Native Americans, but the majority was politically oriented. One such work is *Tears on My Pillow*, a fabric pillow embroidered with "Pat + Dick" that comments on the relationship between the President and his wife during the Watergate scandal, which ultimately ended in August 1974, when impeachment proceedings led to Nixon's resignation from office.(Fig. 5.16) Prior to his resignation, investigations had uncovered a series of illegal activities undertaken by members of the Nixon administration that included surveillance on political enemies and activist groups. Publicly, Pat Nixon stoically stood by her husband, but Cotter's pillow suggests an alternative viewpoint, one that imagines her tears each night after learning about her husband's transgressions.

Although Cotter received no formal art education in the small town in Iowa in which he grew up, his love of hot rods and the *Rat Fink* comics led him to learn how to illustrate, and he made graphic T-shirts and sign paintings on trucks and stock cars. These early interests, combined with practical, hands-on skills learned at Boy Scouts, fueled his interest in making things. When Cotter was recruited to play football in 1963 at Wayne State College in Nebraska, his college advisor encouraged him to take a sculpture class. Cotter doubted his abilities but soon became hooked on art, ultimately receiving his degree in art education and industrial arts.[220]

During the height of the Vietnam War, Cotter attended protests at Wayne State. He had conflicted feelings, however, because his father was a war hero who had been wounded three times in World War II. "In the small town I grew up in, hippies and protests, that wasn't allowed," Cotter recalls. "When you came home, you put on a different face so to speak."[221]

Cotter's path to becoming a jeweler was circuitous and full of chance encounters.(Fig. 5.17) In 1968 Cotter had been on his way to study at the Instituto Allende in San Miguel de Allende, Mexico, when he stopped in Boulder, Colorado. There, he met a woman and ended up staying; he also enrolled in a two-week casting class offered at the University of Colorado with Arthur Pennington. Later that year, he moved to Central City, Colorado. When a local gallery owner discovered that he made jewelry and saw his pieces, she asked if he would like to show his jewelry and work in the gallery.[222] At this point, Cotter was already using found materials and melting change for silver and soup cans for other metals. He was predominantly casting, making minimal-looking rings with etchings or stones as well as pieces with nails. The wedding bands and other more commercially viable rings that he created in Central City paid the bills. This marks the beginning of Cotter's dual career making experimental jewelry along with exquisitely designed and crafted jewelry for more mainstream tastes.

Fig. 5.16

Fig. 5.16
Jim Cotter
Tears on My Pillow, 1973
Neckpiece
Fabric and thread
3 ½ × 3 ½ inches
Collection of the artist

Fig. 5.17
Jim Cotter, late 1960s

Fig. 5.17

In 1969 Cotter moved to Vail, Colorado, where he opened his own jewelry gallery the following year. Vail was a sleepy ski town when Cotter arrived, but its picturesque terrain was already bringing devotees to the valley to settle or vacation. Back then, the town was conservative. Cotter remembers, "Hippies were bad. They would not serve you if you had long hair. It was really politically incorrect to have long hair and a beard here, so I took a plastic bag and took my hair and made a hair bag."[223] About this time, a client asked him to make a necklace using a pearl that she owned. After she rejected a few designs for not being simple enough, Cotter placed the pearl in a plastic bag and hung it, telling his client that he could not make it any simpler. She was dumbfounded; since he obviously understood what she desired, why did he not just make it? "I do know," Cotter answered, "but I can't make it. Go and buy it at Sears." With that, a new series was born.[224]

The plastic-bag series of necklaces allowed Cotter to explore a number of themes that interested him at the time: the Vietnam War, politics, cultural appropriation, branding and consumerism, and the changing nature of America. By combining elements such as a plastic pig, an American flag, dirt, and a farmer working the land framed by two chickens in silver, Cotter could make a love letter to his grandfather's Iowa farm and comment on the struggle of farmers to hold onto their land in the face of large corporations. Another combination of a plastic American Indian toy and a piece of turquoise could point attention to the "authentic" simulated Native American jewelry that was prevalent at that time, made in China and passed off as the real thing. Some of the plastic-bag series contained Nixon campaign buttons, American flags, stars, and pins with sayings such as "I am loved." President Nixon was a popular subject for Cotter. Another of his political works from that time was a bronze belt buckle called *Impeachment with Honor* (1974),(Fig. 5.18) which featured an image of the Disney character Goofy (a stand-in for Nixon) at the center, the stars and stripes of the American flag, and the words "Impeachment with Honor."

Goofy was introduced as a character by Disney in 1932, starring alongside Mickey Mouse and the rest of the early Disney figures in movies and cartoons. His main role was that of the dim-witted, clumsy sidekick, easily duped and without leadership qualities. Cotter's use of Goofy as a stand-in for Nixon equates the two in terms of character traits and would have been easily understood by American viewers.

Metcalf, Woell, Tompkins, and Cotter demonstrate the potential of satire to grapple with the extraordinary times in which they lived. As their works reveal, satire can have a moral purpose, encouraging the censure of those who fail to meet ethical standards. It can punish and reform, using methods such as wit, humor, irony, parody, and caricature. However, satire can also be about inquiry, exploring and provoking its audience to think in a different way. It can embrace fantasy as well as realism, and it can be a kind of play, a rebellious release against authority. Satire must connect with people

Fig. 5.18

and events known to both the satirist and the audience, because this is how it generates its disruptive force. In this manner, it is tethered to the immediate, present-day context in which it is produced. In the case of *Impeachment with Honor*, the satire remains strong because Nixon has survived as a cultural figure; his failings have been repeated in movies, books, and articles, and the suffix "gate" is commonly applied to new scandals.

These American jewelers were part of a boom in American satire that took place after World War II, as sick jokes, black comedy, and radical satire became useful methods to engage with the rapid changes that were reshaping society in the 1950s and 1960s. The media explosion opened up new places to publish and present satirical content, while the growing acceptance of frank attitudes to language and sex pushed boundaries, all fed by the social and political anxieties that accompanied the Cold War. Publications like *Mad* magazine, founded by Harvey Kurtzman in 1954, skewered American icons like Superman and the Lone Ranger, ripping apart the model of American heroism that they represented. Comic strips such as *Pogo* by Walt Kelly attacked President Eisenhower and Senator Joe McCarthy. Then there was the *Realist*, founded in 1958 by Paul Krassner, which was like an adult version of *Mad* magazine—radically outrageous and obscene.

Stand-up comedy also became politically transgressive (attacking McCarthy and J. Edgar Hoover, head of the FBI) and sexually vulgar, moving from casinos and resorts into nightclubs, and spread through TV specials and on LP records featuring groups like the Firesign Theatre. Satire also featured in movies, with films such as *Dr. Strangelove* (1964) and *M.A.S.H.* (1970) offering a savage critique of the military bureaucracy, technology, and U.S. foreign policy.[225]

During the 1960s and 1970s, numerous institutions served as conveners and disseminators of information for American craftspeople. These independent institutions provided professional guidance as well as a place for larger aesthetic, technical, and material issues to be discussed through their publications, exhibitions, and conferences. As such, they played an outsized role in shaping the dialogue around studio craft during this period. This is especially true for the American Craftsmen's Council (ACC, later the American Craft Council), and SNAG, which was the first nationwide professional group for jewelers.

The origins of the ACC can be traced to 1939 when Aileen Osborn Webb created the Handcraft Cooperative League of America to develop markets for rural American craftspeople to sell their work in urban centers. Prior to that, during the Great Depression, Osborn Webb had started Putnam Country Products, a small shop in New York City designed to financially aid farmers and craftspeople in the area by selling their products. Initially, the shop offered agricultural products such as eggs and then expanded its inventory to include needlepoint, woodwork, and other handicrafts, which ultimately became its focus. Osborn Webb realized that the problem for rural craftspeople was finding a year-round market for their goods. Developing a marketing plan for crafts became her lifelong passion.[226]

In 1940 Osborn Webb opened America House, which served as a retail space for the ACC in New York City until 1971. The ACC added a magazine, named *Craft Horizons*, the following year. This publication would become the leading American journal for studio craft. Over the next decade, the organization was granted an

Fig. 5.19

Fig. 5.20

educational charter, merged with other like-minded groups, helped establish the School for American Craftsmen, and inaugurated a series of exhibitions called *Young Americans* and *American Designer-Craftsmen* that would usher in a golden age for American craft promotion and discourse. In 1956 the ACC and Osborn Webb founded the Museum of Contemporary Crafts (MCC) in New York City. The institution had a library, organized exhibitions, and began forming a permanent collection. The next year, the ACC held its first national conference in Asilomar, California.

As the 1960s dawned, the ACC continued its ambitious conference schedule and opened regional offices that organized their own programs. On the retail front, America House continued to support craftspeople, and the organization began to sponsor craft fairs. The ACC changed its name in 1966 to the American Craft Council and also officially incorporated its flagship journal *Craft Horizons* under its umbrella, joining the Museum of Contemporary Crafts as the standard-bearer for the display of and dialogue about American craft. As the ACC told members in 1975, "The Council addresses itself to maintaining an atmosphere in the United States in which the crafts and those who create them can exist with dignity as contributing members of our cultural society."[227]

In addition to Osborn Webb, two other figures were key in shaping the ACC and the larger American craft field during this period. Rose Slivka had joined the organization in 1956 as the managing editor of *Craft Horizons* and became editor in chief in 1959.(Fig. 5.19) Paul J. Smith began working at the MCC to develop exhibitions in 1957 and rose to become its director in 1963.(Fig. 5.20) Slivka and Smith worked closely together for almost two decades. However, they sometimes approached craft from different perspectives, leading to a vastly richer program than if they had been perfectly in sync. "Rose was very aware of what was going on, she was not keeping craft in a closet," recalls Smith. "She was very connected with the hierarchy in the arts, especially in New York. She was at the Cedar Bar, she knew all those famous artists … . I was not connected to that art world. I was always evaluating what was taking place in the broadest sense but also in the sense of studio craft movement."[228]

The evidence of Slivka's diverse viewpoint is borne out in the pages of *Craft Horizons*. In its news department, "The Craftsman's World," professional opportunities and reviews of exhibitions and conferences appeared next to visually exciting, informative articles that included artist profiles, overviews of specific media, techniques, aesthetics, ethnic and international work, and historical objects. Equally important were Slivka's long-form editorials, in which she contextualized the role of the craftsperson, took stock of the field and its challenges and successes, and provided a look into future possibilities in a cogent and persuasive manner. The way she saw it, the battles being fought by studio craft had larger cultural implications. "In his struggle to make ethical connections with his object," she wrote in one editorial from 1965, "the craftsman of our time is making new demands on his knowledge, cultural sources, sensibilities, and

Fig. 5.18
Jim Cotter
Impeachment with Honor, 1974
Belt buckle
Bronze
3 3/8 × 2 3/4 × 7/8 inches
Collection of Mark Bricklin

Fig. 5.19
Rose Slivka, editor of *Craft Horizons* magazine, 1969
Courtesy American Craft Council Library & Archives

Fig. 5.20
Paul J. Smith holds Paul Stanley's boot from the rock band Kiss
Courtesy American Craft Council Library & Archives

Fig. 5.21

experience. He is trying to create not necessarily new objects but new attitudes towards objects, to reinvest the object with its original, intrinsic reality, value, power."[229] Her editorials, and other special projects published in the magazine, such as a roundtable discussion with leading craft artists, gallerists, and educators on "The Decade: Change and Continuity" (1976), were all driven by her belief that "Culture — human value in action and object — has become the decisive moral issue of our time. *Craft Horizons*, as a publication, is and always has been at the crux of this issue."[230]

Meanwhile, Paul J. Smith's program at the MCC was wide-ranging and ambitious. It introduced the public to new makers, contextualized them within the history and trajectory of craft, and placed no boundaries on what could be called craft. Smith asserted, "The museum benefited enormously because it was a new national, specialized museum based in New York that was showing work not being shown in other New York museums. We did have a small permanent collection, but the main focus was being a showplace in New York for this emerging, outstanding innovative work from around the country, and some selected work from abroad."[231] In the 1960s and 1970s, he organized shows that covered the diverse field of American jewelry, including works by Donald B. Wright (1962), Mary Ann Scherr (1963), Ronald Hayes Pearson (1963), John Paul Miller (1964), Stanley Lechtzin (1965), Margaret De Patta (1965), Alice Shannon (1966), J. Fred Woell (1967), Arline Fisch (1968), L. Brent Kington (1968), Olaf Skoogfors (1968), Art Smith (1969), Ken Cory (1970), John Prip (1972), and Ruth Nivola (1977). These exhibitions took place in what was known as the "Little Gallery" at the MCC, a small space with two cases, and Smith was able to publish modest catalogues for each show.(Fig. 5.21)

Smith's choice of jewelers for these solo exhibitions provides a snapshot of his view of prevailing trends in American jewelry during this period. Although the featured jewelers came from across the United States, there was an emphasis on the East Coast. Most were academics and were shaping the field with their technical advancements. By highlighting this type of American jewelry, Smith was placing the museum's imprimatur on a specific aesthetic and set of materials and processes, thereby signaling to the field, museumgoers, and readers of exhibition reviews in *Craft Horizons* that this was what was important in American jewelry.

While Slivka was the editor in chief of *Craft Horizons* and had the ultimate decision-making power about what was published in its pages, she also hired subeditors for specific media whose job was to feed her ideas for content. The metals subeditor in the 1960s and 1970s was Ada Husted-Anderson. She was related to David Anderson, whose jewelry firm in Oslo, Norway, was deeply rooted in the Scandinavian tradition of metals and stones. Husted-Anderson's background and taste were more conservative; not surprisingly, she assigned feature articles on artists who fit that style or whose jewelry celebrated technical accomplishments. *Craft Horizons* profiled artists such as Fred Fenster, Stanley Lechtzin, John Paul Miller, Ruth Nivola, Margaret De

Fig. 5.21
Installation photograph of the exhibition *Jewelry by Art Smith*, held in the Little Gallery of the Museum of Contemporary Crafts in New York, September 12 – October 12, 1969
Courtesy American Craft Council Library & Archives

Patta, Merry Renk, Resia Schor, Olaf Skoogfors, and Bob Winston. It also covered exhibitions such as *American Jewelry 1963*, a national survey of jewelry featuring traditional precious materials and techniques such as lost-wax casting, forging, and granulation; *American Jewelry Today* (1967), a juried exhibition at the Everhart Museum featuring Lechtzin, Albert Paley, and Heikki Seppä, among other more mainstream American studio jewelers; and the MCC's exhibition *The Art of Personal Adornment* (1965), which examined adornment in world cultures over a number of centuries.

The magazine did, however, publish profiles of J. Fred Woell and Ken Cory on the occasion of their MCC solo exhibitions in the late 1960s. The article on Woell, penned by N. J. Loftis in the March–April 1968 issue, reveals the writer's bias. Although Loftis included images of Woell's *Come Alive! You're in the Pepsi Generation* and *The Body Politic* brooches made of found objects and featuring social and political ideas, the article gave more attention to his more traditional small-scale sculptures and jewelry. The author maintained, "While it is the Pop jewelry that has brought Woell's work to the public's attention, his most impressive works are characterized by a more consciously sculptural and poetic approach. These works, primarily brooches, reveal the influence of primitive African sculpture, possessing a profound inwardness and frequently a grotesque, tortuous beauty."[232] Loftis also surprisingly described the work as possessing "a sculptural quality characteristic of the Renaissance and art nouveau."[233] Cory's 1970 exhibition at the MCC merited only a small review with one image in the back of the magazine. At least in this case, the writer, Deborah Waroff, understood Cory's intent, describing his jewelry as "small sculptures rather than badges of wealth" that are not "all intense primitive evocations ... they are ... sometimes coming across as good dirty jokes."[234]

For many American jewelers, *Craft Horizons* was their bible, eagerly read and discussed. Students and their professors, independent studio craftspeople, collectors, and enthusiasts looked to the magazine for information and introductions to new trends, exhibitions, artworks, and opportunities. However, neither the ACC nor the magazine appears to have expressed an official position on studio craft's relationship to the political issues that were rife in public life at the time. Slivka's essays rarely delved into non-art issues and what they might have meant for studio craft. Perhaps Osborn Webb and the ACC board were conservative in their outlook, or perhaps political and social issues were not considered to be within the purview of a craft magazine.

That being said, during the late 1960s and 1970s, it would have been very difficult to completely avoid the issues of the day. For *Craft Horizons*, any reports on these issues were relegated to the news-driven section titled "The Craftsman's World." One such example is the article "No Sex Bias in Craft Horizons Says Art Press Study," published in June 1972. Citing a study conducted in 1970 and 1971 on exhibition reviews in art magazines, *Craft Horizons* was found to be "at the top of the art press for fair and equal coverage of the work of women and men."[235] Whether this equal coverage was due to editorial planning or because so many craft artists were women is beside the point: Slivka thought that readers should know about it, at a time when battles over the Equal Rights Amendment to the constitution were in the news and on the minds of many Americans.

Similarly, discussions of the major issues facing Americans during the 1960s and 1970s and their relation to craft and jewelry rarely appeared on the programs of ACC conferences. In keeping with the ACC's goals, most were workshop-heavy, with maker demonstrations, slide lectures, and talks covering practical matters for the professional craftsperson. Sometimes, though, the turmoil of the period intruded. The program of the "Introspection" conference, held in October 1971 at the Midland Art Center in Michigan, included exhibitions that referred to the students protesting the Vietnam War who had been killed by the National Guard at Kent State University the previous year. In June 1977, the conference "Historical Traditions in the New South," held at Winston-Salem University in North Carolina, included a lecture by the University of Maryland art history professor David Driskell on "America's Black Craftsmen" that addressed the role of a group traditionally marginalized in craft history.

As the ACC grew, it could no longer serve the needs of all craftspeople. As a result, media-specific organizations were established to promote, educate, and support makers who specialized in the different branches of studio craft. For example, the National Council for the Education on the Ceramic Arts was founded in 1966, and the Glass Art Society was established in 1971. Jewelry had SNAG, which began in late 1968 when jeweler Philip Morton, who was teaching at the School for American Craftsman, wondered, as Robert Ebendorf recalls, "Is it not time that we should take responsibility for our own destiny ... our own journey?"[236]

To that end, Morton gathered eight leading American jewelers and metalsmiths for a three-day meeting in Chicago in November of that year to discuss the formation of a professional society. The men—Robert Ebendorf, Phillip Fike, Hero Kielman, L. Brent Kington, Stanley Lechtzin, Kurt Matzdorf, Ronald Pearson, Olaf Skoogfors, and Morton—were all academics, with the exception of Ron Pearson, who was on a break from teaching at the School for American Craftsmen. They agreed to form a "guild, association or organization" that would promote the importance of education, get involved in issues such as the transferability of courses, organize professional exhibitions, and work closely with other groups that had similar goals.[237] It was agreed that a conference and exhibition would be held in January 1970 in St. Paul, Minnesota, focusing on "professional designer-craftsmen and the colleges teaching metalsmithing," and featuring discussions about "aesthetic values and qualities," opportunities to "exchange technical information," and the chance to "evaluate educational programs in metalwork in North America."[238] The group proposed a second planning meeting in Boston in January 1969, to which additional "well-known" jewelers and metalsmiths such as Hans Christensen, Richard Thomas, Harold Stacey, Ronald McNeish, Miye Matsukata, Arlene Fisch, Orland Larson, Fred Fenster, Michael Jerry, Ed Weiner, and John Prip would be invited.[239]

Those who attended the Boston meeting argued over proposed names for the group and suggested activities such as developing an encyclopedia for jewelry, establishing educational standards and a centralized image library, and purchasing and distributing materials and supplies to members. Hero Kielman remembers that Ronald Pearson "expressed his concern for the establishment of an organization which would be too tight and not pursue the high ideals and historic values of this age-old craft. He suggested that our main aim should be to encourage the established craftsmen to pursue the high ideals set by others in the past and to carry on the further development in both design and techniques."[240] These early conversations set the scene for the vein of conservatism that ran through SNAG. While some early members such as Robert Ebendorf and Arline Fisch made jewelry that challenged expectations of scale, expanded the kinds of materials and techniques that jewelers could use, and introduced new artistic strategies, they were outliers in the fledgling organization.

From the beginning, SNAG's membership criteria were onerous and divisive. "Charter members" were invited to join SNAG by the steering committee. These jewelers and metalsmiths were all academics and were also invited to submit work to the 1970 exhibition without having to submit work to a jury. A category for "associate members" was created as a three-year membership for students and unestablished professionals. In this two-tier system, associate members had no voting rights, making many younger jewelers feel unappreciated. For a small organization, with only sixty-four members in 1970, to establish such a hierarchy speaks to the elitism of the founders. Professional makers who wanted to be considered for full membership "would have to submit twenty-five images of work of a professional standard that would be judged by a membership committee of three who would establish 'standard criteria for professionalism both factual or arbitrary.'"[241] Criteria for associate and full membership were initially defined as exhibiting "proven professionalism and outstanding creative achievement in metalwork as well as contributions to the field for other than creative work."[242] After individuals successfully passed the gauntlet of the membership committee, they still required a favorable vote by two-thirds of the general membership.

Given the strictures and arbitrariness of membership acceptance, it is no wonder that the organization in its earliest form was off-putting for many jewelers who worked outside of the academic system. SNAG members were located mostly on the East Coast and in the Midwest, with thirty-seven professional, twenty-five associate, and two honorary members in 1970. By 1972 the number of professionals had grown to fifty-three; the following year it increased to seventy-two. In 1976 SNAG boasted eighty-six professional and two hundred and eighteen associate members, and by the end of the decade it had a total of fifteen hundred members.

SNAG conferences were fairly conservative affairs. The 1970 conference in St. Paul included lectures, artist-led slide shows, films, demonstrations, and meetings on historical international metalwork and techniques. Only Arline Fisch's presentation on "Body Jewellery" diverged from the accepted norm of technical presentations: she discussed her exploration of scale as well as her aesthetic sources. The second SNAG conference took place in 1974 at the Renwick Gallery in Washington, D.C., along with a corollary *Goldsmith '74* exhibition. Again the focus of the conference was on technical talks and historical traditions, but the exhibition was more dynamic, at least in the realm of materials. As Pat Passlof noted in *Craft Horizons*, "No longer were there only a few artists broadening conceptions of jewelry, in this exhibition, a significant amount of work featured scarabs, stones, yarn, fossils, feathers, fur, leather, wood, and plastics, to name a few."[243] She also offered some criticism about the effects of academic standards on American jewelry and metalsmithing. "Is it possible that in the classroom—where one is forced to set up standards which can be submitted to the arbitrary hierarchy of school marks—technical perfection, neatness, and regularity beyond the functional needs of the piece have become too convenient criteria?" asked Passlof. "Some works appear to have been planned to death ... calculated rather than felt; the product of a technical perfectionism and exaggerated crispness which tend to harden form and make it mechanical."[244]

SNAG ultimately focused on professional and technical support rather than serving as a forum for exchanging or encouraging broader conversations about ideas. This focus is most evident in the pages of SNAG's journal *Golddust* (later *Goldsmiths Journal*), which was established in 1975. (Fig. 5.22) Mark Baldridge, a young jeweler from Virginia who had joined SNAG in 1973, became the first editor. He was solely in charge in the journal's early years, deciding what to publish as well as being responsible for printing and mailing it to all members.[245] The journal featured member news and profiles, as well as listings for exhibitions, lectures, workshops, schools, publications, and symposia. It included regular columns titled "Helpful Hints," "Question Corner," and "Idea Corner," among other topics.

Some of the articles asked probing questions, such as "Is goldsmithing an art or a craft (or both) and what is the difference or makes the difference?" (December 1, 1975); "Do many artists feel that they need a gimmick to succeed? Does metalwork of today need some technical or aesthetic twist in order to be noticed?" (February 1, 1976); and "How political is the metal world? Is it who you know and what organizations that you belong to that make the critical difference in achieving a moderate level of success in metalsmithing or is it simply the quality of the work?" (August 1, 1976). They point to an organization (and field) that was struggling to define itself and was insecure about its place in the wider visual arts scene. None of these questions addressed aesthetics or concepts. Likewise, the topics discussed in the letters to the editor veered toward practical and professional matters: disagreements about the role of academic programs versus technical training, and inquiries about exhibitions, jewelry repairs, gallery dealings, and other concerns.

The politics that had the greatest effect on American jewelry in the late 1960s and 1970s was not the social and political revolution being staged by the counterculture but the impact of the field's institutional politics. Judging by exhibition reviews of the period, technically

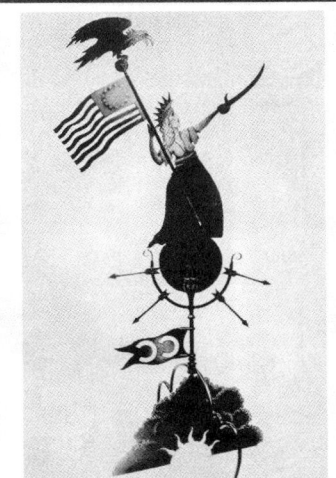

Fig. 5.22
Goldsmiths Journal 5,
no. 1, February 1979, cover image:
L. Brent Kington's *Liberty 76*

sophisticated jewelry made from metals in a sculptural, organic, or geometric form was most likely to be accepted for exhibitions and singled out for awards. However, exhibition jurors who themselves made socially or politically engaged work were more likely to include work in that vein. For instance, Ken Cory, Alvin Pine, and Tio Gaimbruni served as jurors for *The Metal Experience* (1971), held at the Oakland Museum and presented by its Women's Guild and the Metal Arts Guild. The show included jewelry, furniture, sculpture, and painting in metal, and one reviewer concluded that the jurors "admitted precious little that could be even remotely regarded as traditional or conservative."[246]

A similar case was the *American Designer-Craftsmen* exhibition in 1971, at the Richmond Art Center in California. The show was juried by Viola Frey, Phillip Yost, and William Clark, who himself produced narrative and politically engaged jewelry. A review in *Craft Horizons* mentioned that "the mood of the show was in the spirit of the times ... [including] strangely imaginative jewelry" and singled out pieces by Ken Cory and others.[247]

Jurors such as Stanley Lechtzin, John Prip, Olaf Skoogfors, and Robert von Neumann, who worked in a more traditional vein, as well as craft-based executives and curators, tended not to select jewelry reflecting the counterculture. SNAG's own exhibitions also reinforced this tendency, as seen in *Goldsmith '70* and *Goldsmith '74*. Gary Griffin's review of the 1978 SNAG exhibition *American Goldsmiths Now* also reveals that the group's selections continued on a more conservative path. "There is little that is shocking or revolutionary, but elements of the reactionary or retreatist are present," wrote Griffin in *Craft Horizons*. "Craftsmanship and good design prevail, but what remains indistinct is the element of the avant-garde."[248]

Bias could also be found at the annual *Northwest Craftsmen's Exhibition* in Seattle, a city with a thriving jewelry scene of artists using alternative materials, taking inspiration from world travels and ethnic cultures, and commenting on social and political issues in their work. Seattle was a short distance from Ellensburg, home at one point or another to Ramona Solberg, Don Tompkins, Ken Cory, and Merrily Tompkins. Yet these jewelers rarely submitted their work to this prominent exhibition, possibly because they felt that their works did not align with the aesthetics of the jurors.

The *Northwest Craftsmen's Exhibition* was held at the Henry Art Gallery of the University of Washington and organized by the Lambda Rho Alumni Association, the Seattle Weavers Guild, and the Seattle Clay Club. Recognized as one of the most important juried shows in the United States, the exhibition was inaugurated in 1952 to provide local craftspeople with a regular opportunity to show their work, make the public aware of fine craft, and discover new talent. In 1965 the exhibition became a biennial. Each show had jurors for specific media, including jewelry, so the juror's tastes were reflected in the selected works and award winners.

The jurors for jewelry in the 1965 *Northwest Craftsmen's Exhibition* were Pat Maher of Everett, Washington, and Mary Stephens Nelson of Boise, Idaho, two traditionalists who gave awards in the category predominantly to cast, forged, and hammered works. The jeweler and enameler John Paul Miller was the juror for the 1967 show, giving awards and citations to traditional forms such as gold rings with stones or pearls, silver necklaces, teakettles, and other examples of hollowware. The following year, the jurors Gervais Reed, Harold Balazs, and Rudy Autio selected works by Ken Cory, and his "group

Fig. 5.23

of four pins designed in interesting combinations of fabricated and electroformed copper or brass with glass beads, plastics, and wood" was highlighted in a review.[249] Among the necklaces with pearls and other traditional forms, Cory's jewelry indeed must have stood out.

Jewelry is barely mentioned in *Craft Horizons*' review of the 1969 exhibition, juried by Eudorah Moore, the force behind the important *California Design* annual exhibition at the Pasadena Art Museum. The following year, the journal praised Ramona Solberg's *Ecology* necklace for its "charming content."[250] The 1973 *Northwest Craftsmen's Exhibition* included works by the Pencil Brothers and Merrily Tompkins. Tompkins received an award for her jewelry and garnered accolades for her "mind-tripping, storybook pendants," and for her "refreshing, unsophisticated fun."[251] In comparison, the work of George Sherotsky, the other award winner, was described as "too elemental and decorative."[252] By that time, the tide was starting to turn, and the establishment, at least in the Northwest, was beginning to accept and even prefer the work of alternative jewelers aligned with Funk.

University-based exhibition venues also had a significant impact on the field by showcasing narrative jewelry that engaged political, social, or cultural issues. The type of jewelry shown in such venues directly correlated with the philosophy of the university's jewelry and metalsmithing program. For example, under the direction of Ken Cory, Central Washington University (CWU) held one-person exhibitions of progressive jewelers such as Jim Cotter, Lane Coulter, Richard Mawdsley, Linda Ross, and J. Fred Woell, among others, thereby reinforcing his teaching methodology with examples by like-minded makers. Cory also organized the 1975 jewelry invitational *Symbolism and Imagery* at CWU, which included works by his predecessor Don Tompkins, his former student Merrily Tompkins, Woell, and Mawdsley, as well as his own jewelry made as part of the Pencil Brothers.

Other jewelry artists leading academic programs with an affiliated museum also made an effort to curate exhibitions that featured alternative jewelry. One example is Gary Knoffke, who arrived at the University of Georgia to replace Robert Ebendorf in 1971. Knoffke was unorthodox, challenging established and authorized techniques in metalwork and working in a style that rejected the smooth surfaces and subtlety to which American jewelry audiences were accustomed. The three *National Ring Exhibition*s that he organized in the late 1970s and early 1980s with Jim Cotter, Lane Coulter, and Elliot Pujol were an opportunity to emphasize the trends that he personally appreciated and pursued in his own jewelry. He selected and exhibited rings with inexpensive and unconventional materials featuring humor and social commentary.[253]

In 1980 the jeweler Karen McCreary made a neckpiece titled *Environmentally Safe*. (Fig. 5.23) Fabricated from bronze sheet with industrial paint, the neckpiece is divided in half. The right side is about solar power: a circular solar cell illuminates three green LEDs when activated by sunlight. The left side is about nuclear power: a battery hidden in the bronze base powers red LEDs that illuminate the resin with iridescent powder and runs a flicking Geiger counter to measure radiation. An accompanying silhouette of a nuclear cloud is made of sterling silver, overlaid by a nickel-silver border forming the international prohibition sign. At the base of the neckpiece is the fluke of a disappearing whale, a symbol of a popular cause in the 1970s as well as shorthand for a kind of general environmental consciousness. McCreary's commentary was reflected not only in these symbols but also in the materials: the wires feeding from the solar into the nuclear side of the neckpiece are resistant to corrosion from oil and gas, while the cord is made of an FDA-approved nontoxic vinyl tubing.

McCreary's jewelry picked up on the widespread concerns of the environmental movement, which in the 1960s became a mass social movement that adopted the political activism and protest used so successfully by the civil rights and anti-war movements. The following decade saw popular and government responses to the urgent question of environmental protection. The first Earth Day was held on April 22, 1970, and organized by the Wisconsin senator Gaylord Nelson as a way to send a message to politicians that Americans supported environmental legislation. Schools and universities around the country took part, and an estimated twenty million Americans participated in some way. That same year, the National Environmental Policy Act was passed into law, requiring the government to consider the environmental impact of all major federal actions. The Endangered Species Act was passed in 1973, and the Federal Land Policy and Management Act in 1976, which included preservationist measures.

Immediately relevant to McCreary's neckpiece was the Comprehensive Environmental Response, Compensation, and Liability Act of 1980, which was designed to help control toxic hazards by creating a superfund that would clean up contaminated waste sites and spills. This act was the last in a series of legislation passed in the 1970s that tried to deal with the threats of pollution. McCreary's neckpiece is a personal tool, a wearable machine to symbolically track toxic radiation and monitor the environment, perfect for the thousands of Americans who joined environmental organizations like the Sierra Club and the Environmental Defense Fund.

Karen McCreary was born in Los Angeles in 1953. She grew up in Southern California but spent summers with her extended family in a small town in North Carolina. Her parents had moved to the West Coast for work; her mother was employed as a secretary, and her father was a pilot and built helicopters. Craft activities were a familiar part of McCreary's domestic life. Both her mother and grandmother sewed and had an interest in

Fig. 5.23
Karen McCreary
Environmentally Safe, 1980
Neckpiece
Bronze, industrial paint, sterling silver, nickel silver, solar cell, vinyl tube, electric wires, LEDs, electronic circuits, and battery
15 × 11 × 2 inches
Collection of the artist

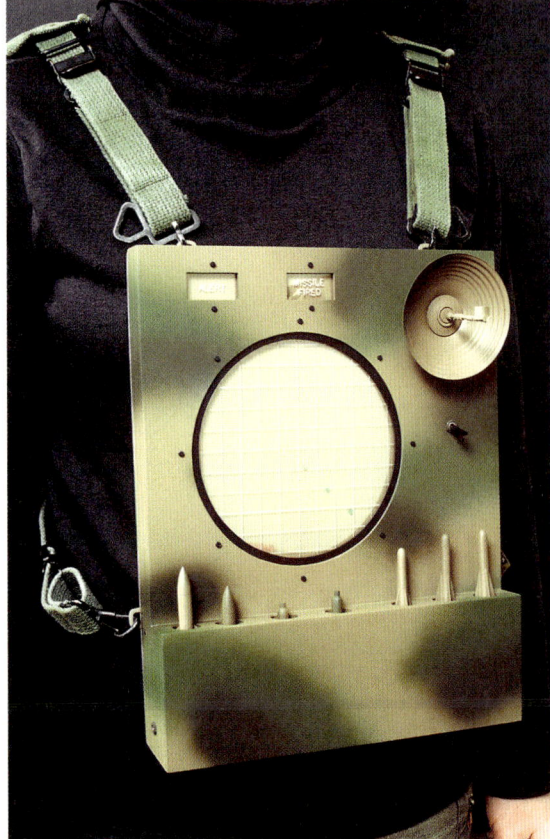

Fig. 5.24   Fig. 5.25

handicrafts of different kinds. McCreary was taught how to make her own clothes, and it was a natural extension for her to make her own jewelry, too. Her first jewelry experiments were rings cut out from sheets of felt and laminated with glue, which would match her homemade outfits. The years in which McCreary was a teenager marked a period when people were keen to make interesting things that they could wear. She and her friends would tie-dye and distress their clothes: they would buy new jeans and then individualize them by bleaching, washing repeatedly, rubbing the denim on the street or other rough surfaces, and adding beads and other stitched designs. She was a high school hippie.[254] (Fig. 5.24)

When McCreary graduated from high school in 1971, her male friends lived in fear of being drafted and going overseas to fight in the Vietnam War. That same year, McCreary was actively involved in the movement to get the voting age lowered from twenty-one to eighteen. She wrote letters to congressmen and senators, arguing that if the government was going to send people her age overseas to die in the Vietnam War, they deserved to have the right to vote and have their voices heard. In March 1971, both houses of Congress adopted the proposal, and the Twenty-Sixth Amendment to the Constitution was ratified by the states and became official in July. The Vietnam War ended in 1973, which was cause for celebration, but not long after, the political controversy of the Watergate scandal revealed the corruption of the government and fed the sense of distrust toward official institutions and the older generation. Environmental causes became more prominent, and recycling began to become a feature of life in Southern California. In 1974 McCreary began studying jewelry at California State University in Long Beach, which had just established a recycling program for students and staff. For her, being involved in such activities felt important and necessary.[255]

During the three years that McCreary studied at California State University with Alvin Pine and Dieter Muller-Stach, the price of silver rose to fifty dollars an ounce, making it, like gold, beyond the reach of students. This economic factor hastened the search for alternative materials, which was also being fed by developments in the contemporary jewelry field. Southern California was a flourishing industrial center, especially for the aerospace industry, which provided a rich source of alternative materials such as aluminum, titanium, and resin, plus access to sophisticated industrial processes like anodizing, which produced a range of colors and effects. McCreary wanted to make jewelry for and about her time, and these industrial materials and processes were key to an overt engagement with the period in which she was living.

The politically and socially engaged jewelry that McCreary produced in the late 1970s was made after she graduated from California State University in 1977. She was working for a jewelry manufacturer, and she had a studio at home in her garage. McCreary's then-husband, Bob Duckson, was an electronics enthusiast and designed the electrical systems that literally powered her work in the late 1970s and early 1980s.[256]

McCreary believed in the role of contemporary jewelry as a way to communicate. The *Environmentally Safe* neckpiece had a message that was clear to anyone who saw it. But despite her interest in grappling with urgent political and social problems, she gave little thought to the precise ways in which her jewelry might contribute to change. Although McCreary occasionally wore this neckpiece to parties and art openings, for the most part she showed it in exhibitions or in photographs (sometimes on the body) and then stored it in the studio. McCreary believed that exhibitions provided an opportunity for more people to see her work than a single owner wearing these objects every now and then. In any case, the opportunity to find owners for such works was rare; mass-produced buttons and pins provided a more accessible and affordable means for most people to promote their sociopolitical beliefs.

In 1982 McCreary made a large wearable object called *MAD*. (Fig. 5.25) The title stands for *Mutually Assured Destruction,* a military doctrine of deterrence that relies on both sides of a nuclear conflict having sufficient weapons to destroy the other. McCreary's object is a personal protection device, falling somewhere between a piece of jewelry and a garment. Fabricated from acrylic, which allowed her to work at a larger scale, *MAD* features a radar display, with LEDs around the circumference that flicker on and off in a sequence, a metal radar dish, counters, and a bank of missiles at the base that appear ready to be launched at anyone who penetrates the wearer's personal space. The work is suspended on a strap that McCreary purchased at an army surplus store.

MAD goes beyond the concerns of environmentalism to tackle the problem of nuclear war, but both issues could be traced to President Ronald Reagan. When Reagan was elected in 1980, he declared war on the environmental movement's achievements of the previous decade. A conservative, pro-business Republican, Reagan wanted to set American corporations free from the web of regulation that protected the environment. His administration tried to paint environmentalists as radicals far outside the mainstream of American social and political life, and he gutted the Environmental Protection Agency that was responsible for enforcing federal regulations.

Reagan also swerved from a decade of U.S. foreign policy by rejecting the policy of détente that saw America and the Soviet Union pursue trade relations, cultural exchanges, and arms-control agreements. He thought that arms control made the United States weak and vulnerable to attack, and that it only encouraged the Soviets to expand their influence around the globe. He massively increased the Pentagon's budget, hoping to bankrupt the Soviet Union in a new arms race, and he stepped up the anti-Communist rhetoric, culminating in his infamous statement that the Soviet Union was an evil empire, and the Cold War a struggle over right and wrong, good against evil.

In June 1982, the year McCreary made *MAD*, more than five hundred thousand people crowded into Central Park in New York City to protest Reagan's policies. In a protest at the Hollywood Bowl in Los Angeles, President Reagan's own daughter spoke out against the escalating arms race. Activists from all over the country formed a massive social movement seeking a "nuclear freeze" on the testing and use of the American nuclear arsenal. Two senators, one from each political party, introduced a plan to implement a freeze to the U.S. Senate. All of these events must have fed into McCreary's decision to produce a personal deterrent system. In a time of complete political madness, it must have seemed like one of the saner things a jeweler could do.

Fig. 5.24
Karen McCreary, 1975

Fig. 5.25
Karen McCreary
MAD, 1982
Wearable object
Acrylic, metal, fabric, LEDs, electronic circuits, and battery
12 × 9 × 1½ inches
Collection of the artist

Civil Rights and Body Politics

Civil Rights and Body Politics

Starting in the 1960s and becoming more organized in the 1970s, the push for equal rights for all American citizens took complicated and contradictory paths. Inherent racism and traditional conservative values pushed back hard against changes advocated by women and people of color. Many people were fearful of the outcome of letting women and Black people have the same rights as white men. Yet several groups formed to advance those rights; although these groups had different goals, they shared the desire for individuals and groups to define their own identities. These Americans wanted the government and their fellow citizens to give them equal rights under the law.

The second wave of feminism was underway, with women protesting, writing influential books, and organizing to gain equal rights. The movement was spurred on by the publication of *The Second Sex* by Simone de Beauvoir in 1949 and Betty Friedan's *The Feminine Mystique* in 1963. Friedan went on to organize the National Organization of Women (NOW) in 1966. The passing of the Civil Rights Act in 1964 was supposed to have ended segregation and prohibit discrimination based on race, color, religion, sex, or national origin in the workplace, but its failure to enact real change in the lives of women drove the establishment of NOW and other similar organizations that pursued political policies to support women in the workplace and in society.

It was under these conditions that Sharon Church enrolled at Skidmore College in Saratoga Springs, New York, in 1968. She had wanted to study fine art, but when she realized that making a living as an artist would be difficult, maybe impossible, she decided to pursue jewelry and studied under Earl Pardon. Skidmore was a women-only college when Church was there, and some of its students were paying attention to the developing

Fig. 6.1

feminist movement. Both at school and in her family, Church could see the way men and women were treated differently. She also got mixed messages from her mother, who was a feminist but worked hard to keep her husband happy, sometimes subjugating her own desires.[257]

Church graduated with a BS in art in 1970. She went on to study at the School for American Craftsmen (SAC) at the Rochester Institute of Technology (RIT), graduating with an MFA in 1973. While there, Church did not get along with Hans Christensen, the master Danish silversmith who oversaw the metals department. Yet Albert Paley, who was also teaching at SAC, had a strong impact on Church. His large-scale and frankly sexy jewelry with its Art Nouveau-like flourishes was acclaimed at the time. Although she admired Paley, Church wanted to make jewelry that was beautiful and that she could wear, which was often not the case with Paley's work. She was always interested in looking good and making an impression.[258]

Church found a way to assert herself in the metalsmithing department at SAC. As she recalls, "We worked with fire, we worked with magic things, we forced metal to do things it didn't want to do."[259] By working metal the way she did, and using fire and tools to bend it to her will, she created a path to self-expression. Her method of challenging the patriarchal system was to be undeniably good at making jewelry; then, she thought, it would be obvious that she was equal to her male peers.

Church was never a hippie. She always dressed nicely in her version of well-tailored bohemianism.(Fig. 6.1) But the issues of the day were personal to her; she traveled to Washington, D.C., with some friends from school to talk to William Roth, the senator from Delaware, about the war in Vietnam. She had friends who were Marxists, although she was not really one of them. Church was deeply affected by the assassination of the civil rights leader Martin Luther King, Jr., in 1968, and the massacre of student protestors against the Vietnam War by the National Guard at Kent State University in 1970. She was aware of the swirl of political ideas and social and cultural changes going on around her and was very sympathetic, but she did not get passionately involved enough to act. Rather, she was an observer.

Church had friends who were having sex and taking the birth-control pill, and sometimes they still got pregnant. Some sought abortions, which were illegal until the landmark Supreme Court judgment in the *Roe v. Wade* case in 1973. Before that, the women Church knew had to leave town and travel to Washington, D.C., to get an illegal abortion, which would cost around six hundred dollars, and then there was the worry as to whether they would survive the experience.

About 1969–70 Church made her *No. 2 Pin*, which was connected to the Zero Population Growth (ZPG) movement, a political movement fed by feminism and environmentalism.(Fig. 6.2) ZPG activists argued that "a constantly increasing population is responsible for many of our problems: pollution, violence, loss of values and of individual privacy."[260] Church's sympathy with women's liberation and sexual freedom led her to being sexually active but responsible. She did not want to reproduce without consideration for the effects of population growth, and the silver brooch was her way of taking part in the campaign to raise awareness. The number 2 referred to how many children a couple could have, enough to replace themselves but not cause an increase in the world's population. The idea was most (in)famously promoted by Paul R. Ehrlich and Anne Ehrlich in *The Population Bomb*, a book published in 1968 that predicted worldwide famine and major social upheaval due to overpopulation. Ehrlich became notorious for statements such as "The mother of the year should be a sterilized woman with two adopted children." The book appealed to Church, and she became interested in promoting the ZPG movement and its beliefs. She gave copies of *No. 2 Pin* to friends who shared her ideals.

Barry Merritt, like Church, was a graduate of the School for American Craft. He was one of the few male jewelry artists to take up the cause of feminism in his work. Born in Modoc, South Carolina, in 1941, Merritt lived the majority of his life in western New York, particularly in the Rochester area. He studied metalsmithing at SAC from 1960 to 1962 during a period of transition: America House no longer showed student work, and the metalsmith's identity was shifting from craftsman to artist. However, this transition was not reflected in the SAC curriculum, which focused on theory, tools, and techniques, as well as marketing and other professional practices. As John Prip, a faculty member from 1948 to 1954, recalls, "The purpose of the school was to send people into the world to survive, not to become artists."[261] Even after Hans Christensen replaced Prip, the metals program continued to prioritize making hollowware and preparing students for the practicalities of life as a craftsperson.

Yet some aspects of the program were in flux due to the influence of the counterculture. As Albert Paley said, in the 1960s "traditional values changed and hollowware became a symbol of the lifestyle that many were rejecting. Contemporary jewelry, on the other hand, allowed you to express yourself as an individual. It projected an image of nonconformity which was an important aspect of the '60s social revolution."[262] While this mindset did not fully take hold at SAC until the late 1960s under the teaching of Paley, the seeds were sown during the time Merritt studied there.

After graduation, Merritt spent the rest of the 1960s teaching, working in the jewelry industry, and working for the metalsmith Ronald Pearson. He also maintained his own studio practice making jewelry from precious metals. Not until the end of the decade was he able to focus on his own career, developing and presenting workshops and lectures and participating in invitational exhibitions. Merritt furthered his national connections by becoming a founding member of the Society of North American Goldsmiths (SNAG) in 1969, attending the first conference in St. Paul in 1970 and

Fig. 6.1
Sharon Church, Linda Stanley, and Linn Perkins, in downtown Saratoga Springs, New York, 1970

Fig. 6.2

being accepted into the *Goldsmith '70* exhibition, where he showed conventional jewelry shaped by his education. Through SNAG and his other activities, Merritt became known to a larger community of metalsmiths, which resulted in national opportunities. His anti-war and feminist positions led him to be invited to participate in Summervail's metalsmithing conference in 1977 and 1978.

In 1968 Merritt began investigating working with alternative materials and combining them in assemblages. He was inspired by the Funk movement emanating from the Bay Area, and particularly the use of satirical humor to comment on issues of the time. Merritt's jewelry in this vein initially took the form of humorous badges with double entendres and puns; they were not necessarily political, but more for people to enjoy.[263] This is certainly how they

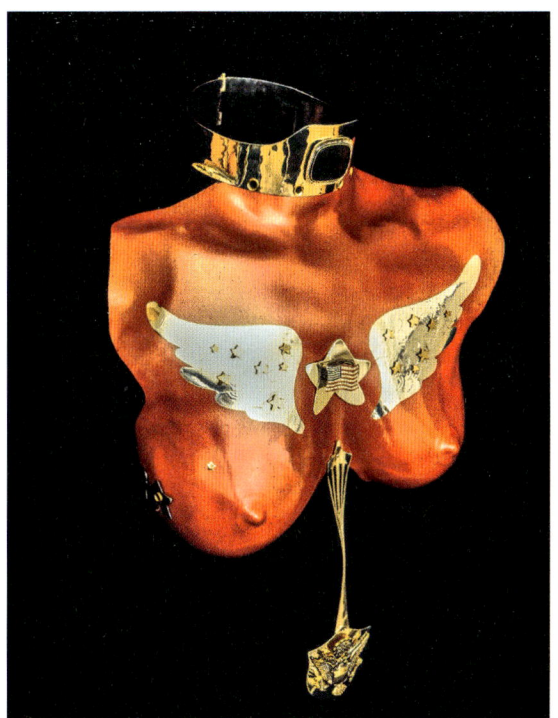

Fig. 6.2
Sharon Church
No. 2 Pin, 1969–70
Silver
1 × ⅞ inches
Collection of the artist

Fig. 6.3
Barry Merritt
Wonder Woman, 1972
Torso piece
Fiberglass, silver, enamel, copper, and sardonyx

Fig. 6.3

were reviewed at the time. Merritt's *Buffalo Bill Badge*^(Fig. 5.11) was exhibited in 1972 at Fairtree Gallery in New York City in a show of contemporary American silversmiths and goldsmiths curated by the jewelers Tom Markusen and Robert Ebendorf. Merritt's badges were exhibited alongside some of Don Tompkins's *Commemorative Medals*, ^(Fig. 1.4) and a review of the exhibition published in *Craft Horizons* drew a contrast between them. While Tompkins's jewelry was divided between memorials to artists and satirical commentary, Merritt's brooches—including *Little Orphan Annie's Secret Society Brownie Baking Badge*, *Nancy Drew*, and *Buffalo Bill Badge*—were described as "reminders of a gentler era."[264]

By 1972 Merritt had begun to expand his notion of scale, creating body adornment that covered the upper torso. These fiberglass forms were augmented with found objects, leather, metal, and other materials. For the *Torso Pieces* series, Merritt's inspirations ranged from artistic movements such as Art Deco to feminism. *Wonder Woman* (1972) was most likely inspired by a July 1972 cover of *Ms.* magazine. Under a banner proclaiming "Wonder Woman for President," the cover art pictured a distraught superhero rescuing an American city from a rain of bombs; a billboard on one of the buildings states "Peace and Justice in '72." Merritt's *Wonder Woman* is a full upper-body cast of a female torso made from fiberglass and embellished with gold wings and a star that form a kind of breastplate, with a futuristic collar, and a suspended medallion bearing the seal of the United States.^(Fig. 6.3) Stars and the American flag also decorate the torso. For Merritt, an anti-war activist who was also concerned with issues of equal rights for women, his choice of Wonder Woman was unsurprising. As Gloria Steinem wrote in *Ms.*, "Wonder Woman symbolizes many of the values of the women's culture that feminists are now trying to introduce into the mainstream: strength and self-reliance for women; sisterhood and mutual support among women; peacefulness and esteem for human life; a diminishment both of 'masculine' aggression and of the belief that violence is the only way of solving conflicts."[265]

In 1977 Merritt opened his own jewelry gallery in Rochester, called the Gallery of Contemporary Metalsmithing. Deborah Norton, a contemporary jewelry collector, was its first manager. Together, they showed a wide range of work, from affordable rings, earrings, brooches, and necklaces to more significant pieces by leading jewelers of the time, including Sharon Church, Jim Cotter, Louis Mueller, Gary Noffke, and others. Merritt and Norton also took on the role of activists in the contemporary jewelry field, publicly addressing SNAG members about issues that were facing America and encouraging jewelers to get involved.

In a letter to the editor of SNAG's *Goldsmiths Journal*, published in December 1978, they wrote, "We think SNAG is long overdue in joining the campaign to boycott states that have not passed the ERA [Equal Rights Amendment]. We feel it was an insult to all the women members of this organization to have held this year's conference in Missouri, a state that has not ratified the amendment. We are assuming that it is not necessary for us to justify our stand on this issue. We would feel proud to be able to add SNAG to NOW's long list of organizations that have joined the boycott."[266] As the name suggests, the Equal Rights Amendment was a proposed amendment to the United States Constitution that would guarantee equal legal rights for all American citizens, regardless of sex. Buoyed by the growing power of what is now called "second-wave feminism," the ERA was approved by the House of Representatives in 1971,

Fig. 6.4

Fig. 6.5

Fig. 6.4
Carolyn Kriegman
Kinetic Necklace, 1969
Polymethyl methacrylate
and metal rings
19 ¾ × 15 ¾ × 10 ½ inches
Los Angeles County Museum of Art,
gift of Lois and Bob Boardman,
M.2015.31

Fig. 6.5
Mary Ann Scherr, c. 1970s
Courtesy Scherr family

and then the United States Senate in 1972, after which it went to the fifty states for ratification. Requiring the agreement of thirty-eight states to pass, the ERA did not achieve that number before the ratification deadline expired in 1982, despite the efforts of those like Merritt and Norton who worked hard to lobby on its behalf. There is no record of SNAG's response.

Like Merritt, the jeweler Carolyn Kriegman was also creating torso works, though hers were more akin to a cross between body armor and a spacesuit. Kriegman had become known for her plastic jewelry that related to the "space age" trend in industrial design, incorporating the unsettling visual effects of Op Art.[267] They were made from plexiglass, a ubiquitous, disposable material in 1960s American consumer culture and a fairly new addition to the materials of studio craft. An article about Kriegman published in 1969 relished the image of this "housewife from East Orange" working on her earliest pieces in the kitchen rather than the studio, using improvised techniques and heating the plastic in her oven.[268] It was a subversive twist on the classic trope of the American housewife. Her *Kinetic Necklace* (1969), with its acrylic stars, stripes, and red, white, and blue color scheme, also evokes Wonder Woman as an ideal of liberated womanhood, but in a more abstract manner than Merritt's piece.(Fig. 6.4)

Kriegman was born in Orange, New Jersey, in 1933 and attended Yale University, Drew University, and Haystack Mountain School of Crafts. She studied with Josef Albers at Yale University and Olaf Skoogfors at the Philadelphia College of the Arts and was particularly interested in architecture, which came in handy when she and her husband Sam built a house in Maine. She loved wearing her jewelry and was a beautiful woman of elegance and exquisite taste.[269] Her artist statement in the *Objects: USA* catalogue sheds light on her perspective as a woman and a jewelry artist: "I believe in individual rather than multiple choice, and am convinced there are many who choose jewelry as they would sculpture, and wear it as an eclectic identification badge, lavishing upon it as much aesthetic consideration as they would upon the art which surrounds them in their homes. I'm sure that my hands in some way produce a comment upon the recent sum of my continuing experiences, and I hope they act as the realization of the better world seen by my inner eye."[270]

For Mary Ann Scherr, the politics of the body and its relationship to society and the environment fueled her jewelry. Born in Akron, Ohio, in 1921, Scherr (neé Weckman) was the youngest of three daughters and the only one interested in the arts.(Fig. 6.5) Her father was a skilled mechanic and inventor who was employed by B.F. Goodrich Company, while her mother was a classical pianist and dressmaker who designed and made clothing for influential Akron families. Design was an essential part of Scherr's youth, from the clothes she designed for herself to the maternity fashion prototypes that she and her mother designed in 1956–57 for Lord & Taylor department store. Perhaps her most important collaboration with family was when her father, upon his retirement, taught Scherr mechanical bench skills and helped her complete a commission (1965–69) from the United States Steel Company to design and fabricate a jewelry collection that would demonstrate the beauty and durability of stainless steel.[271]

Scherr had taken art classes in high school and began making jewelry soon afterward. Although she studied art and art history at the University of Akron, when the United States became militarily involved in World War II she left school to work at the Goodyear Aircraft Corporation in the cartography department, where she made war posters and visual evaluations of aircraft. Scherr moved to Chicago in 1943 to work for the Burton Browne Advertising Agency but soon after left to join the one-year national tour of a dance show directed and performed by a friend. In San Francisco, an old friend challenged her choice, telling her, "You've got to get out of this; you're an artist. You're not a dancer by training. Get out of here." She listened, and returned to Chicago, but was itinerant for a few years, moving back to Cleveland, reconnecting with her high-school

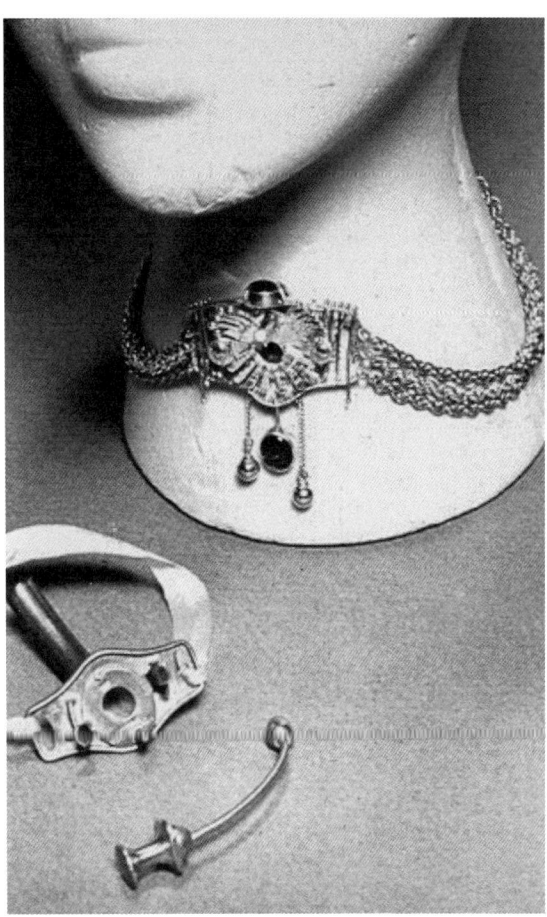

Fig. 6.6

Fig. 6.6
Mary Ann Scherr
Trach Necklace, c. 1979
Gold, silver, sapphire, opal, and hospital-issued standard base tracheotomy tube

Fig. 6.7
Mary Ann Scherr, in collaboration with Harry Hosterman
Heart–Pulse Sensor Bracelet, 1971
Gold, silver, and electronic devices
3 × 4 inches

friend Sam Scherr (whom she would later marry) and moving with him to Detroit, where they both worked as designers in the automotive industry. Finding the scope of their jobs limiting, they moved back to Akron and opened their own industrial design company, Scherr and McDermott, which counted among its clients Tappan appliances, Hoover vacuums, and Rubbermaid. From 1954 to 1969, they also were awarded a product development contract with the U.S. government to work in underdeveloped countries in South America as well as in Korea and Japan. Scherr designed jewelry, as well as clothing and toys, that could be made elsewhere and distributed internationally. The ACC became an important partner in identifying craftspeople who would then work for Scherr and McDermott.[272]

Working full-time as a designer and raising a family, Scherr recalls that she "backed into becoming a metalsmith."[273] She took her first course in jewelry in 1949 at the Akron Art Institute as a young mother looking to escape her apartment. She also began teaching design, product design, and metalsmithing at Kent State University in 1950, ultimately steering the department until 1978 and seeing it grow into a significant program that offered undergraduate and graduate studies in jewelry, enameling, and metalsmithing. By the late 1960s, it was a vibrant scene. "The students and other young people were concerned with remaining independent of authority and creating a world in which they felt comfortable,"

she recalled in 2001. "The *Whole Earth Catalog*, describing ways to survive with less mechanical assistance, became the how-to bible, and life returned to hand tools for building houses and making objects."[274]

Scherr's own response to the new world imagined by the counterculture began in 1969. It was a two-part endeavor, but each aspect dovetailed with the other in respect to Scherr's desires to help people cope with medical issues and the potential effects of the environment on their health. The first part of the project occurred serendipitously. While teaching a workshop in North Carolina, Scherr had a meaningful encounter with one of her students. As she recalls, "A woman at Penland School of Craft walked toward me and her scarf fell away from her throat, exposing an ugly piece of equipment. I was troubled with the image of her embarrassment as she moved her head allowing the trach to roll around inside her neck. I asked her about the device. Her reaction to the staring of others caused her to wear scarves to mask the device. I made her a decorative trach cover."[275] This "cosmetic cover-up," as Scherr called it, hid the ugly hospital devices for throat and esophagus issues. The simple design, a one-by-two-inch plane of gold and silver, was studded with precious stones and gave the wearer the confidence she needed to deal with an otherwise uncomfortable situation.(Fig. 6.6) With the satisfaction of providing an alternative, Scherr continued to make trach covers for women all over the country.

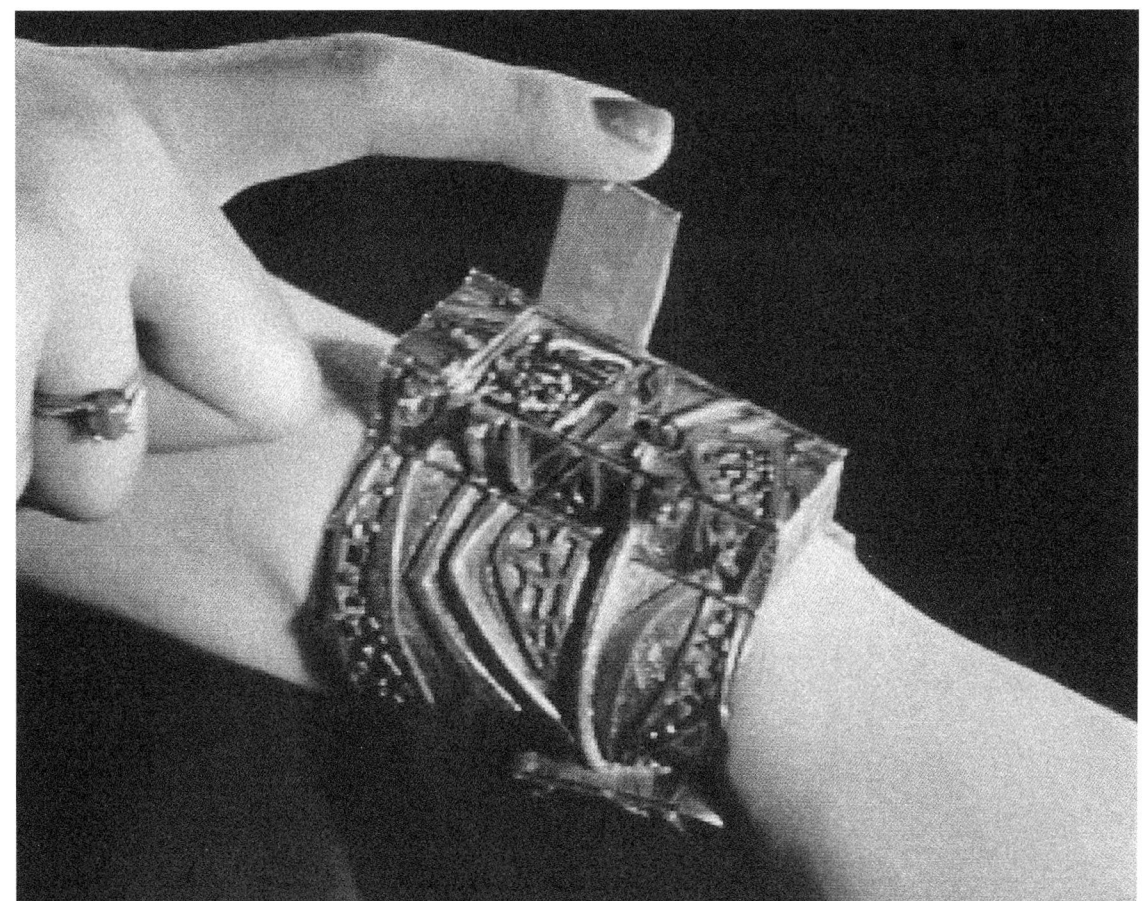

Fig. 6.7

The second part of the project grew from a commission to design the costume for the Miss Ohio representative to the Miss Universe competition. Scherr accepted the commission, even though she philosophically disagreed with beauty contests. Since one of the first astronauts, John Glenn, was from Ohio, the costume was based on a spacesuit. As she recalls:

> During one of those all-night working sessions ... I watched the awesome, still chilling, moon landing. I was making a stainless steel belt for the costume. It simulated the devices that might measure the astronaut's heartbeat and other vital areas of the body.... The TV screen showed a chart and recorded the beep-sounds that registered the results of the monitoring.... Amazing!... It occurred to me that we could measure the body in a similar way on our own planet. The following Monday ... I went on campus, talking to different department people, asking questions about the possibilities. I wanted to make a pendant that measured the air, so that in bad air, something could alert the wearer. I was advised that I was looking at an 11 by 15 foot wall that measured air quality ... . The wall was filled with massive mechanical and electronic devices measuring air. The professor smiled when I commented that I wanted a device small enough to wear as jewelry.[276]

Scherr quickly realized that if she could make works that could help people monitor the environment and its impact on health issues, then she could help a wide range of people, as with the trach covers. After visiting many Kent State University labs without success, she connected with an electronic engineer named Harry Hosterman, who was a consultant at her husband's office. During a month of hard work, Hosterman was able to reduce the size of the air-quality-measuring wall to a seven-by-three-inch area, which Scherr then turned into her first body-monitor pendant. A bracelet that covered a pulse monitor with an LED that displayed the wearer's pulse beat followed soon after.

By 1979 Scherr had designed, patented, and made numerous monitors that measured air, posture, heartbeat, and pulse; detected smoke; recognized sleep deprivation; and covered oxygen masks. Perhaps most significantly, she developed a portable electrocardiogram device.[(Fig. 6.7)] Scherr received national and international press for her devices, appearing on television shows such as *Today* and *The Tonight Show Starring Johnny Carson*, as well as in newspaper articles and documentaries. Doctors, scientists, and engineers wanted to collaborate with her, demonstrating the validity of her ideas from a medical perspective. Scherr hoped that the devices would be put into production. However, for many reasons, including financial and legal ones, they never went further than the prototype stage.

Civil Rights and Body Politics

Fig. 6.8

Fig. 6.9

Fig. 6.8
Mary Ann Scherr
Electronic Oxygen Belt Pendant, 1974
Sterling silver, electronics, amber, and oxygen mask
12 × 4 × 1 inches
Museum of Arts and Design, New York, gift of Mary Lee Hu, through the American Craft Council, 1979

Fig. 6.9
Back cover of the exhibition catalogue for *Portable World* held at the Museum of Contemporary Crafts in New York City, October 5, 1973 – January 1, 1974
Courtesy American Craft Council Library & Archives

Scherr utilized her design and metalsmithing skills to create works whose ornament was often inspired by African and Byzantine art. The earliest pieces, such as the heart-rate monitor bracelet and an oxygen-supply-holder pendant feature bold graphic patterns rendered in gold and silver. By the time that she created the *Electronic Oxygen Belt Pendant* (1974), she was augmenting these surface patterns with additional materials such as amber and decorative hanging elements. (Fig. 6.8)

Other monitors in the series were larger-scale, body-conscious, stainless-steel pendants. Scherr had worked with stainless steel for her submissions to the United States Steel Company competitions between 1965 and 1969, but now she combined the metal with liquid crystals and peacock feathers to create futuristic necklaces that monitored air temperature, air pollution, and body temperature. Scherr's body monitors addressed a host of issues that were becoming important in the 1970s, from climate change and its health repercussions to the effects of technology on daily lives. Her jewelry envisaged a world in which people with health conditions could be free to go about their daily lives untethered to bulky equipment. As such, they were exhibited and heavily promoted in Barbara Bullock and Paul J. Smith's *Portable World* exhibition in 1973 at the Museum of Contemporary Crafts in New York, an exhibition that explored the idea that the "portable person is the development of the 'technoself' through 'technological refinement.'"[277](Fig. 6.9) Scherr's monitors were displayed under the "Body Extension" section, though they could have easily been a part of the "Portable Person" section, whose description included the following: "Portable person is performance based. All system elements are integrated into a whole performance technoself. Individual performance needs result in a personal exoskeleton that results in a personal style."[278] The element of personal style speaks to the adornment provided by Scherr for her monitoring devices, without which their impact might not have been as strong.

Aside from Scherr, the *Portable World* exhibition included four other jewelers: the Pencil Brothers (Ken Cory and Leslie LePere), Don Tompkins, and Merrily Tompkins. The show featured futuristic machines, body extensions, shelters, vehicles, and other forms of portability. By the early 1970s, humans had ventured into space and landed on the moon, and, even on Earth, people were traveling more than ever. Barbara Bullock, one of the curators of *Portable World*, thought the time was right to show a large variety of objects related to this adaptability. "There are two extremes of mobility," she wrote in the catalogue. "An obsession with materialism and gadgets ... with all the accoutrements of a suburban community, contrasted with a desire for minimal possessions, represented by the youth in blue-jeans who travels the world with his needs in a backpack." This is a clear description of the split in American society between the adults who were interested in material wealth, and the youth of the counterculture who rejected it and were traveling

Civil Rights and Body Politics

135

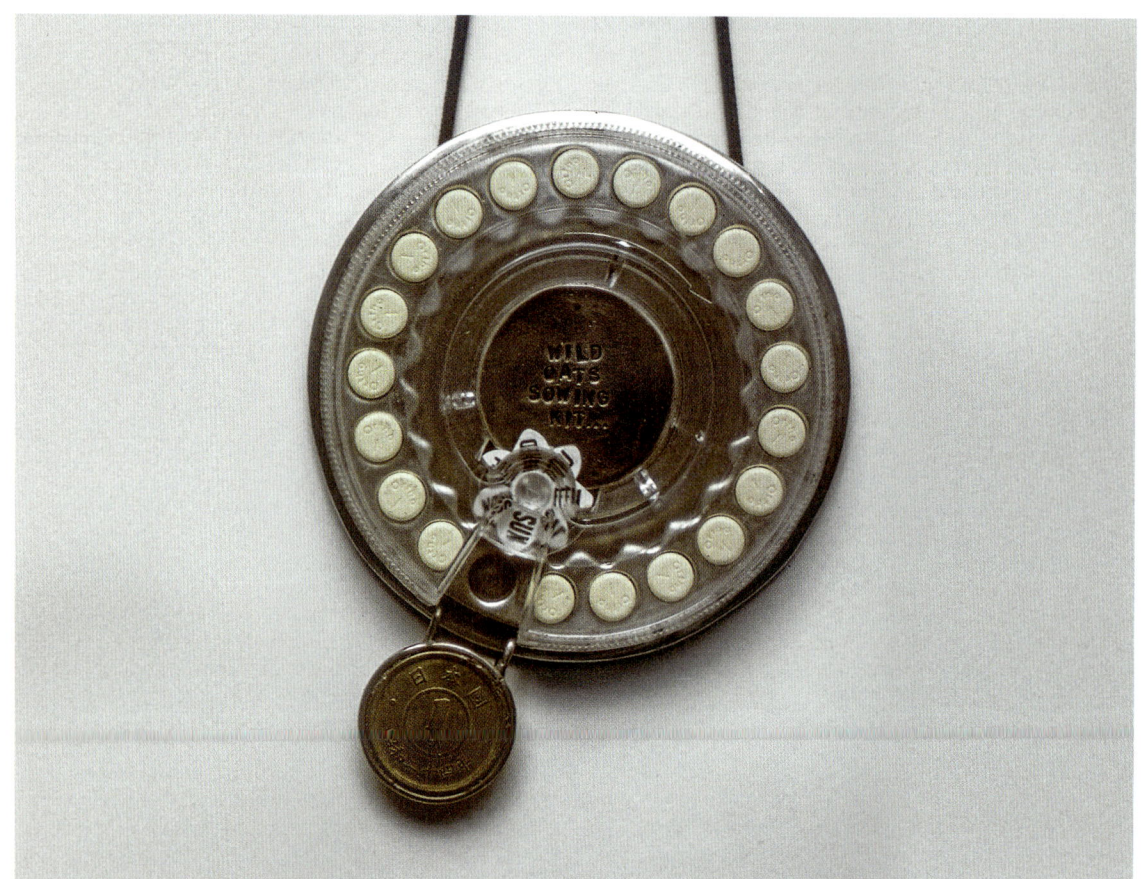

Fig. 6.10

the world to find a different answer. By including both in the exhibition, Bullock established a kind of nostalgic futurism that looked backward as much as forward. Mobility led to an individual's need to personalize and decorate items to hold on to an identity: "In the same way nomadic tribes ornamented both the interiors and exteriors of their yurts, tipis and tents, modern travelers decorate their vans, backpacks or blue-jeans."[279]

Merrily Tompkins was represented in the *Portable World* exhibition by a large pendant called *Wild Oats Sowing Kit* (1971).[Fig. 6.10] In the center of a Dialpak birth-control pill dispenser, Tompkins stamped the title on the brass backing plate, replacing the pharmaceutical logo of the original unit. The opening that enables each day's pill to be removed has been extended into a lever that incorporates a Japanese one-yen brass coin as a pun. To "have a yen for" something means to crave, and Tompkins offers the new sexually liberated woman of the 1970s, who refuses to accept that biology is destiny, a symbolic way to satisfy all her urges without fear of reproductive consequences.

Tompkins was living an unconventional life as a hippie in the Pacific Northwest when she made the *Wild Oats Sowing Kit*, and she was deeply affected by the youthful experiments related to sex, freedom, and individual expression and the search for meaning that were going on all around her. The Pill, as birth control was popularly called, played a key role in the mantra of "free love" that fed the social revolution of the late sixties and early seventies. Now women could have sex without the risk of pregnancy, so it was not necessary to postpone sexual activity until marriage.

By turning the Pill into a piece of jewelry that is proudly worn around the neck, Tompkins riffs off the Pill as a useful tool for American women. With its days-of-the-week labeling and set number of tablets, the "fool-proof" packaging also helped drug companies reassure conservative doctors that women would be able to safely use the medication, a concern raised by doctors who were fighting against the increasing number of young and unmarried women demanding contraceptive advice. Tompkins's pendant suggests that, by the early 1970s, that battle had been resoundingly won.

Fig. 6.10
Merrily Tompkins
Wild Oats Sowing Kit, 1971
Pendant
Birth-control dial, sterling silver, brass, and found object
3 × 3 × ⅜ inches
Courtesy American Craft Council Library & Archives

The jeweler Nancy Worden also addressed issues of feminism in her jewelry of the late 1970s.(Fig. 6.11) Worden was born in 1954 in Boston, Massachusetts. When she was eleven, her parents divorced; the following year, she and her mother moved to Ellensburg, Washington. Her mother remarried, and her stepfather and mother were both professors at Central Washington University and deeply involved in politics. "I was constantly around politics," recalls Worden. "Politics at the dinner table, politics nationally, politics about what was going on at the university where they taught. My mother was very active in George McGovern's campaign—she was a delegate to the Miami Convention. She was also active in Eugene McCarthy's anti-war campaign in 1968. She and my step-dad were very strongly opposed. She had a brother who was bombing Cambodia over there in Vietnam. He did two tours and they didn't speak for ten years. I think it divided our whole country."[280]

Worden was a strong feminist. She purchased the very first issue of *Ms.* magazine in November 1971, and she was a member of the feminist club at CWU, even before she became a student. Her mother was ambitious and a role model as to how a woman could be educated and pursue a career: "My generation had the pill. Big deal, very big deal. We didn't have to have children, we could choose. We were able to work, you didn't have to stay at home…. I had the advantage of a very ambitious and professional mother, and so this was expected of you."[281] Worden started collecting jewelry when she was thirteen in the belief that, if you wore interesting jewelry and clothes, people might think you were an interesting person. In 1972, when she was seventeen and still attending high school, she went to Central Washington State and asked Ken Cory if she could join his jewelry class. He said she could if she brought her own tools, and so she did, learning both basic techniques as well as jewelry history. Subsequently, in the spring of 1973, while the Watergate hearings were dominating the news, she took a design class from Cory.

Worden started using found objects in her jewelry because she did not have much access to stones. She hated enameling but wanted to introduce color into her work; found objects were the answer. *Initiation* (1977) demonstrates her deft use of found objects as messengers of meaning.(Fig. 6.12) Worden made the necklace in response to a class assignment from Cory asking his students to make a work responding to traditional Native American jewelry forms. Worden decided to use hair curlers as her base material. Many women had shag haircuts, or got perms and used curlers, so she found some curlers that looked like bones to her. Worden wrapped some in copper wire, electroformed others, and left a few in their pristine, pink form. The use of pink was a political statement, inspired by the feminist icon Gloria Steinem. This necklace conveys Worden's personal experiences as a woman, as well as fertility, hair, and other aspects tied to femininity.

During World War II, women joined the workforce, but when the men came home from fighting, women's roles reverted to working in the home and raising children. This idea was reinforced by advertisements and corporate slogans, which were crafted to develop a consumer base of women to buy their products. The companies selling labor-saving mixers, washing machines, ovens, and other appliances also developed the image of the perfect housewife. These ideals rang hollow to many women and resulted in a delayed reaction, known as second-wave feminism. Many magazine and newspaper articles at the time discussed "Women's Libbers" with contradictory interpretations about what women's liberation meant. Yet there was a real need for women to work in order to augment household income, as jobs shifted from blue-collar to service-sector positions and as the oil embargo in 1973 raised the price of gas exponentially.[282] The flagging economy caused a huge upheaval in the social structure of the country.

Like Worden, Harriete Estel Berman(Fig. 6.13) created jewelry that addressed gender roles. In addition, it concentrated on the way commercialism affected those roles. "From about 1967 to the present, I collected old tin cans," recalls Berman. "Originally, for 20 years or so I never cut up the tins…. I just collected them. I liked to study the advertising. Color, images, patterns, and words in advertising, and in this case tin cans, reveal a lot about society."[283] Berman loved the graphics and clever language used in advertisements for children's toys and was interested in how the selling of all kinds of consumer goods, including toys, toolboxes, and chemistry sets, reinforced specific gender roles and ideas of domesticity.

Berman's jewelry had strong feminist messages, which she developed in reaction to her own family experiences. Berman was born in Harrisburg, Pennsylvania, to a middle-class Jewish family. During summers, she worked for her father's office supply and furniture store. It was there that she learned her work ethic. Her mother was a stay-at-home mom, which she resented. As a rebellious teenager, Berman longed to escape her parents as soon as possible. In the spring of 1970, while she was in high school, Berman visited Syracuse University for a few days. At the time, heated demonstrations were occurring at colleges all over the United States, and Berman witnessed some in Syracuse, New York. These demonstrations closed down some of these universities and colleges until the end of the school year.

A few months later, Berman joined a summer class at Syracuse University just before the start of her freshman year at college. After graduating in 1974, she began working for Syracuse Jewelry and Manufacturing, a commercial jeweler, where she sized rings. Between 1974 and 1978, she lived in Charleston, West Virginia, with her future husband and worked at Galperin Jewelry, a traditional jeweler. From 1978 until her graduation in 1980, she pursued an MFA in jewelry and metalsmithing at the Tyler School of Art, studying under Stanley Lechtzin. She had heard about him and his program through craft magazines. He had an excellent reputation and had mentored many well-known graduates, so she thought that he would help her find her voice.

In 1979, at Lechtzin's suggestion, Berman submitted a piece, *Silver Iron*, for a competition sponsored by Sterling Silver Design and held at the Lever House in New York City.(Fig. 6.14) It was rejected for being untraditional. In *Silver Iron*, a full-sized, constructed iron opens to reveal a woman standing at an ironing board, holding a hammer. Her dress features a grid pattern (what Berman calls a gridiron pattern) intended to make fun of the

Fig. 6.11
Nancy Worden
Self-Portrait, 1975
Black-and-white photograph

Fig. 6.12
Nancy Worden
Initiation, 1977
Necklace
Silver, rhodonite, copper, pills set in epoxy, and hair curlers
12 ¾ × 10 ¼ × 1 inches
Tacoma Art Museum,
gift of the artist, 1999.5 A–B

Fig. 6.13
Harriete Estel Berman, 1983

Fig. 6.14
Harriete Estel Berman
Silver Iron, 1979
Sterling silver, epoxy resin, copper flooring, nickel silver, lacquer, and color Xerox
Dimensions when open:
7 × 4 × 7 inches
Collection of Leonard
and Phyllis Berman

Fig. 6.15

Fig. 6.15
Harriete Estel Berman
Buns in the Oven, 1982
Copper, paint, sterling silver or silver-plated, and candelabra
11 × 10 × 11 inches
Collection of the artist

Fig. 6.16
Harriete Estel Berman
Womanizer, Kitchen Queen, 1982
Paint, copper, brass, plastic container, doll, and lamination with wind up mechanism
15 × 5 × 5 ½ inches
Collection of the artist

Minimalist modern art of the 1970s. *Silver Iron* is a satirical shrine to the woman as homemaker; the figure appears within a space shaped like an altar, as a goddess of domestic chores.

Silver Iron led Berman to create The Family of Appliances You Can Believe In series. Her anger about women being discouraged by society from becoming professionals was one of the driving forces behind it, as was her fear about getting married, having children, and therefore having to stop being a metalsmith. Berman speculates that the idealization of the housewife was developed against the background of World War II, when normal life was on hold. After the war, everyone wanted to get married, have children, and live the American Dream. The fantasy of happiness and convenience was a way to return women to their traditional roles and tie them ever more tightly to the home with the promise of modern appliances.

The Family of Appliances You Can Believe In series comprises twenty-four objects made between 1981 and 1988. To add more humor to the series, and at the same time to have the series taken more seriously, Berman created a spoof video to accompany a show of the work at the California Crafts Museum in 1982, which promoted the range of "appliances," including *Silver Iron*, that she had created. She appears in an apron and long dress going into a storefront. Inside the store, she describes how each appliance is made, demonstrating them and describing what they do for women.

One of the works in the series, *Buns in the Oven*, embodies the fears and anger that Berman felt about marriage and women's role in that arrangement. Berman saw the *Birth Project* (1980 – 85) by Judy Chicago around the time that she was working on this piece, and it influenced her, even though she had issues with some aspects of Chicago's work. *Buns in the Oven* takes the shape of a miniature stove called a "Georgia O'Keefe" (perhaps a play on the O'Keefe & Merritt brand).(Fig. 6.15) Inside one of the two ovens, she has misquoted Chicago with the phrase "Project Birth," and the drawer below it contains a miniature marriage bed. The other oven holds a cross, indicating the sacrifice a woman makes when she is married. The back of the stove looks like the front of a bank building with the words "Infidelity Trust and Savings" and a small slot above to deposit coins. The doors to the bank are slightly ajar, and inside is a reproduction of Georgia O'Keeffe's painting *Sky Above Clouds IV* (1965), although there is no blue sky here for women. The title, referencing a "bun in the oven," a colloquial phrase for pregnancy, indicates that the anxiety about matrimony included a fear of being trapped by maternity.

Another work in the series, *Womanizer, Kitchen Queen* (1982), is a blender with a crown on top and a ballerina inside.(Fig. 6.16) The nu-gold crown bears a script that says "Misstress of the Home," misspelled on purpose to evoke Miss America–type beauty competitions and because the name Harriete means "mistress of the home." The blender button panel reads: LOVE, HONOR, OBEY, CHERISH, MIX, BLEND, STIR, CREAM, SPREAD, BEAR — ten activities prescribed for women. The ballerina wind-up doll, like those used in jewelry

140

Fig. 6.16

boxes, spins to the tune "When You Wish Upon A Star." The work undermines girlhood dreams of dancing and being a queen with the blender-button burdens of an adult woman's world. In this manner, Berman highlights the absurd fantasy of a perfect life promised by advertisers looking to sell such appliances.

Berman says, "As an artist, wife, and mother suffocating in 'domestic bliss,' my work is embedded with the mundane of everyday life and the relentless messages of 'satisfaction guaranteed.' The second-class status of women who care for home and children bears a strong relationship to the second class status of craft and handmade objects in the art world … . The irony of handmade objects replicating the status symbols of manufactured domestic appliances is an important aspect of their cultural meaning."[284]

Berman's clever titles are satirical, many taken directly from ads from the 1960s and 1970s that she had collected. In one, "The Promise of an Easier Way" floats above a dishwasher encircled by a sparkling, magical loop; in another, two small girls sitting at a table in front of a small refrigerator are accompanied by the words "I see a future of savings and convenience for you." Yet another features an image of a woman split in half; on one side she is a homemaker standing in her kitchen with an appliance in her hand, while on the other she wears a gown, and her tuxedo-clad husband stands in the background. Women were expected to lead double lives. These ads presented clearly defined roles and no moral dilemmas, and those who did not buy into them ultimately rebelled against their unreal expectations.

In the 1960s, African Americans also were campaigning for the legal and social rights that they had been historically denied. Even though the South had lost the American Civil War in 1865, and slavery had officially been abolished, Southern politicians continued to defend discrimination and racism through local and state laws that prevented African Americans from voting in the Deep South. "Jim Crow" laws upheld segregation in schools, public transportation, and the army. When Rosa Parks refused to give up her seat on a bus to a white man in 1955, a bus boycott led by the Montgomery Improvement Association and its leader, Martin Luther King, Jr., marked the beginning of the modern civil rights struggle in the United States. Sit-ins at lunch counters began in 1960, and "Freedom Riders" on buses traveling south tested the government legislation that supposedly ended segregation.

Over the next few years, Martin Luther King, Jr., promoted nonviolent resistance, specifically in his "I Have a Dream" speech during the 1963 March on Washington, in which more than two hundred thousand Americans protested to put pressure on President John F. Kennedy to push civil rights legislation through Congress. Even though the Civil Rights Act was passed the following year, the push to outlaw discrimination and segregation based on race, nationality, or gender, violence surrounding civil rights issues continued. In 1965 King led a march from Selma to Montgomery, the state capital of Alabama, to highlight the lack of voting rights for African Americans. More than thirty thousand people gathered on the steps of the state capitol. As a result, in late 1965 Congress passed the Voting Rights Act, which outlawed literacy tests for voting access and sent thousands of government officials into the South to supervise voter registration. Tragically, King was assassinated on April 4, 1968, by James Earl Ray, a white man, in Memphis, Tennessee.[285]

Yet, for the most part, African American studio jewelers did not make work that reflected the struggle for civil rights. Rather, commercial jewelry artists took on the subject. African American magazines and newspapers such as *Jet*, *Ebony*, and the *New York Amsterdam News* regularly featured editorials, news items, images, and advertisements for commercial jewelry that represented Black Power and Freedom Fists.[286]

One African American maker who did create work relating to political issues facing Black Americans during the period was Evangeline J. Montgomery. She completed a BFA at the California College of Arts and Crafts in 1969 and was active as a promoter of Black artists and craftspeople. In 1968, while she was still in college, she held a position at the Oakland Museum of California as an art consultant under the museum's Cultural and Ethnic Affairs Guild. From 1968 to 1974, she organized eight exhibitions of established and emerging African American artists and encouraged the museum in its efforts to collect work by key Black artists of the time, including Betye Saar and Raymond Saunders.[287] In association with Mills College in Oakland, Montgomery created a craft show that toured the Western Association of Art Museums. The exhibition participants were asked to create one work that explored their relationship to ancestors.

Two cast metal boxes that Montgomery created as part of her *Ancestor Box* series in the early 1970s are *Justice for Angela* (1970) and *Marcus Garvey Box* (1973). She based the series on African reliquary containers that provided a means to connect with ancestors. Her contemporary take on this tradition was to create boxes that would "connect" to important African Americans. The subject of *Justice for Angela* was Angela Davis, a member of the Black Panthers and the Communist Party, as well as a feminist and anti-war protestor. (Fig. 6.18) Davis was a former professor of philosophy at the University of California, Los Angeles, at the time that this work was made. In 1970 she famously armed citizens who were staging a hostile takeover of a courtroom in Marin County, outside of San Francisco, where four people were killed. Montgomery, who was in Oakland at the time, was well aware of Davis and the events surrounding her arrest and jail sentence. *Justice for Angela* features a large Ashanti symbol for justice. By using this symbol, Montgomery further connects African heritage to the Black American present.

Likewise, in the Marcus Garvey Box, also known as *Red, Black, and Green*, Montgomery created a reliquary box in the spirit of Marcus Garvey, featuring a Jamaican flag and abstract decorations. (Fig. 6.19) Garvey was a Jamaican-born political activist, journalist, and the founder and first president-general of the Universal Negro Improvement Association and African Communities League, an organization that promoted African Americans moving back to Africa and other separatist views that were adopted by the Nation of Islam and the Black

Fig. 6.17
Mills College gallery, *California Black Craftsmen*, 1970,
Courtesy Mills College Library

Fig. 6.18
Evangeline J. Montgomery
Justice for Angela, 1970
Box
Bronze
4½ × 2 × 1½ inches
Collection of Martha Jackson Jarvis

Civil Rights and Body Politics

Power Movement, among other groups. Garvey's controversial opinions were shared by the Klu Klux Klan, with whom he collaborated, earning him the suspicion of many Americans.

Montgomery's interest in Garvey stems from her pride in her African ancestry, and the promotion of African heritage in her own work and curatorial projects was strongly connected to the reigning motivations behind African American craft in the 1960s and 1970s. At the time, historically Black colleges and universities such as Howard University, Hampton College, Tuskegee, and Fisk University, as well as the National Conference of Artists (NCA) and AfriCobra (African Commune of Bad Relevant Artists), hosted lectures and exhibitions about African art, and Black craftspeople, like their colleagues in the fine arts, focused on African art and its creativity.[288] This moment has been described as "the second phase of recovery of the ancestral period."[289] For the jeweler Akosua Bandele, after bearing witness to the rise of Black nationalism and the politics of the Black Panthers in the 1960s, this meant turning toward Africa. "The ancestors spoke, and I listened," she recalls. "I realized that my life's mission was to lift up the spirit of the ancestors and the African cultural tradition in my art."[290]

Because of the focus on African heritage, and because Black craftspeople studied in African American schools, the field of African American studio craft largely occupied a parallel universe to that of mainstream American craft. Black makers sold their work annually at fairs organized by the NCA or at special exhibitions rather than through channels developed by organizations such as the American Craft Council (ACC) or the Society of North American Goldsmiths (SNAG).[291] For many, if not most, African American craftspeople, jewelers included, becoming members of the ACC or SNAG held little interest. Some leading scholars, such as Dr. David Driskell from the University of Maryland, were members specifically to receive *Craft Horizons*; others, especially professors, became members because it looked good on their résumés. Driskell's talk at the 1977 ACC conference held in Winston-Salem, North Carolina, on "America's Black Craftsmen" was one of many lectures that he gave across the country in the 1970s promoting the art of African American craftspeople, and the only lecture on Black artists at an ACC conference during the period. Largely dealing with ceramists and woodworkers, and well received by the audience, it did not have much of an impact on the ACC's future activities, including the inclusion of African American artists in *Craft Horizons* magazine.[292]

There were never many jewelers or metalsmiths in the African American craft community. One reason was the high cost of materials.[293] Another reason was that the art programs at historically Black colleges and universities did not emphasize jewelry or metals. With the exception of Howard University in Washington, D.C., which had a metals program beginning in the 1920s, and an art education program, led in the 1960s and 1970s by Catherine Pitchfork, that incorporated metals, no other institution offered a separate jewelry program. At Texas Southern University in Houston, Professor Carroll Harris Simms, a jeweler and ceramicist who was the first African American graduate of the Cranbrook Academy of Art, joined the faculty in 1950 and wanted to teach

Fig. 6.19
Evangeline J. Montgomery
Marcus Garvey Box, also known as *Red, Black, Green Ancestral box*, 1973
Silver and enamel
2 ¼ × 1 ⅝ × 1 ⅞ inches
Collection of Cledie Collins Taylor

jewelry; however, the university's concerns about enrollment and the necessary investment in equipment prevented him from doing so.[294]

The parallel universe for African American craftspeople extended to exhibitions and conferences. Perhaps the earliest exhibition, and possibly the first show dedicated to Black craftspeople at a public museum, was *California Black Craftsmen* (1970), (Fig. 6.17) curated by Evangeline J. Montgomery and held at the Mills College Art Gallery in Oakland, California.[295] Although only one jeweler, Carole Allen Ward, was mentioned in *Craft Horizons*, four others, Manuel Albert Gomez, Vernita Henderson, Bob Jefferson, and William Maxwell, took part, as did two makers working in metal, Montgomery and Harry S. Richardson.[296]

In 1979 the *Contemporary African American Crafts* exhibition was held at the Brooks Memorial Art Gallery in Memphis, Tennessee. Sponsored by the National Endowment for the Arts and organized by Driskell and Richard Hunt, the show included works by twenty-three craftspeople in all media, and its purpose was to proselytize an overlooked history. "The black craftsman remains obscure in the contemporary art world," noted the curators in the catalogue. "No single exhibition can rectify the omission of black craftsmen from exhibitions, but it is both timely and proper that the rich visual heritage and cultural contributions of the black artist be presented in a manner that will permit proper recognition of his talents as a craftsman and an artist."[297]

Only three jewelers were included in the exhibition: Montgomery, Joyce J. Scott, and Winifred Brown. Montgomery and Scott were well-established artists at the time, and Brown was working as an art teacher in the school system of St. Paul, Minnesota, while working on her MFA from the University of Wisconsin, Madison. Brown's practice followed the trajectory of many Black craftspeople in the 1970s: "As I worked on, the burning question became, 'what did I have to say with my craft as a black artist?' This led to a trip to Africa in 1973 and lo, a metamorphosis. Being black is an important dimension in my life that can't be denied or repressed."[298]

Contemporary African American Crafts was timed to coincide with a conference called "Toward Artistic Self-Sufficiency," the first African American crafts conference to take place in the United States. With a national advisory board of artists and scholars, the conference broadly examined African American history, aesthetics, traditions, and values in craft. In his keynote address, David Driskell delivered a call to arms. "Scholars of the crafts, historians of material and popular culture, art historians and practitioners of the arts, we as a people, greatly concerned with our own cultural survival in a hostile assimilationist racist society, must go all the way in every sense of the word to affirm our presence as

Fig. 6.19

Fig. 6.20
Joyce J. Scott at Haystack, 1973

Fig. 6.21
Joyce J. Scott
The White Boy's Gone Crazy, from the *Jonestown Massacre* series, 1980
Brooch
Beads, photos, pins, and bones
9 ½ × 3 ¼ × 1 ¼ inches
Philbrook Museum of Art, Tulsa, Oklahoma, museum purchase, 1991.21.4

African Americans," he told the audience. "We must not permit our image, the most visible one in this borrowed land, to be erased through acts of partial documentation and poorly conceived anomalies from sociologist types who write of black curiosities and call it scholarship."[299]

Joyce J. Scott is one of the only African American jewelers whose career straddled the parallel universes of the mainstream and African American craft communities during the 1970s.[Fig. 6.20] Scott graduated from the Maryland Institute College of Art in Baltimore in 1970 on a full four-year work/study scholarship. She was one of twelve African Americans there. She went on to earn an MFA at the Instituto Allende in San Miguel de Allende, Guanajuato, Mexico, in 1971. She wanted, she said, "to go someplace that was different and new and a challenge to myself. I also wanted to go to a place where there were indigenous people who were still living and having a real grasp on their history and that the history was alive in their country."[300] While she was there, she traveled to Guatemala, the San Blas Islands in Panama, and Peru.

In 1979 Scott began working on a series about the Jonestown massacre, which had horrified Americans the previous year. Nine hundred and eighteen people were killed in Guyana at a commune organized by Jim Jones, the founder of a religious group called the Peoples Temple. Jones was white, but the majority of his followers were Black. It was a mass suicide, or murder-suicide, in which Jones and the members of the Peoples Temple drank Kool-Aid mixed with cyanide. Jones called it a "revolutionary suicide." It was a result of his paranoid mental state, drug use, and declining health, as well as his worry about the exposure of his religious community in Africa by U.S. Congressman Leo Ryan, who was following up on disturbing reports from some of the relatives of the followers. Ryan arrived in Guyana with a group of eighteen people, including reporters and a camera crew, to question some of the Peoples Temple members. When a group of defectors decided to leave the compound with Ryan, chaos ensued. The whole horrific story was broadcast around the world when Ryan and five others were shot on the landing strip near the compound. The shooting led Jones to completely freak out and instruct his followers to drink the Kool-Aid.

"I made these works to exorcise the rage and despair I felt after reading about this tragedy," Scott recalls.[301] She could not believe that so many people would so easily end their lives because someone told them to do so. The *Jonestown Massacre* series is a quartet playing to the emotions that she felt at the time.

The first of these brooches is *The White Boy's Gone Crazy* (1980). A figure made of tree bark with bone extremities has a head featuring a photograph of Jim Jones, while a picture of Congressman Ryan with outstretched hands is crudely cross-stitched to the figure's chest.[Fig. 6.21] A photograph of a cup of poison, a single-edged razor blade, and innumerable stickpins with beaded heads complete the composition. The violence of the piece explicitly recalls Macumba, a blend of Christianity and voodoo that is widespread in northern Brazil. Razor blades are important in Macumba ceremonies to separate the soul from its ties to earth. Scott intended for this piece to sever Jones's body and soul so they could never return.[302] The violence of this exorcism is visceral.

Another brooch in the series, *The Double Cross* (1980), takes the form of a cross with a figure made from pigs' knucklebones wired together.[Fig. 6.22] The head is a photograph of a person crying out, and a heart shape hangs over the chest. A beaded rosary hangs around the figure. The cross combines a budded cross, which symbolizes an immature Christian or someone who is new to the faith, and a Celtic cross with a circle in the middle that symbolizes eternity. Scott intended both symbols and their meanings to be present in the work. The title also refers to how Jim Jones double-crossed the innocent souls who followed his beliefs and then his orders to drink the poisoned Kool-Aid.

Kool-Aide Kocktail (1980) refers to the way in which the Peoples Temple members were killed.[Fig. 6.23] Followers gave the drink to their children; others refused but were forced to take it. This brooch's shape is defined by a photograph of one of the metal tubs used to mix the lethal Kool-Aid. Over it, Scott superimposed a cutout photograph of a dead person in a fetal position, as though floating in the tub, tied up with crisscrossed

Fig. 6.21

Fig. 6.22

Fig. 6.23

thread. The brooch is coated in clear plastic as if to preserve it, then rimmed with bright-red beads and fringed with stiff, dark-brown hair like a scary vibrating halo.

The fourth and last piece in the *Jonestown Massacre* series is called *For the Souls* (1980). It comprises three black stones encased in shiny plastic that dangle from a larger stone bearing a tiny silver frame showing the face of a Black baby—one of the innocents massacred.[Fig. 6.24] In some religious traditions, stones are placed on graves to keep the spirits from rising up; in others, stones are thought to be made from crushed souls. Some Africans who were taken as slaves swallowed stones so that they could bring a piece of their land with them when forced to cross the Middle Passage to America. For Scott, "These souls are floating over Guyana. Because when you die of violence your soul cannot rest."[303]

Scott wants the viewer to engage with the beauty of the stones before realizing the horror of what is being depicted. She has said, "Being an artist is a political statement. After all, in a world where families can't feed their kids and people are homeless, to choose to be an artist is a political act. I can't be complacent about the world I live in. It's important for me to use art in a manner that incites people to look and then carry something home—even if it's subliminal—that might make a change in them."[304]

Fig. 6.22
Joyce J. Scott
The Double Cross, from the
Jonestown Massacre series, 1980
Brooch
Beads, photos, pins, bones, copper, and wood
9 ½ × 5 ¼ × 1 ½ inches
Philbrook Museum of Art, Tulsa, Oklahoma, museum purchase, 1991.21.3

Fig. 6.23
Joyce J. Scott
Kool-Aide Kocktail, from the
Jonestown Massacre series, 1980
Brooch
Beads, photo, pins, hair, and elastic
5 ½ × 4 ½ × ¼ inches
Philbrook Museum of Art, Tulsa, Oklahoma, museum purchase, 1991.21.1

Civil Rights and Body Politics

Fig. 6.24

Fig. 6.24
Joyce J. Scott
For the Souls, from the *Jonestown Massacre* series, 1980
Brooch
Beads, photos, pins, hair, and plastic
10 ½ × 5 ½ × 1 ¼ inches
Philbrook Museum of Art, Tulsa, Oklahoma, museum purchase, 1991.21.2

The End of an Era

Conclusion

The End of an Era

Richard Mawdsley's neckpiece *Wonder Woman in Bicentennial Finery* (1975–76) is a slightly unsettling object. (Fig. 8.1) A naturalistic female head and shoulders—Wonder Woman, as the title suggests—is joined to a machine-like torso, constructed of silver tubes, spheres, and curving forms that evoke a woman's body (breasts, narrow waist, hips, and legs). Two "arms," created from curving arcs of silver like the ornamental struts of a nineteenth-century bridge, terminate in cabochon-cut smoky quartz in elaborate settings that look like lamps or torches. In particular, they evoke the torch held aloft in the right hand of the Statue of Liberty, a connection reinforced by the exaggerated spikes of the tiara that Mawdsley's Wonder Woman sports on her head. This is Wonder Woman in costume, as if dressed up as the Statue of Liberty for a Bicentennial fancy dress party.

The year 1976 was America's Bicentennial, marking two hundred years since the signing of the Declaration of Independence. What should have been a time of pride and patriotism, a celebration of democracy in the world's most powerful country, was in fact a muted and conflicted affair. It had been a bruising decade. The Vietnam War and the struggle for civil rights had revealed stark and possibly irreconcilable fault lines in American society. Words like "people" and "revolution," so central to the Bicentennial, were almost impossibly complicated in the mid-1970s. A long history of discrimination meant that many Americans felt excluded from the famous phrase "We the people" in the U.S. Constitution, and "revolution" held contradictory meanings depending on what side of the political divide you stood.

The financial might and sense of security that had buoyed postwar America was challenged by a series of economic shocks that forced economists to coin a new term, "stagflation," to describe the combination of rising prices (inflation) and low economic growth and decline (stagnation), which was not supposed to be possible, according to conventional economic theory.

Mawdsley recalls, "After the horrific mess of the Vietnam War, to try to celebrate what America stood for seemed to be inappropriate. Or to ignore what happened and celebrate it like nothing had happened was offensive to a lot of people."[305] Mawdsley's neckpiece captures these mixed emotions. The image of the Statue of Liberty was everywhere during the Bicentennial, so it is not surprising that Mawdsley has Wonder Woman masquerading as another powerful lady who stands for truth, justice, and the American way. His choice of Wonder Woman also seems to share in the desire to reclaim wholesome and unambiguous symbols of American culture. Her lower torso and

Richard Mawdsley
Wonder Woman in Bicentennial Finery, 1975–76
Neckpiece
Silver, pearls, and smoky quartz
13 ¾ × 5 ½ × ¾ inches
Los Angeles County Museum of Art, gift of Lois and Bob Boardman, M.2015.252.69

The End of an Era

155

legs have the sleek appearance of a machine, a fitting tribute to the technological advancement and ingenuity that allowed the United States to win the space race and land a man on the moon just seven years earlier.

Yet each element is undercut in some way. This Statue of Liberty is not the real thing but rather someone dressed up in a costume. Wonder Woman, who debuted in *All-Star Comics* in 1941, was essentially propaganda for feminism and women's rights, so she stands for the disruption to social norms and American values that were so confronting and confusing to many Americans. Mawdsley further complicates things by the strange inclusion of two silver plates of salad topped with pearls that sit inside the figure's chest cavity. It is as if Wonder Woman, dressed as the Statue of Liberty, is catering a Bicentennial barbeque rather than fighting fascism and injustice with her Amazonian superpowers.

All these conflicting signals combined in Richard Mawdsley's neckpiece make it a perfect symbol of the late 1970s. Rather than fulfilling the utopian dream of the counterculture, the decade resulted in confusion and uncertainty, and a creeping sense of crisis, loss, limits, and failure.

American society might have been experiencing a late 1970s hangover from the wild party of the previous decade, but American jewelry—like the wider studio craft movement—was very successful in this period. The popularity and prominence of studio craft in America in the 1970s came about precisely because it embodied so much of what the counterculture had been seeking: self-expression, self-reliance, and environmental, social, and political awareness.

The field saw the establishment of professional practices and commercial venues through which to sell and promote jewelry, along with educational opportunities beyond universities and countercultural stances that challenged or outright rejected conventional norms. It was a heady period filled with excitement and with the sense that jewelers could make a difference and forge their own path, creating work that spoke to their specific interests and concerns.

Whereas some American jewelers used found objects and techniques appropriated from the fine arts, such as collage or assemblage, others remained true to hand-forming their materials but imbued their work with humor, satire, narrative, symbols, or other meanings. Jewelry as a means to tell stories and communicate ideas revolutionized the field and provided an alternative to the more aesthetically and materially accepted jewelry of most American jewelers at the time. It also contributed to a strong move away from the preciousness of traditional jewelry and claimed a whole new set of materials.

The most obvious legacy of this jewelry is the way it gave permission for American jewelers to open their work up to specific kinds of content. It could be political, dealing with events, ideas, or movements in the nation and the rights and responsibilities of its citizens; it could be cultural, dealing with personal stories and identities; or it could be emotional or nostalgic, tackling ambiguous concepts like "America." As American jewelers broke with the values that underpinned conventional jewelry—swapping the economic value of precious materials for other kinds of value based on artistic expression, subject matter, or social identity—they created new opportunities. They invigorated the field through their use of found objects, pop-cultural references, humor and satire, personal narratives, and figurative images. These qualities are what make American jewelry from the 1960s and 1970s seem novel and distinctive—and they set the tone for the inventive jewelry that would follow in the subsequent decades.

This book project began with a series of questions. What makes American jewelry "American"? Is it to do with a particular willingness to embrace political or cultural content? Who are the jewelers that most represent whatever qualities mark "American jewelry" as distinctive, and how do they fit into the American jewelry canon? The answers to these and other questions in this book represent an alternative history of American jewelry, one tied to the incredible period of the 1960s and 1970s, with all of its attendant political, social, and cultural issues. These jewelers and their work belong to a unique and truly American story, one without parallel anywhere else in the world.

Further Readings

A number of surveys of American jewelry provide a great overview of this branch of the studio craft movement. Janet Koplos and Bruce Metcalf's *Makers: A History of American Studio Craft* (University of North Carolina Press, 2010) is a decade-by-decade survey of the entire movement, with jewelry covered in pithy summaries that are both focused and alert to the wider cultural and social currents. *Jewelry by Artists in the Studio, 1940–2000*, a catalogue edited by Kelly H. L'Ecuyer about the Daphne Farago Collection at the Museum of Fine Arts, Boston, is probably the best survey of American jewelry. Starting with modernist jewelry of the 1940s and continuing through until the early 2000s, L'Ecuyer and her fellow authors use the Farago Collection to track the developments in American jewelry over six decades, weaving a national story into an international one, as American makers began to increasingly interact with their European colleagues from the 1970s onward. *Ornament as Art: Avant-Garde Jewelry from the Helen Williams Drutt Collection*, edited by Cindi Strauss and published by the Museum of Fine Arts, Houston, in 2007, is another excellent source. While not focused on American jewelry, its short but informative essays and the detailed biographies introduce the leading figures in the American jewelry movement. *Beyond Bling: Contemporary Jewelry from the Lois Boardman Collection* (Los Angeles County Museum of Art, 2016), edited by Rosie Chambers Mills and Bobbye Tigerman, not only is a rich source of images and information but also includes an essay by Tigerman focused on the West Coast jewelers who play such an important role in this book.

Monographs are the primary building blocks of art history, and telling the story of American jewelry's relationship to the counterculture has been made possible by many different publications that track the lives and careers of individual American jewelers. These include *The Miniature Worlds of Bruce Metcalf* (Palo Alto Art Center, 2008), *Robert W. Ebendorf: The Work in Depth* (Racine Art Museum, 2014), *Elegant Fantasy: The Jewelry of Arline Fisch* (San Diego Historical Society and Arnoldsche, 1999), *Thomas Mann: Metal Artist* (Guild Publishing, 2001), *Joyce J. Scott: Harriet Tubman and Other Truths* (Grounds for Sculpture, 2018), *Findings: The Jewelry of Ramona Solberg* (University of Washington Press, 2001), *Loud Bones: The Jewelry of Nancy Worden* (Tacoma Art Museum, 2009), and *J. Fred Woell: Art Is an Accident* (Metal Museum, 2015).

One particular monograph, *The Jewelry of Ken Cory: Play Disguised*, written by Ben Mitchell and published by Tacoma Art Museum in 1997, has been especially significant for this book. Mitchell's lively and playful text, which does not just tell the reader about Cory but embodies the same Funk characteristics that inform Cory's jewelry, has been an inspiring example of how to write about American jewelry and its various connections to the counterculture in the 1960s and 1970s.

One of the best sources for information about American jewelry in the 1960s and 1970s are the pages of *Craft Horizons*. First published in 1942, by the sixties the magazine had become the leading studio craft publication in America, adroitly guided by the editor Rose Slivka. It contains feature articles about many of the jewelers discussed in this book, as well as exhibition reviews and reports from conferences, workshops, and other events. These not only document what happened but also reveal the attitudes and opinions of the authors. As a whole, the magazine is an extraordinary representation of the studio craft movement in America and offers fascinating insights into the complex and sometimes contradictory relationship between craft and the counterculture. *Craft Horizons* has been digitized by the American Craft Council, and is available on its website (https://digital.craftcouncil.org/digital/collection/p15785coll2).

Many of the jewelers featured in this book have been written about in *Metalsmith* magazine, which began in 1975, first as *Golddust*, then as *Goldsmiths Journal*, and then as *Metalsmith* in 1980. It would be impossible to write any history of American jewelry without the research supported by this magazine over the past four decades. Some of its articles can be found online on the Ganoksin website (www.ganoksin.com).

The Smithsonian Archives of American Art is an excellent place to search for information about American jewelry (https://www.aaa.si.edu/). Its collection of oral histories with American jewelers is a superb resource, providing detailed insights into the attitudes, lives, and work of leading makers, including many who feature in this book. Most interviews have transcripts that can be downloaded as well. The American Craft Council archives are the other essential resource for anyone who wants to know more about American jewelry and American studio craft (https://craftcouncil.org/library/archives). They hold material from the American Craft Council, the Museum of Contemporary Crafts, the World Crafts Council, and the Craft Students League of New York. An extraordinary number of these archives have been digitized and are accessible online, and the librarians are extremely helpful and quick to respond.

One of the most insightful books about the counterculture is Theodore Roszak's *The Making of a Counter Culture: Reflections on the Technocratic Society and Its Youthful Opposition*, first published in 1969, and widely available in a 1995 edition from the University of California Press. Roszak was writing while the various forms of the counterculture were unfolding in real time, and he balances a rich sense of the aesthetics, events, and politics of the late sixties with a deeper analysis of what kind of revolution young Americans were seeking to create.

Danny Goldberg's *In Search of the Lost Chord: 1967 and the Hippie Idea*, published by Akashic Books in 2017, does a wonderful job of conjuring the textures, moods, and values of the hippie movement. This book brings to life such events as the Summer of Love in San Francisco in 1967, documenting the people, events, and movements in music, art, politics, and psychoactive substances that informed hippie culture and its beliefs. Goldberg writes in a breezy style that is supported by solid research, creating an affectionate and detailed portrait of an era and its legacies.

Hippie Modernism: The Struggle for Utopia, edited by Andrew Blauvelt and published by the Walker Art Center in 2015, accompanied an exhibition of the same name and serves as a fascinating guide to the intense and unexpected connections between the hippie movement and certain currents in fine art, design, and architecture. Blauvelt and his fellow authors roam widely, not just in terms of the cultural, social, and political movements that they cover but in terms of geography and locations, moving beyond major centers and outside the white cube of galleries and museums to track the radical visual experiments taking place between 1964 and 1974.

A similarly inspiring book is *West of Center: Art and the Counterculture Experiment in America, 1965–1977*, edited by Elissa Auther and Adam Lerner and published by the University of Minnesota Press in 2012. Like *Hippie Modernism*, *West of Center* is a survey of cultural and social experiments deeply connected to the counterculture that do not fit into conventional categories of fine art, making them largely invisible in most art histories of the period. Demonstrating that the counterculture collapsed the gap between lifestyle and art form, this book makes an important argument for the significance of handmade objects in the counterculture, as well as showing how culture and politics were intertwined in dynamic and radical ways.

Some wonderful publications from the period provide insights into how handmaking and American jewelry as part of the studio craft movement were implicated with the counterculture. Donald J. Willcox, an American craftsperson living in Denmark, published *Body Jewelry: International Perspectives* with the Henry Regnery Company in 1973, bringing together a selection of jewelers from around the world to illustrate his point that the radical experimentation that had shaped contemporary jewelry in the 1960s and continued to remake it in the 1970s was driven by the same counterculture impulses that were convulsing society during the same period.

A year later, Alexandra Jacopetti published *Native Funk and Flash: An Emerging Folk Art* (Scrimshaw Press, 1974), a richly illustrated documentation of what she described as a "contemporary folk art" taking place in the San Francisco Bay Area. Many different kinds of making were being utilized by the tribes of the counterculture to express their individuality as well as their tribal belonging. They developed a complex venacular of invented and appropriated symbols, which they embroidered on jeans, jackets, and headbands, or applied to shirts, skirts, and blankets, or carved in wood or shaped in clay. It is a wonderful record of the aesthetics of the counterculture, and the important role of making in the counterculture, outside and beyond the studio craft movement.

At the end of the decade, *Craftsman Lifestyle: The Gentle Revolution* was published by California Design in 1979. A survey of California-based craftspeople, with texts by Olivia H. Emery and photographs by Tim Andersen, this book reveals the extraordinary sympathy between the values of the counterculture and the beliefs and practices of studio craft. Jewelers feature alongside potters, weavers, glass blowers, and furniture makers, living lives deeply dedicated to the profound authenticity of the handmade, and demonstrating the variations of social arrangements and connections to nature that flourished on the West Coast in the sixties and seventies.

Notes

Acknowledgments

[1] Janet Koplos and Bruce Metcalf, *Makers: A History of American Studio Craft* (Chapel Hill: University of North Carolina Press, 2010), 182.

[2] Theodore Roszak, *The Making of a Counter Culture: Reflections on the Technocratic Society and Its Youthful Opposition* (Berkeley: University of California Press, 1995 [1969]), 149.

Introduction
Objects and Politics

[3] Teresa A. Carbone, "Exhibit A: Evidence and the Art Object," in Teresa A. Carbone et al., *Witness: Art and Civil Rights in the Sixties* (Brooklyn and New York: Brooklyn Museum and Monacelli Press, 2014), 81, 89–90.

[4] William C. Seitz, *The Art of Assemblage* (New York: Museum of Modern Art, 1961), 83.

[5] Ibid., 87–89.

[6] J. Fred Woell, "The Impact of the University of Wisconsin Art Metals Program," unpublished typed document, 2007, J. Fred Woell Archive, Maine.

[7] J. Fred Woell, "Statement of Influences Upon My Work," unpublished typed document, July 24, 1996, J. Fred Woell Archive, Maine.

[8] J. Fred Woell, "The Impact of the University of Wisconsin Art Metals Program," unpublished typed document, 2007, J. Fred Woell Archive, Maine.

[9] J. Fred Woell, letter to Kirstie McDermott, November 4, 1994, J. Fred Woell Archive, Maine.

[10] J. Fred Woell, "A Brief Narrative Account of My Career," unpublished typed manuscript, 1983, J. Fred Woell Archive, Maine.

[11] Kathleen Kriegman, email to Damian Skinner, September 20, 2016.

[12] J. Fred Woell, "A Brief Narrative Account of My Career," unpublished typed manuscript, 1983, J. Fred Woell Archive, Maine.

[13] Paul J. Smith et al., *The Art of Personal Adornment* (New York: Museum of Contemporary Crafts, 1965), 44.

[14] J. Fred Woell, interview with Donna Gould, June 6 and 11, 2001, and January 9, 2002, Nanette L. Laitman Documentation Project For Craft and Decorative Arts in America, Archives of American Art, Smithsonian Institution.

[15] J. Fred Woell, untitled comments about *Fetish* pendant, unpublished typed document, c. 1988, J. Fred Woell Archive, Maine.

[16] Eleanor Moty, "In Memory of J. Fred Woell," *Art Jewelry Forum*, April 13, 2015, https://artjewelryforum.org/articles-series/in-memory-of-j-fred-woell.

[17] Kathleen Kriegman, email to Susan Cummins, October 12, 2018.

[18] J. Fred Woell, letter to Helen Drutt, December 28, 2001, J. Fred Woell Archive, Maine.

[19] Ibid.

[20] J. Fred Woell, letter to John Cage, January 26, 1987, J. Fred Woell Archive, Maine.

[21] Susan Cummins, "In Conversation with Robert Shetterly," *Art Jewelry Forum*,

January 29, 2018, https://artjewelryforum.org/in-conversation-with-robert-shetterly.

22   J. Fred Woell, letter to Helen Drutt, December 28, 2001, J. Fred Woell Archive, Maine.

23   Kathleen Kriegman, email to Susan Cummins, October 12, 2018.

24   J. Fred Woell, "A Comment About My Work," unpublished typed document, c. 1969, J. Fred Woell Archive, Maine. Although this statement is not dated, it is a more refined version of the statement published in the catalogue to his 1967 exhibition at the Museum of Contemporary Crafts in New York City.

25   Ben Mitchell, "Heart and Head: The Life and Work of Don Tompkins," *Metalsmith* 23, no. 3 (Summer 2003): 29–30.

26   Ibid., 33.

27   Ibid.

28   "Cognitive Dissonance: Paul Krassner's 'Fuck Communism' Banner, 1963," Dangerous Minds website, October 10, 2014, https://dangerousminds.net/comments/cognitive_dissonance_paul_krassners_fuck_communism_banner_1963.

29   Kurt Vonnegut, in Paul Krassner, *The Winner of the Slow Bicycle Race: The Satirical Writings of Paul Krassner* (New York: Seven Stories Press, 1997), 15.

30   Michael Dumas, "The Life and Times of J. Fred Woell," *Metalsmith* 7, no. 1 (Winter 1987): 27.

31   J. Fred Woell, "Artist Statement," in *Jewelry by Fred Woell* (New York: Museum of Contemporary Crafts, 1967), unpaginated.

32   J. Fred Woell, "Artist Statement," in "J. Fred Woell: Epoxy and Metal Sculpture," press release, Lee Nordness Galleries, December 1969, J. Fred Woell Archive, Maine.

33   Merrily Tompkins, "My Bro + Me," handwritten unpublished text, Merrily Tompkins Archives, Ellensburg.

34   J. Fred Woell, "Artist Statement," in Lee Nordness, ed., *Objects: USA — Works by Artist-Craftsmen in Ceramic, Enamel, Glass, Metal, Plastic, Mosaic, Wood, and Fiber* (New York: Viking, 1970), 226.

35   Olaf Skoogfors, excerpt from *The American Contemporary Jewelry Exhibition* catalogue, 1968, as reprinted in *Olaf Skoogfors 20th Century Goldsmith 1930–1975* (Philadelphia: The Falcon Press, 1979), 5.

36   Albert Paley, interview with Cindi Strauss, January 13, 2005.

37   Stanley Lechtzin, "Juror's Statement," in *Goldsmith '70* (St. Paul: Minnesota Museum of Art, 197), unpaginated.

38   Ibid.

39   John Prip, "Juror's Statement," in *Goldsmith '70*.

40   Glenn Adamson, "Objects: USA," in *Shows and Tales: On Jewelry Exhibition Making*, ed. Benjamin Lignel (Mill Valley, CA: Art Jewelry Forum, 2015), 43–44.

41   J. Fred Woell, "Artist Statement," in *Objects: USA*, 226.

42   Paul J. Smith, interview with Cindi Strauss, April 9, 2018.

43   Lee Nordness, "Approaches to the Object," in *Objects: USA*, 11.

44   Robert Hilton Simmons, "Objects: USA — The Johnson Collection of Contemporary Crafts," *Craft Horizons* 29, no. 6 (November/December 1969): 27.

45   Ibid., 66.

Chapter One
Making in the Counterculture

46   Arthur Korb, quoted in Olivia H. Emery, *Craftsman Lifestyle: The Gentle Revolution* (Pasadena: California Design Publications, 1979), 71.

47   Merry Renk, quoted in Emery, *Craftsman Lifestyle*, 128.

48   Eudorah M. Moore, introduction, in ibid.

49   Ibid.

50   Donald Willcox, *Body Jewelry: International Perspectives* (Chicago: Henry Regnery Company, 1973), x.

51   Ibid.

52   Ibid., viii.

53   Elissa Auther, "Craft and the Handmade at Paolo Soleri's Communal Settlements," in Elissa Auther and Adam Lerner, eds., *West of Center: Art and the Counterculture Experiment in America, 1965–1977* (Minneapolis: University of Minnesota Press, 2012), 123–24.

54   Greg Castillo, "Counterculture Terroir: California's Hippie Enterprise Zone," in Andrew Blauvelt, ed., *Hippie Modernism: The Struggle for Utopia* (Minneapolis: Walker Art Center, 2015), 93.

55   Janet Koplos and Bruce Metcalf, *Makers: A History of American Studio Craft* (Chapel Hill: University of North Carolina Press, 2010), 293.

56   Thomas Mann, email to Susan Cummins, November 25, 2019.

57   Joni Mitchell, Woodstock, from Ladies of the Canyon, 1970. Woodstock lyrics © Sony/ATV Music Publishing LLC

58   Ibid.

59   Ibid.

60   Amy Azzarito, "Libre, Colorado, and the Hand-built Home," in Auther and Lerner, eds., *West of Center*, 96.

61   Roberta Price, *Huerfano: A Memoir of Life in the Counterculture* (Amherst and Boston: University of Massachusetts Press, 2004), 68.

62   Lloyd Kahn, *Shelter* (Bolinas, CA: Shelter Publications, 1973), 107.

63   Azzarito, "Libre, Colorado, and the Hand-built Home," 99–100.

64   Blauvelt, ed., *Hippie Modernism*, 268.

65   *The Last Whole Earth Catalog* (Menlo Park, CA: Portola Institute, 1972), 156.

66   Paulus Berensohn, *Finding One's Way with Clay: Pinched Pottery and the Color of Clay* (New York: Simon and Shuster, 1972), 38–41.

67   Jane Holtz Kay, "ACC/Northeast Regional Conference," *Craft Horizons* 29, no. 5 (September/October 1969): 4.

68   Danny Goldberg, *In Search of the Lost Chord: 1967 and the Hippie Idea* (New York: Akashic Books, 2017), 30–62.

69   "Back to Nature," *ACC Outlook* 12, no. 3 (April 1971): 2.

70   Jessica Shaykett, "This Month in American Craft Council History: July 2012," American Craft Council website, July 2, 2012, https://craftcouncil.org/post/month-american-craft-council-history-july-2012.

71   Clotilde Barrett, "Colorado Craft-in," *Craft Horizons* 32, no. 6 (December 1972): 3.

72   Christina Smith, interview with Damian Skinner and Susan Cummins, August 13, 2018.

73   Jim Cotter, interview with Cindi Strauss, August 8, 2017.
74   Lynda Watson, interview with Susan Cummins, August 14, 2018.
75   Jan Brooks, interview with Cindi Strauss, November 14, 2018.
76   Robert Ebendorf, interview with Cindi Strauss, November 13, 2018.
77   Jim Cotter, interview with Cindi Strauss, August 8, 2018.
78   Eleanor Moty, interview with Susan Cummins, January 28, 2019.
79   Jan Brooks, interview with Cindi Strauss, November 14, 2018.
80   Lane Coulter, interview with Cindi Strauss, November 12, 2018.
81   Jim Cotter, interview with Cindi Strauss, August 7, 2018.
82   Randy Milhoan, interview with Cindi Strauss, August 7, 2018.
83   *Summervail Workshop*, brochure (Vail: Summervail Workshop, 1975).
84   Randy Milhoan, interview with Cindi Strauss, August 7, 2018.
85   Jim Cotter, interview with Cindi Strauss, August 8, 2017.

Chapter Two
Counterculture Jewelers

86   Theodore Roszak, *The Making of a Counter Culture: Reflections on the Technocratic Society and Its Youthful Opposition* (Berkeley: University of California Press, 1995 [1968]), 66.
87   Danny Goldberg, *In Search of the Lost Chord: 1967 and the Hippie Idea* (New York: Akashic Books, 2017), 13 – 14.
88   Ibid., 17 – 18.
89   Lynda Watson, interview with Susan Cummins, July 1, 2018, and February 23, 2018.
90   Lynda Watson, interview with Susan Cummins, February 23, 2018.
91   Ibid.
92   Lynda Watson, email to Susan Cummins, May 27, 2018.
93   Lynda Watson, interview with Susan Cummins, July 14, 2018.
94   Lynda Watson, quoted in Olivia H. Emery, *Craftsman Lifestyle: The Gentle Revolution* (Pasadena: California Design Publications, 1979), 94.
95   Diane Kuhn, William Clark Biography, unpublished typed document, November 6, 2009, Diane Kuhn Collection, Berkeley and San Diego, CA.
96   Ibid.
97   William Clark, notes written by Diane Kuhn, 2005, the Diane Kuhn Collection, Berkeley and San Diego, CA.
98   William Clark, notes by Diane Kuhn, Diane Kuhn Collection, Berkeley and San Diego, CA.
99   Paul R. Ehrlich, prologue to *The Population Bomb* (New York: Ballantine Books, 1968), xi.
100 Thomas Albright, "May's Animals, Birds, Figures," *San Francisco Chronicle*, February 27, 1971, 34.
101 Kuhn, William Clark Biography.
102 William Clark, résumé from Velvet da Vinci Gallery, 2005, the Diane Kuhn Collection, Berkeley and San Diego, CA.
103 Connie Fukuda, "Exhibits at Palo Alto Cultural Center Cover Wide Range of Interests," *Palo Alto Times*, November 20, 1973; Penny Smith, "Jewelry of Social Comment," *Artweek* (1974), the Diane Kuhn Collection, Berkeley and San Diego, CA.
104 Laurie H. Glass, "Sculpture to Wear," *Artweek* (n.d.), the Diane Kuhn Collection, Berkeley and San Diego, CA.
105 Louis Mueller, interview with Susan Cummins, September 29, 2018.
106 Ibid.
107 Ibid.
108 Ibid.
109 Andrew Blauvelt, ed., *Hippie Modernism: The Struggle for Utopia* (Minneapolis: Walker Art Center, 2015), 11.
110 Alexandra Jacopetti, *Native Funk and Flash: An Emerging Folk Art* (San Francisco: Scrimshaw Press, 1974), 5, 23.
111 Allen Ginsberg, quoted in Goldberg, *In Search of the Lost Chord*, 228.
112 Arline Fisch, interview with Sharon Church, July 29 – 30, 2001, Smithsonian Archives of American Art, Washington, D.C.
113 Ida Katharine Rigby, "The Tributaries of Memory," in *Elegant Fantasy: The Jewelry of Arline Fisch* (San Diego and Stuttgart: San Diego Historical Society and Arnoldsche, 1999), 14 – 17.
114 Robert Bell, "The Language of Woven Metal: The Influence of Textile and Thread in the Work of Arline Fisch," in *Elegant Fantasy*, 21.
115 Lori Talcott, conversation with Damian Skinner and Susan Cummins, July 31, 2018.
116 LaMar Harrington, "Master Metalsmith Ruth Penington," *Metalsmith* 6 (Winter 1986), available online at https://www.ganoksin.com/article/master-metalsmith-ruth-penington/ (accessed September 5, 2019).
117 Quoted in Vicki Halper, *Findings: The Jewelry of Ramona Solberg* (Seattle: Bank of America Gallery and the University of Washington Press, 2001), 6 – 7.
118 Ibid., 8.
119 Ibid., 10.
120 Ramona Solberg, "Artist Statement," in *Objects: USA*, 205.
121 Ben Mitchell, *The Jewelry of Ken Cory: Play Disguised* (Seattle: University of Washington Press, 1997), 78 – 80.
122 Leslie LePere, interview with Damian Skinner, April 26, 2018.
123 Sandra Alfoldy, *Crafting Identity: The Development of Professional Fine Craft in Canada* (Montreal and Kingston: McGill-Queens University Press, 2005), 163 – 64.
124 Rose Slivka, "People/Talk/Travel/Work," *Craft Horizons* 28, no. 6 (November/December 1968): 19 – 21, 51 – 55.
125 James S. Plaut, "A World Family," in *In Praise of Hands: Contemporary Crafts of the World* (Greenwich, CT: New York Graphic Society, 1974), 9.
126 Ibid., 10 – 11.
127 Ibid., 12.
128 "Bennington Plays Pivotal Rose in Crafts History," This Is Vermont, https://www.thisisvermont.com/TIV/bennington-crafts-history/ (accessed December 3, 2019).

129 Thomas Mann, interview with Susan Cummins, October 20, 2019.
130 Bennett Bean, interview with Susan Cummins, September 9, 2019.
131 Connie Mettler, "A Walk Through History: The Roots of the Craft Show Business," *Art Fair Insiders*, January 13, 2010, https://www.artfairinsiders.com/profiles/blogs/a-walk-through-history-the.
132 Conrad Brown, "Shop One," *Craft Horizons* 16, no. 2 (March/April 1956): 19–21.
133 Yoahiko Uchida, "A San Francisco Jewelry Shop: It Buys to Sell," *Craft Horizons* 17, no. 4 (July/August 1957): 12–13.
134 "Sheinbaum Tells Why Fairtree Closes in New York," *Craft Horizons* 36, no. 1 (February 1976): 7.
135 Larry Grobel, "Profile: Fairtree's Stan Reifel," *Craft Horizons* 35, no. 3 (June 1975): 10.
136 Ibid.
137 Jean Cacicedo and Ana Lisa Hedstrom, *Obiko Artwear Archive Project* (San Francisco: Textile Arts Council Fine Arts Museums of San Francisco, 2014), unpaginated. Available online at http://www.textileartscouncil.com/wp-content/uploads/2014/09/Obiko_Archive_screen.pdf (accessed December 30, 2019).
138 Paul J. Smith, "Fur and Feathers," press release, 1971, American Craft Council Archives.
139 Paul J. Smith, *The Art of Personal Adornment* (New York: Museum of Contemporary Crafts, 1965), 1.
140 Helen W. Drutt English, interview with Cindi Strauss, February 9, 2005.
141 Helen W. Drutt English, email to Cindi Strauss, January 27, 2020.
142 Helen W. Drutt English, interview with Cindi Strauss, February 9, 2005.
143 Bella Neyman, "Robert Lee Morris: Staying Power," *Metalsmith* 40, no. 1 (2020): 45.
144 Gloria Lieberman, "Sculpture to Wear: Artist Jewelry and Joan Sonnabend," *Skinner Auctioneers and Appraisers*, August 16, 2012, https://www.skinnerinc.com/news/blog/joan-sonnabend-artist-jewelry-sculpture-to-wear-2/.
145 Dorothy Spencer, "Robert Lee Morris: The End of an Era," *Metalsmith* (Spring 1994): 43.
146 Ettagale Blauer, *Contemporary American Jewelry Design* (New York City: Springer, 1991), 35.

Chapter Three
Funk Jewelry

147 Quoted in Lisa Phillips, "Beat Culture: America Revisioned," in Lisa Phillips, ed., *Beat Culture and the New America: 1950–1965* (Paris and New York: Flammarion and Whitney Museum of American Art, 1996), 29.
148 Ibid., 29–33.
149 Toni Greenbaum, *Messengers of Modernism: American Studio Jewelry 1940–1980* (Montreal and Paris: Museum of Decorative Arts and Flammarion, 1996), 15–17.
150 Ibid., 17.
151 Quoted in Kelly H. L'Ecuyer, "Abstraction to Assemblage: Studio Jewelry Begins, 1940–1970," in Kelly H. L'Ecuyer, *Jewelry by Artists in the Studio, 1940–2000* (Boston: MFA Publications, 2010), 68.
152 Greenbaum, *Messengers of Modernism*, 22.
153 Quoted in L'Ecuyer, "Abstraction to Assemblage," 46.
154 Ibid., 49.
155 Ibid., 66; Greenbaum, *Messengers of Modernism*, 90.
156 Rebecca Solnit, "Heretical Constellations: Notes on California, 1946–61," in Phillips, ed., *Beat Culture and the New America*, 73.
157 Ibid.
158 Quoted in Thomas Albright, *Art in the San Francisco Bay Area 1945–1980: An Illustrated History* (Berkeley: University of California Press, 1985), 86.
159 Daniel Macchiarini, quoted in Marbeth Schon, *Form & Function: American Modernist Jewelry, 1940–1970* (Atglen, PA: Schiffer Publishing, 2008), 169.
160 Greenbaum, *Messengers of Modernism*, 23.
161 Ibid., 18.
162 Blanche Brown, quoted in Janet Koplos and Bruce Metcalf, *Makers: A History of American Studio Craft* (Chapel Hill: University of North Carolina Press, 2010), 193.
163 Albright, *Art in the San Francisco Bay Area 1945–1980*, 89.
164 Solnit, "Heretical Constellations," 71, 85.
165 Thomas Crow, *The Rise of the Sixties: American and European Art in the Era of Dissent 1955–1969* (London: Calmann & King, 1996), 25, 27.
166 Beverly Cory, quoted in Ben Mitchell, *The Jewelry of Ken Cory: Play Disguised* (Tacoma: Tacoma Art Museum, 1997), 34.
167 Mitchell, *The Jewelry of Ken Cory*, 51.
168 Ibid., 49.
169 Judith Tannenbaum, "Outside the Looking Glass," in Dan Nadel, ed., *What Nerve! Alternative Figures in American Art, 1960 to the Present* (New York: D.A.P., 2014), 13–14.
170 Peter Selz, "Notes on Funk," in *Funk* (Berkeley: University of California, 1967), 3.
171 Ibid., 5.
172 Robert Arneson, quoted in Alfred Frankenstein, "The Ceramic Sculpture of Robert Arneson: Transforming Craft into Art," *ARTnews* 75, no. 1 (January 1976): 48.
173 Hilarie Faberman, *Fired at Davis: Figurative Ceramic Sculpture by Robert Arneson, Visiting Professors, and Students at the University of California, Davis* (Stanford, CA: Iris & B. Gerald Cantor Center for Visual Arts, 2005), 18–19.
174 Albright, *Art in the San Francisco Bay Area 1945–1980*, 122–23.
175 Matthew Kangas, "Ellensburg Funky," *Metalsmith* (Fall 1995): 15.
176 Leslie LePere, interview with Damian Skinner, April 26, 2018.
177 Quoted in Mitchell, *The Jewelry of Ken Cory*, 59.
178 Ken Cory, Notebook, 1969, Beverly Cory Collection, San Carlos, CA.
179 Mitchell, *The Jewelry of Ken Cory*, 70.
180 Leslie LePere, interview with Damian Skinner, April 26, 2018.
181 Leslie LePere, "Standard Objects as the Subject" (MA thesis, Washington State University, 1971), Leslie LePere Archives, Harrington, WA.

182 LePere, quoted in Mitchell, *The Jewelry of Ken Cory*, 72.
183 Ibid.
184 Ibid., 73.
185 Leslie LePere, interview with Damian Skinner, April 26, 2018.
186 Ibid.
187 Ken Cory, Notebook 2, 1973, Beverly Cory Collection, San Carlos, CA.
188 Mitchell, *The Jewelry of Ken Cory*, 78.
189 Ken Cory, Notebook 1969–71, Beverly Cory Collection, San Carlos, CA.
190 Ken Cory, Notebook 3, 1973, Beverly Cory Collection, San Carlos, CA.
191 Merrily Tompkins, quoted in Ben Mitchell, "Merrily Tompkins: Over Yonder," *Metalsmith* (Winter 2006): 45.
192 Merrily Tompkins, email to Ben Mitchell, April 16, 2006, Merrily Tompkins Archive, Ellensburg, WA.
193 Nancy Worden, email to Susan Cummins, May 16, 2019.
194 Albright, *Art in the San Francisco Bay Area 1945–1980*, 111, 119–21.
195 Merrily Tompkins, interview with Helen Williams Drutt English, March 10, 2006, Hirsch Library and Archives, the Museum of Fine Arts, Houston.
196 Mitchell, *The Jewelry of Ken Cory*, 64.

Chapter Four
The Politics of American Jewelry

197 Robert Ebendorf, interview with Cindi Strauss, November 13, 2018.
198 Ibid.
199 Ibid.
200 Theodor Roszak, *The Making of a Counter Culture: Reflections on the Technocratic Society and Its Youthful Opposition* (Berkeley: University of California Press, 1995 [1968]), 124.
201 Elissa Auther and Adam Lerner, "The Counterculture Experiment: Consciousness and Encounters at the Edge of Art," in Elissa Auther and Adam Lerner, eds., W*est of Center: Art and the Counterculture Experiment in America, 1965–1977* (Minneapolis: University of Minnesota Press, 2012), xxviii.
202 Thomas Mann, email to Susan Cummins, November 22, 2019.
203 Advertisement, *Democrat and Chronicle*, February 18, 1966, 10.
204 Leslie LePere, interview with Damian Skinner and Susan Cummins, May 26, 2019.
205 David LaPlantz, interview with Cindi Strauss, November 14, 2018.
206 Richard Mawdsley, interview with Cindi Strauss, May 30, 2018.
207 Ibid.
208 Ibid.
209 Ibid.
210 Mary Ann Scherr, interview with Mary Douglas, April 6–7, 2001, The Nanette L. Laitman Documentation Project for Craft and Decorative Arts in America, Archives of American Art, Smithsonian Institution, Washington, D.C.
211 Crosby, Stills, Nash and Young, Ohio, from 4 Way Street, 1970. Ohio lyrics © WMG (on behalf of Reprise); EMI Music Publishing, Sony/ATV Music Publishing LLC
212 Bruce Metcalf, interview with Damian Skinner, May 19, 2019.
213 Ibid.
214 Bruce Metcalf, email to Damian Skinner, August 25, 2016.
215 Kathleen Kriegman, email to Susan Cummins, October 12, 2018.
216 Joan Mondale, *Politics in Art* (Minneapolis: Lerner Publications, 1972), 22.
217 Kathleen Kriegman, email to Susan Cummins, October 12, 2018.
218 Frank Zappa, Son of Orange Country, from Roxy & Elsewhere, 1974. Son of Orange County lyrics © A·k Company Limited, Munchkin Music Co
219 Shirley Marein, "Contemporary American Silversmiths and Goldsmiths," *Craft Horizons* 33, no. 1 (February 1973): 62.
220 Jim Cotter, interview with Cindi Strauss, August 8, 2017.
221 Ibid.
222 Ibid.
223 Jim Cotter, interview with Cindi Strauss, March 16, 2018.
224 Ibid.
225 Jonathan Greenberg, *The Cambridge Introduction to Satire* (Cambridge: Cambridge University Press, 2019), 253–62.
226 Stephen Brandon Hintze, "Cultivating the Crafts: Aileen Osborn Webb and the Instituting of American Craft 1934–1964" (MFA thesis, Corcoran College of Art + Design, 2008), 16.
227 American Craft Council Membership Kit, Rose Slivka Papers, Box 2, Folder 2.12, 1975, Archives of American Art, Smithsonian Institution, Washington, D.C.
228 Paul J. Smith, interview with Cindi Strauss, April 8, 2018.
229 Rose Slivka, "The Object: Function, Craft and Art," *Craft Horizons* 25, no. 5 (September/October 1965): 10.
230 Rose Slivka, "Affirmation: The American Craftsman 1971," *Craft Horizons* 30, no. 6 (December 1970): 10.
231 Colin E. Fanning, interview with Paul J. Smith, April 24, 2013, Bard Graduate Center Craft, Art, and Design Oral History Project, New York.
232 N. J. Loftis, "The Jewelry of Fred Woell," *Craft Horizons* 28, no. 2 (March/April 1968): 56.
233 Ibid., 37.
234 Deborah Waroff, "Ken Cory," *Craft Horizons* 30, no. 3 (May/June 1970): 59.
235 "No Sex Bias in Craft Horizons Says Art Press Study," *Craft Horizons* 32, no. 3 (June 1972): 3.
236 Robert Ebendorf, interview with Tacey Rosolowski, April 16–18, 2004, Nanette L. Laitman Documentation Project for Decorative Arts and Craft, Archives of American Art, Smithsonian Institution, Washington, D.C.
237 Hero W. Kielman, "Meeting of the Planning Committee for the Contemporary Jewellers Conference," November 16, 1968, Box 1, Society of North American Goldsmiths Records, Archives of American Art, Smithsonian Institution, Washington, D.C.
238 Ibid.

239 Ibid.
240 Hero W. Kielman, "To All Members—Contemporary Jewellers Conference," February 1, 1969, Box 1, Society of North American Goldsmiths Records, Archives of American Art, Smithsonian Institution, Washington, D.C.
241 Ibid.
242 Ibid.
243 Pat Passlof, "Metal Arts North America," *Craft Horizons* 34, no. 5 (October 1974): 43.
244 Ibid., 45.
245 Mark Baldridge, interview with Cindi Strauss, August 22, 2018.
246 "Letter from San Francisco," *Craft Horizons* 31, no. 5 (October 1971): 54.
247 Alan Meisel, "Letter from San Francisco," *Craft Horizons* 31, no. 3 (June 1971): 60–61.
248 Gary Griffin, "American Goldsmiths Now," *Craft Horizons* 38, no. 7 (October 1978): 54.
249 LaMar Harrington. "Letter from Seattle," *Craft Horizons* 28, no. 1 (January/February 1968): 43.
250 David Mendoza, "Review: Northwest Craftsmen's Exhibition," *Craft Horizons* 31, no. 3 (June 1971): 57.
251 David Mendoza, "Northwest Craftsmen's Biennial," *Craft Horizons* 33, no. 3 (June 1973): 39; Jeanne Metzger, "Five Award Winners," *Craft Horizons* 33, no. 8 (December 1973): 53.
252 Ibid.
253 Ashley Callahan, "Renegade Tradition: None Decades of Jewelry and Metalwork at the University of Georgia," *Metalsmith* 38, no. 4 (April 2018): 38.
254 Karen McCreary, interview with Damian Skinner and Susan Cummins, October 26, 2018.
255 Ibid.
256 Ibid.

Chapter Five
Civil Rights and Body Politics

257 Sharon Church, interview with Susan Cummins and Damian Skinner, May 23, 2019.
258 Ibid.
259 Ibid.
260 "ZPG—A New Movement Challenges the U.S. to Stop Growing," *Life* (April 27, 1970): 12.
261 John Prip, interview with Deborah Norton, September 10, 1984, as quoted in Deborah Norton, "The School for American Craftsmen," *Ganoksin*, https://www.ganoksin.com/article/school-american-craftsmen-sac/ (accessed August 16, 2019).
262 Albert Paley, quoted in Marbeth Schon, *Form & Function: American Modernist Jewelry, 1940–1970* (Atglen, PA: Schiffer Publishing, 2008), 35.
263 Barry Merritt, "Artist Statement," in Ralph Turner, *Contemporary Jewellery: A Critical Assessment 1945–75* (Worthing, UK: Littlehampton Book Services, 1976), 174.
264 Shirley Marein, "Contemporary American Silversmiths and Goldsmiths," *Craft Horizons* 33, no. 1 (February 1973): 62.
265 Gloria Steinem, "A Personal Report from Ms.," *Ms. Magazine* 1, no. 1 (July 1972): 4.
266 Deborah L. Norton and Barry S. Merritt, "Letter to the Editor," *Goldsmiths Journal* 4, no. 6 (December 1978): 28.
267 Pat Gleeson, "Essex Jewelry Designer Keeps Space Age Pace," *Newark Evening News*, 1970, Collection of Kathleen Kriegman, La Jolla, CA.
268 "Bennington Fair," *The Sunday News and Tribune*, July 6, 1969, 30.
269 Kathleen Kriegman, interview with Susan Cummins, January 22, 2019.
270 Carolyn Kriegman, "Artist Statement," in Lee Nordness, ed., *Objects: USA — Works by Artist-Craftsmen in Ceramic, Enamel, Glass, Metal, Plastic, Mosaic, Wood, and Fiber* (New York: The Viking Press, 1970), 235.
271 Mary Ann Scherr, interview with Mary Douglas, April 6–7, 2001, the Nanette L. Laitman Documentation Project for Craft and Decorative Arts in America, Archives of American Art, Smithsonian Institution, Washington, D.C.
272 Ibid.
273 Ibid.
274 Ibid.
275 Ibid.
276 Ibid.
277 Barbara Bullock, as quoted in Jean Libman Block, "A Packetful of World," *Craft Horizons* 33, no. 6 (December 1973): 19.
278 Jeffrey Hannigan and Robert Mangurian, "Portable Person," in Barbara Bullock and Paul J. Smith, *Portable World* (New York: Museum of Contemporary Crafts, 1973): unpaginated.
279 Bullock and Smith, *Portable World*.
280 Nancy Worden, interview with Susan Cummins, January 9, 2019.
281 Ibid.
282 Beth Bailey, "She 'Can Bring Home the Bacon,'" in Beth Bailey and David Farber, eds., *America in the 70s* (Lawrence: University of Kansas Press, 2004), 110–26.
283 Harriete Estel Berman, email to Susan Cummins, February 5, 2018.
284 Harriete Estel Berman, email to Susan Cummins, September 4, 2016.
285 "Civil Rights," in Kate Bush, ed., *Everything Was Moving: Photography from the 60s and 70s* (London: Barbican Art Gallery, 2012), 335.
286 Dick Edwards, "Black Business: Soul in Gold," *New York Amsterdam News*, July 11, 1970, 26, and *Freedom Fist Ring and Watch* advertisement in *Ebony* 30, no. 1 (November 1974): 95.
287 Sean Dickerson, "E. J. (Evangeline) Montgomery: Oakland African American Artists' Advocate," Oakland Public Library blog, January 6, 2018, https://oaklandlibrary.org/blogs/library-community/ej-evangeline-montgomery-oakland-african-american-artists-advocate (accessed September 21, 2019).
288 Alvia Wardlaw, interview with Cindi Strauss, December 12, 2019.
289 Nkiru Nzegwu, "A Circle of Dibias: Making Vessels of Memory and Life," in *Uncommon Beauty in Common Objects: The Legacy of African-American Craft* (Wilberforce, OH: National Afro-American Museum and Cultural Center, 1993), 12.
290 Akosua Bandele, quoted in *Uncommon Beauty in Common Objects*, 26.
291 Alvia Wardlaw, interview with Cindi Strauss, December 12, 2019.
292 Dr. David Driskell, interview with Cindi Strauss, December 12, 2019.

[293] Ibid.
[294] Alvia Wardlaw, interview with Strauss, December 12, 2019.
[295] "Letter from San Francisco," *Craft Horizons* 30, no. 3 (May/June 1970): 67.
[296] California Black Craftsmen listing, *Craft Horizons* 30, no. 3 (May/June 1970): 67.
[297] David Driskell, quoted in Patti Lechman, *Contemporary African American Crafts* (Memphis: Shelby State University and the Brooks Memorial Art Gallery, 1979), unpaginated.
[298] Winifred Brown, quoted in Lechman, *Contemporary African American Crafts*.
[299] David C. Driskell, "The Appointed Time: Hands and Mind" (keynote address, "Toward Artistic Self-Sufficiency" conference, Memphis, Tennessee, May 30, 1979).
[300] Joyce J. Scott, interview with Robert Silberman, July 22, 2009, Smithsonian Archives, Washington, D.C.
[301] Joyce J. Scott, quoted in Kim Carlin, ed., *Kickin' It with the Old Masters* (Baltimore: Baltimore Museum of Art, 2000), 26.
[302] Joyce J. Scott, interview with Susan Cummins, September 29, 2018.
[303] Joyce J. Scott, quoted in Marcia and Tom Manhart, eds., *The Eloquent Object* (Tulsa: The Philbrook Museum of Art, 1987), 129.
[304] Jo Ann Lewis, "The Wit and Anger of Joyce Scott," *The Washington Post*, January 30, 2000, G1.

Conclusion
The End of an Era

[305] Cindi Strauss, interview with Richard Mawdsley, May 30, 2018.

Copyright and Photo Credits

All effort was made to research and credit copyright and Photo credits for this book. Any errors are the authors.

Listed by figure number as they appear in the book:

^{Cover} © Estate of J. Fred Woell; Photo credit: John Bigelow Taylor
^{p. 2} Photo credit: Leslie LePere
^{Fig. 1.1} © Tamara Karla Surendorf
^{Fig. 1.2} © Estate of J. Fred Woell; Photo credit: Bridgeman Images
^{Fig. 1.3} © Estate of J. Fred Woell; Photo: Gene Young
^{Fig. 1.4} © Estate of Don Tompkins
^{Fig. 1.5} © Paul Krasser and John Francis Putnam
^{Fig. 1.6} © Estate of Don Tompkins
^{Figs. 1.7–1.9} © Estate of J. Fred Woell; Photo: Gene Young
^{Fig. 1.10} Courtesy American Craft Council Library & Archives
^{Fig. 1.11} Courtesy Betty Tompkins
^{Fig. 1.12} © Estate of Olaf Skoogfors; Photo credit: Thomas R. DuBrock
^{Fig. 1.13} © Stanley Lechtzin; Photo credit: Thomas R. DuBrock
^{Fig. 1.14} © Albert Paley, Paley Studios Ltd.; Photo credit: Thomas R. DuBrock
^{Fig. 1.15} © Estate of J. Fred Woell; Courtesy American Craft Council Library & Archives
^{Fig. 1.16} © L. Brent Kington; Courtesy American Craft Council Library & Archives
^{Fig. 1.17} © David LaPlantz; Courtesy American Craft Council Library & Archives
^{Fig. 1.18} © Richard Mawdsley; Courtesy American Craft Council Library & Archives
^{Fig. 1.19} © Estate of J. Fred Woell; Photo credit: John Bigelow Taylor, 2008
^{Fig. 2.1} © Arthur Korb; Photo credit: Jay Ahrend
^{Fig. 2.2} Photo credit: Richard Gross
^{Fig. 2.3} Courtesy Thomas Mann
^{Fig. 2.4} © Thomas Mann; Photo credit: Thomas Mann
^{Fig. 2.5} Photo credit: Roberta Price © 2004, 2010 / All Rights Reserved
^{Fig. 2.6} Courtesy American Craft Council Library & Archives; Photo credit: Lois Moran
^{Fig. 2.7} Photo credit: Rimas VisGirda
^{Fig. 2.8} Courtesy SummerVail Archives
^{Fig. 3.1} Courtesy the Artist
^{Fig. 3.2} © Lynda Watson; Photo credit: Eva Heyd
^{Fig. 3.3} © Lynda Watson
^{Fig. 3.4} © Estate of William Clark; Photo credit: John Bigelow Taylor, 2008
^{Fig. 3.5} © David Fenton / Getty Images
^{Fig. 3.6} © Ted Streshinsky / CORBIS / Corbis via Getty Images
^{Figs. 3.7–3.10} © Estate of William Clark; Courtesy Diane Kuhn
^{Fig. 3.11} Photo credit: Phoebe Knapp
^{Fig. 3.12} © Louis Mueller
^{Figs. 3.13–3.14} © Louis Mueller; Photo credit Marty Doyle
^{Fig. 3.15} © Arline Fisch; Photo credit: William Gullette
^{Fig. 3.16} © Arline Fisch; Photo credit: Ed Watkins, 2008
^{Fig. 3.17} © Ramona Solberg; Courtesy Sharon Dwinnel-Smith
^{Fig. 3.18} © Ramona Solberg; Photo credit: John Bigelow Taylor, 2008

Fig. 3.19 © Beverly Cory; Photo credit: Thomas R. DuBrock
Fig. 3.20 Courtesy American Craft Council Library & Archives; Photo credit: Ferdinand Boesch
Fig. 3.21 Photo credit: Thomas Mann
Fig. 3.22 Courtesy American Craft Council Library & Archives; Photo credit: Raphael Warshaw
Fig. 3.23 Courtesy Ruth Snyderman
Fig. 3.24 Photo credit: Jerry Wainwright
Fig. 3.25 Courtesy Helen Williams Drutt English; Photo credit: Daniel Kron / Laurie Seniuk
Fig. 4.1 © Estate of Sam Kramer; Photo credit: Chad Redmon
Fig. 4.2 © Charles L. Russell; Photo credit: Thomas R. DuBrock
Fig. 4.3 © Fred W. McDarrah / Getty Images
Fig. 4.4 © Beverly Cory
Fig. 4.5 © Beverly Cory; Photo credit: Doug Yaple
Fig. 4.6 © Hairy Who; Courtesy Jim Nutt and Gladys Nilsson
Fig. 4.7 © 2020 Estate of Robert Arneson / Licensed by VAGA at Artists Rights Society (ARS), NY
Fig. 4.8 © Beverly Cory
Fig. 4.9 © Estate of Don Tompkins; Photo credit: Thomas R. DuBrock
Fig. 4.10 Courtesy Beverly Cory
Fig. 4.11 Courtesy Leslie LePere
Fig. 4.12 © Leslie LePere
Fig. 4.13 © Pencil Brothers; Photo credit: Richard Nicol
Fig. 4.14 © Beverly Cory Digital Image © 2020 Museum Associates / LACMA. Licensed by Art Resource, NY
Fig. 4.15 © Pencil Brothers
Fig. 4.16 Courtesy Merrily Tompkins Estate, Ellensburg
Fig. 4.17 © Merrily Thompkins Estate, Ellensburg; Photo credit: Lynn Thompson
Fig. 4.18 © Merrily Tompkins Estate, Ellensburg; Photo credit: Thomas R. DuBrock
Fig. 4.19 © Merrily Tompkins Estate, Ellensburg
Fig. 4.20 © William T. Wiley; Photo credit: Michael Tropea, Chicago
Fig. 4.21 © Merrily Tompkins Estate, Ellensburg; Photo credit: Thomas R. DuBrock
Fig. 5.1 © Robert Ebendorf
Fig. 5.2 Courtesy Leslie LePere
Fig. 5.3 © Richard Mawdsley
Fig. 5.4 © Irving Petlin, Jon Hendricks, Frazer Dougherty, and Ronald L. Haeberle
Figs. 5.5–5.6 © Richard Mawdsley; Photo credit: Thomas R. DuBrock
Figs. 5.7–5.10 © Bruce Metcalf
Fig. 5.11 © Barry Merritt; Photo credit: 2020 John Griebsch
Fig. 5.12 © Estate of Fred Woell Photo: Gene Young
Fig. 5.13 © Estate of Don Tompkins
Fig. 5.14 © John Filo / Getty Images
Fig. 5.15 © Estate of Don Tompkins
Figs. 5.16–5.17 © Jim Cotter
Fig. 5.18 © Jim Cotter; Photo credit: Justin Klocke
Fig. 5.19 Courtesy American Craft Council Library & Archives; Photo credit: Edith Dugmore
Figs. 5.20–5.21 Courtesy American Craft Council Library & Archives
Fig. 5.22 Courtesy Moderne Gallery, Philadelphia
Figs. 5.23–5.25 © Karen McCreary
Fig. 6.1 Courtesy Sharon Church
Fig. 6.2 © Sharon Church; Photo credit: Aengus McGiffin
Fig. 6.3 © Estate of Barry Merritt; Photo credit: 2020 John Griebsch
Fig. 6.4 © Estate of Carolyn Kriegman; Digital image © 2020 Museum Associates / LACMA. Licensed by Art Resource, NY
Fig. 6.5 Courtesy Scherr Family
Figs. 6.6–6.7 © Archives of American Art, Smithsonian Institution
Fig. 6.8 © Scherr Family; Photo credit: John Bigelow Taylor, 2008
Fig. 6.9 Courtesy American Craft Council Library & Archives; Photo credit: Bob Hanson
Fig. 6.10 © Merrily Tompkins Estate, Ellensburg; Courtesy American Craft Council Library & Archives
Fig. 6.11 Courtesy Nancy Worden
Fig. 6.12 © Beverly Cory; Photo credit: Doug Yaple
Fig. 6.13 Courtesy Harriet Estel Berman
Figs. 6.14–6.16 © Harriet Estel Berman
Fig. 6.17 Courtesy Mills College Library
Fig. 6.18 © E.J. Montgomery; Photo credit: Martha Jackson Jarvis
Fig. 6.19 © E. J. Montgomery; Photo credit: Senghor Reid
Fig. 6.20 © Photo credit: Michael Fields
Figs. 6.21–6.24 © Joyce J. Scott
p. 155 © Richard Mawdsley Digital Image © 2020 Museum Associates / LACMA. Licensed by Art Resource, NY
Back Cover © Merrily Tompkins Estate, Ellensburg

Index

A

Aaron Faber Gallery, New York City, 73
abortion, 127
Abraham, Erick, at Summervail Workshop for Art & Critical Studies, 1976 or 1977 (Fig. 2.8), *42*
Abstract Expressionism, 14, 27, 77, 84, 90
Adventures of Superman (television show), 24
African Americans
    crafts conferences of, 144, 146
    as craftspeople, 40, 78, 117, 144, 146
    discrimination against, 31, 98, 126, 142, 144, 146
    education of, 144
    separatist movements, 142, 144
    as studio jewelers, 142, 144
African art, 79, 117, 135
African Communities League, 142
African heritage, 142, 144
AfriCobra (African Commune of Bad Relevant Artists), 144
Albers, Josef, 131
Albright, Thomas, 53
Alexander, Bill, 41
Alex and Lee, 70, *70*, 71
Allen Ginsberg, reading poetry at the Five Spot Cafe, New York City, February 22, 1964 (Fig. 4.3), *79*
Allrich Gallery, San Francisco, 54
All-Star Comics, 156
amateurism, 19, 31
America House, New York City, 65, 114, 115, 127
American Craft Council (ACC)
    and African American craftspeople, 144
    conferences of, 40, 41, 66–67, 102, 114, 115, 117, 144
    educational charter of, 114–15
    networking benefits of, 132
    and visibility of jewelers, 9
American Craft Council South Central Conference on July 21–25, 1971, in Steamboat Springs, Colorado, participants at a craft-in, 1971 (Fig. 2.6), 40, *40*, 41
American Craft Enterprises, 67
American Craftsmen's Cooperative Council, 65
American Designer–Craftsmen exhibition (Richmond Art Center, California, 1971), 119
American Designer–Craftsmen exhibitions, 115
American Dream, 66, 76, 140
American Goldsmiths Now exhibition (1978), 119
American jewelers. *See also* American studio jewelry; Beat movement; Funk movement; *and specific artists*
    artistic philosophies of, 25, 26
    in counterculture, 8, 9, 10, 34–37, 48, 53–54
    creativity and innovation as markers of value, 9–10, 28–29, 36
    in-jokes of, 20, 95
    material palette of, 25, 26, 36, 39, 85, 118, 156
    narrative compositions of, 29, 72, 87, 102, 121, 156
    political and social concerns of, 26, 31, 35, 98–103, 105–9, 111–14, 121, 156
    priorities of, 28
    and traditional jewelry, 9, 15, 17, 19, 25, 26, 27, 29, 31, 36, 49, 53, 71, 82, 117, 119, 121, 137, 156
    and university programs, 9, 26, 28, 35, 156
    and wearable objects, 10, 17, 26, 51, 53, 58, 70, 87, 118
American Jewelry 1963 exhibition, 117
American Jewelry Today exhibition (Everhart Museum, 1967), 117

American South, 109, 142
American studio craft movement
    American studio jewelry within, 8–9, 10, 28, 37–38, 69, 70–73, 117, 156
    in counterculture, 9, 10, 31, 35–37, 38, 40, 41–42, 65–67, 71, 156
    craft fairs and markets, 66–68, 69, 73, 115
    craft galleries and shops, 68–73, 79
    and craft schools, 41
    cultural implications of, 115
    exhibitions of, 29–31
    and Funk movement, 82–83
    growth of, 8, 9
    and individuality, 65
    innovation in techniques and materials, 30, 31
    market for, 65–73
    Lee Nordness on, 31
    in Philadelphia, 26
    and political and social issues, 117
    and professionalism, 31
    publications of, 39–40
    tradition of, 31
    in West Coast, 35
    and *Whole Earth Catalog*, 39
American studio jewelry
    and African Americans, 142, 144
    and American studio craft movement, 8–9, 10, 28, 37–38, 69, 70–73, 117, 156
    identity of, 9
    and professionalism, 35, 156
    and Olaf Skoogfors, 26
    and Ramona Solberg, 62
Anderson, David, 116
Anholtz Ranch (now Ford Park and Betty Ford Gardens), 42–43
Anti-Jewelry jewelry, 17
Appalachia, 69
Aquino, Pete, 41
Arentzen, Glenda, 73
Arneson, Robert
    and Funk movement, 82–84, 92
    works of
        Busts, 83
        Crisco, 83
        His and Hers, 1964 (Fig. 4.7), 82, 83
        Oreo, 83
        Toilets, 83
        Trophies, 83
        Urinals, 83
Arp, Hans, 72
Arrowmont School of Arts and Crafts, Gatlinburg, Tennessee, 41
Art Deco, 129
Art Nouveau, 26, 27, 117, 127
The Art of Assemblage exhibition (Museum of Modern Art, 1961), 14
The Art of Personal Adornment exhibition (Museum of Contemporary Crafts, 1965), 17, 71, 117
Arts and Crafts movement, 35
Art Team, 86
Art USA Now exhibition, 30
Artwear Gallery, New York, 72
Artweek, 54
Art Workers' Coalition, 102

Ashanti symbols, 142
assassinations
    Robert Ebendorf on, 98–99
    of 1960s, 8, 14, 67, 98, 103, 127, 142
    J. Fred Woell on, 21, 24
assemblage
    and Beat movement, 80
    and Robert Ebendorf, 98–99
    and Thomas Mann, 39
    and Barry Merritt, 128
    and political and social concerns, 14–15
    and Don Tompkins, 19, 27, 85, 99
    and Merrily Tompkins, 92
    and West Coast, 72
    and J. Fred Woell, 14, 17, 19, 21, 25, 27, 29, 31, 99, 117
astrology, 34, 42
Autio, Rudy, 119

B

baby boomer generation, 48
"Back to the Earth" festivals, 38
Bailey, Clayton, 92
Bakker, Gijs, 72
Balazs, Harold, 119
Baldridge, Mark, 118
Bandele, Akosua, 144
Barrett, Clotilde, 41
Bean, Bennett, 67–68
Beatles, 106
Beat movement, 42, 76–80, 90
Beatty, Talley, 78
Bellas Artes, San Miguel de Allende, 61
Benaki Museum, Athens, Greece, 58
Benderson, Nanny, 69
Bennett, Jamie, 43, 73
Bennington College, 40
Berensohn, Paulus, 40
Berkeley Art Museum, 82
Berkeley Free Speech Movement, 106
Berman, Harriete Estel
    on gender roles, 137, 140, 142
    photograph of, 1983 (Fig. 6.13), 139
    works of
        Buns in the Oven (Fig. 6.15), 140, *140*
        The Family of Appliances You Can Believe In series, 140
        Silver Iron, 1979 (Fig. 6.14), 137, *139*, 140
        Womanizer, Kitchen Queen, 1982 (Fig. 6.16), 140, 141, 142
Bicentennial of U.S., 154, 156
Bilderback, Carolyn, 40
Bindy Bazaar, Woodstock Festival, 1969 (Fig. 3.20), 66, 67
biodiversity, 8
Birmingham Gallery, 109
birth control pill, 57, 127, 136, 137
Bitz, Grace, 41
Black Panthers, 142, 144
Black Power, 142, 144
Bloody Sunday, 8
body ornaments, 53–54, 78, 129
Botticelli, Sandro, 80
Brand, Stewart, 39

Breckenridge, Bruce, 43
Breckenridge, Colorado, 41
Breis, Marta, 72
Bremner, Stuart, at Summervail Workshop for Art & Critical Studies, 1976 or 1977 (Fig. 2.8), 42
Brenner, Jules, 77
Brooks, Jan, 43
Brooks, Lee, photograph of (Fig. 3.24), 70, 70, 71
Brown, Blanche, 79
Brown, Judith, 71, 72
Brown, Winifred, 144
Brynner, Irena, 69, 77, 79
building forms, experiments with, 39
Bullock, Barbara, 135–36
Burroughs, William, 77
Bury, Claus, 72
Byzantine art, 135

C

Cage, John, 17–18
Calder, Alexander, 72
California Black Craftsmen exhibition (Mills College Art Gallery, Oakland, 1970) (Fig. 6.17), 142, 143, 144
California College of Arts and Crafts (CCAC), Oakland, 52, 57, 80–82, 84
California Crafts Museum, 140
California Design, 34–36
California Design annual exhibitions (Pasadena Art Museum), 34, 121
California Institute of the Arts, 44
California National Guardsmen
 surrounding a Vietnam War protester during the People's Park riot in Berkeley, California (Fig. 3.6), 52, *52*
 view as they close off a street near People's Park, Berkeley, California, mid-1969 (Fig. 3.5), 52, *52*
California School of Fine Arts, 79
Calley, William, 105
Cambodia, 100, 101, 102, 105, 137
Camp George West in Golden, Colorado, 43
capitalism, 19, 37
Carson, Rachael, 66
Central Washington University (CWU), 20, 85, 121, 137
Cherokee Nation, 69
Chicago, Judy, *Birth Project* (1980–85), 140
China, 20, 56, 100, 113
Christensen, Hans, 26, 28, 49, 54, 117, 127
Church, Sharon
 in downtown Saratoga Springs, New York, 1970 (Fig. 6.1), *126*
 and feminism, 126–27
 and Gallery of Contemporary Metalsmithing, 129
 works of, *No. 2 Pin*, 1969–70 (Fig. 6.2), 127, *128*
Cirino, Antonio, 39
City Lights Bookstore, San Francisco, 79
Civil Rights Act (1964), 126, 142
civil rights movement
 assassinations of, 14, 24, 98, 103, 127, 142
 boycotts of, 142
 marches of, 98, 142
 protests of, 8, 121
 sit-ins of, 142

and Lynda Watson, 50
Clark, William
 in a bubble, 1971 (Fig. 3.10), 54, *54*
 and counterculture values, 51
 Dancers in Muir Woods in California wearing body ornaments, early 1970s (Fig. 3.9), 53–54, *54*
 education of, 51–52
 as juror for *American Designer-Craftsmen* exhibition, 119
 political views of, 51, 54
 and wearable objects, 51, 53
 works of
  Necklace for the American Taxpayer, 1971 (Fig. 3.8), 53, *53*
  Police State Badge, 1969 (Fig. 3.4), 51, *52*
  Survival Necklace, 1971 (Fig. 3.7), 52–53, *53*
Clemmer, Phyllis, 41
climate change, 135
Cody, William Frederick "Buffalo Bill," 108
Cold War
 "better dead than red" slogan, 20–21
 and military-industrial complex, 103, 105
 as political and social concern, 8, 76, 100, 114
 Ronald Reagan on, 123
 and reputation of U.S., 31
Colette, 69
collage, 14, 36, 156
Colorado Mountain College, 42, 43
comic-book-style images, 81
communes, 8, 9, 39, 41–42, 51, 58, 65
Communism, 20–21, 52, 76, 100, 107, 123
Communist Party, 142
Comprehensive Environmental Response, Compensation, and Liability Act, 121
Concord Festival of the Arts, Civic Arts Gallery, 54
Conner, Bruce, 80
conscientious objectors, 38
consciousness-raising events, 40
Constructivism, 79
consumerism
 and Ken Cory, 62
 and Jim Cotter, 113
 and countercultural values, 37
 and marketing strategies, 66, 137
 and Louis Mueller, 56
 and Pencil Brothers, 87
 and plexiglass, 131
 and Don Tompkins, 20, 85
 and J. Fred Woell, 19, 25, 56
Contemporary African American Crafts exhibition (Brooks Memorial Art Gallery, Memphis, Tennessee, 1979), 144, 146
corporations, 66, 83, 113, 123
Correll, Leslie, 71
Corso, Gregory, reading poetry at the Five Spot Cafe, New York City, February 22, 1964 (Fig. 4.3), *79*
Cory, Ken. *See also* Pencil Brothers
 with balsawood boat in the shape of a pencil, *2*
 and Beat movement, 80
 Craft Horizon profile of, 117
 exhibitions of, 116, 117, 119, 121
 and Funk movement, 84, 85, 89–90
 as juror for *The Metal Experience* exhibition, 119
 and Leslie LePere, 62, 85–87, 101

narrative jewelry of, 87
from the *Objects: USA* catalogue, 1968 (Fig. 4.10), 85, *85*
in Pioneer Square, Seattle (Fig. 4.11), 85, *85*
teaching career of, 62, 89–90, 121, 137
and Merrily Tompkins, 90, 92–93, 95
works of
    Fish, c. 1962 (Fig. 4.4), *81*
    How to Fix Your Snake, 1976 (Fig. 4.14), 88, *88*
    Squash Blossom necklace, 1974 (Fig. 3.19), 62, *64*
    Tongue, 1967 (Fig. 4.8), *83*, 84
    (Untitled) Drain, 1968 (Fig. 4.5), *81*
Cory, Robert, 80
Cory, Susan, 80
Cotter, Jim
  exhibitions of, 121
  and Gallery of Contemporary Metalsmithing, 129
  jewelry gallery of, 113
  and Richard Nixon, 109, 112, 113–14
  plastic-bag series of necklaces, 113
  portrait, late 1960s (Fig. 5.17), *113*
  and Summervail Workshop for Art & Critical Studies (Fig. 2.8), 42, *42*, 43, 44
  works of
    I*mpeachment with Honors*, 1974 (Fig. 5.18), 113–14, *114*
    Tears on My Pillow, 1973 (Fig. 5.16), 112, *112*
Coulter, Lane, 43, 121
counterculture of 1960s and 1970s
  American jewelers' place in, 8, 9, 10, 34–37, 48, 53–54
  American studio craft movement in, 9, 10, 31, 35–37, 38, 40, 41–42, 65–67, 71, 156
  and Beat movement, 78
  experiments of, 9, 54
  fantasy and exotic clothing of, 58, 61, 62, 71, 72
  and Funk movement, 82
  hippies associated with, 9, 35, 36, 39, 49, 85, 106, 113
  lifestyles of, 9, 37, 38, 39, 50, 54, 58, 65–66, 70, 71, 127, 135–36
  and music, 9, 38, 48, 105
  and *Objects: USA* exhibition, 31
  and pre-modern and pre-industrial cultures, 58, 61, 62, 65, 72
  rejection of mainstream values, 37, 48, 65–66
  revolutionary goals of, 52
  values of, 8, 14, 25, 31, 34–37, 38, 40, 41–44, 48, 51, 65, 71, 89, 121, 122, 127, 135–36, 156
Craft Horizons
  and African American craftspeople, 40, 144
  on craft-ins, 40, 41
  equal coverage of men and women, 117
  exhibition reviews in, 31, 116, 118, 119, 121, 129, 144
  founding of, 65, 114
  and political issues, 117
  profiles of artists, 116–17
  Rose Slivka as editor of, 115–16, 117
  on Don Tompkins, 111
  and visibility of jewelers, 9
  on J. Fred Woell, 102
craft movement. *See* American studio craft movement
Craftsman Lifestyle: The Gentle Revolution (California Design), 34–36
Croninger, Cara, 71, 72
Cronkite, Walter, 103
Crosby, Stills, Nash and Young, 105

Cubism, 14, 79
cultural appropriation, 113
Cuyàs, Ramon Puig, 72

D

Dada, 14, 79, 82, 93
Dale, Julie Schafler, 71
Daley, William, 69
Davis, Angela, 142
Day, Russell, 19, 20
de Beauvoir, Simone, 126
De Forest, Roy, 92
democratic symbols, 14
Denmark, 54, 58, 127
De Patta, Margaret, 79, 116, 117
Derrez, Paul, 72
Designer/Craftsman '71 exhibition (Richmond Art Center), 54
diamonds, 15, 36, 79
Dougherty, Frazer, Irving Petlin, and Jon Hendricks, *Q. And babies? A. And babies*, 1970 (Fig. 5.4), 102, *103*
Dow Chemical Company, 19, 66
Driskell, David, 117, 144, 146
Dr. Strangelove (film), 114
Drutt, Helen
  gallery of, 71–72
  in the Helen Drutt Gallery, Philadelphia, c. 1979 (Fig. 3.25), *71*
Duckson, Bob, 122
Dude Ranch Dada, 93
Duke Ellington Society, 78

E

Earth, Air, Fire, Water gathering, Grass Valley, California, 1974 (Fig. 2.7), *41*, 42
Earth Day, 121
Earthlight Supply Natural Foods, 39
East Coast
  galleries of, 70, 72, 80
  hierarchies of, 35
  and modernism, 81, 90
  trends in jewelry, 25, 82, 90, 116, 118
  urban environment of, 20
East Village Other, 100
Ebendorf, Robert
  and aesthetic juxtapositions, 100
  and Fairtree Gallery, 70, 129
  as founder of SNAG, 28, 117, 118
  and found-object assemblage, 98–99
  on Summervail Workshop for Art & Critical Studies, 43
  teaching career of, 121
  and J. Fred Woell, 99–100
  works of
    Canned Heat, 98
    Dig It Bigot, 99, 100
    Population Explosion, 1967 (Fig. 5.1), 98, *99*, 100
    Ebony, 142
Ehrlich, Anne, 127
Ehrlich, Paul R., 53, 127

Eikerman, Alma, 26
Eisenhower, Dwight D., 103, 105, 114
electroforming technique, 27
Electrum Gallery, London, 72
Ellensburg, Washington
    and Funk movement, 84, 85, 89, 90, 95
    jewelers centered in, 20, 25, 62, 84–86, 91, 92, 119, 137
Ellington, Duke, 78
Emmons, Wesley, 20
Endangered Species Act, 121
Environmental Defense Fund, 121
environmental issues. *See also* nature
    and biodiversity, 8
    Rachel Carson on, 66
    and William Clark, 51
    climate change, 135
    and countercultural values, 9, 37, 38, 121, 122, 156
    and craft exhibitions, 71
    and Funk movement, 83
    and Allen Ginsberg, 78
    and Karen McCreary, 121–23
    and population growth, 53, 98, 100, 127
    and Mary Ann Scherr, 132, 133, 135
    and Lynda Watson, 50
    and J. Fred Woell, 17, 19, 25
Environmental Protection Agency, 123
Equal Rights Amendment, 117, 129, 131
Ernst, Max, 72

F

Faber, Edward, 73
Faber, Patricia Kiley, 73
Fairtree Fine Crafts Institute, 70
Fairtree Gallery, New York City, 70, 129
Falconer, James, 81
Falkenstein, Claire, 69
Federal Land Policy and Management Act, 121
feminism, 126–29, 131, 137, 140, 142, 156
Fenster, Fred, 116, 117
Fike, Philip, 26, 28, 117
Filo, John, *Mary Ann Vecchio (kneeling) with the body of Jeffrey Miller*, May 4, 1970 (Fig. 5.14), 111, *111*
Firesign Theatre, 114
First World Congress of Craftsmen (New York City, 1964), 65
Fisch, Arline
    artistic philosophy of, 26
    exhibitions of, 116
    as founder of SNAG, 28, 117, 118
    on Museo del Oro, 65
    and Lee Nordness, 70
    and wearable objects, 58, 118
    works of
        Halter and Skirt, 1968 (Fig. 3.16), 58, *60*
        Peacock and Dragonfly, 1969 (Fig. 3.15), 58, *59*
        Textile Techniques in Metal for Jewelers, Sculptors, and Textile Artists, 39
Fisher, Margaret, 54
Fisk University, 144
folk art, 91–92
found images, 14
found objects
    American jewelers experimenting with, 36, 39, 156
    and William Clark, 51
    and Ken Cory, 80
    and Robert Ebendorf, 98, 99
    in *Goldsmith '70* exhibition, 29
    and Ramona Solberg, 62
    and Don Tompkins, 19, 27, 85, 99
    and J. Fred Woell, 14, 17, 19
    and Nancy Worden, 137
Freedom Fists, 142
Freedom Riders, 142
Freedom Trash Can, 8
Frey, Viola, 119
Frid, Tage, 69
Friedan, Betty, 126
Frith, Don, 15
Frost, David, 111
Fulbright, William, 19
Funk exhibition (Berkeley Art Museum, 1967), 82
Funk movement, 81–85, 89–90, 92–93, 95, 121, 128
Fur and Feathers (Museum of Contemporary Crafts, New York City, 1971), 71

G

Gaimbruni, Tio, 119
Galeria del Sol, Santa Barbara, 70
Gallery of Contemporary Metalsmithing, Rochester, New York, 129
Gallo, Frank, 16, 17, 21
Gallo Gold Museum, Lima, 58
Galperin Jewelry, 137
Gardiner, Michael T., 92
Garvey, Marcus, 142, 144
gay community, 8, 70
Gentille, Thomas, 39, 72
Getty, Nilda, 41
G.I. Bill (Serviceman's Readjustment Act), 8–9, 61
Gilhooly, David, 83, 92
Ginsberg, Allen
    at the Five Spot Cafe, New York City, February 22, 1964 (Fig. 4.3), *79*
    poetry of, 40, 58, 77, 78, 80
Glass Art Society, 117
Glenn, John, 133
Golddust (later *Goldsmith's Journal*), 118
Goldsmith '70 exhibition (Minnesota Museum of Art, St. Paul, 1970), 28–29, 31, 103, 117, 119, 128
Goldsmith '74 exhibition (Renwick Gallery, Washington, D.C., 1974), 118, 119
Goldsmith's Hall, London, 72
Goldsmiths Journal, 129
Goldsmiths Journal 5, no. 1, February 1979 (Fig. 5.22), 118, *119*
Gomez, Manuel Albert, 144
Gonzalez, Kay, 41
Goofy (Disney character), 113
Gottlieb, Adolph, 77
Graham Gallery, New York City, 16
Grateful Dead, 41
Great Depression, 80
Green, Art, 81
Gregorius, Jane, 43–44
Griffin, Gary, 72, 119

H

Haida art and culture, 53
Hairy Who, 81
Hairy Who exhibition at the San Francisco Art Institute in 1968, poster (Fig. 4.6), *81*
Hall, Laurie, 71, 72
Hallman, Ted, 69
Hampton College, 144
Handcraft Cooperative League of America, 114
Handcraft Trails, Maine, 69
Harper, William, 43
Hawes, Ed, 62
Hawes, Juanita, 62
Haystack Mountain School of Crafts in Deer Isle, Maine, 41
Hedrick, Wally, 80
Helen Drutt Gallery, Philadelphia, 71–72, *71*
Henderson, Vernita, 144
Hendricks, Jon, Irving Petlin, and Frazer Dougherty, Q. And babies? A. And babies, 1970 (Fig. 5.4), 102, *103*
Hendrie, Ken, 41
Hendrix, Jimi, 67
Henry Art Gallery, University of Washington, 119
Hertz, Bernhard, 58
hippies
  beads of, 58, 61, 67
  counterculture associated with, 9, 35, 36, 39, 49, 85, 106, 113
  do-it-yourself jewelry of, 62
  and Haight–Ashbury district, 71
  mainstream opinions of, 48
  on selling out, 51
historically black colleges and universities, 144
"Historical Traditions of the New South" conference (Winston-Salem University, North Carolina, June 1977), 117, 144
Hitler, Adolf, 69
Ho Chi Minh, 100
Hofmann, Hans, 77
Holocaust, 76
Hoover, J. Edgar, 114
Hopi culture, 62
Hosterman, Harry, in collaboration with Mary Ann Scherr, *Heart–Pulse Sensor Bracelet*, 1971 (Fig. 6.7), 133, *133*
House Committee on Un-American Activities, 76
Howard University, 144
Hu, Mary Lee, 43
Hughes, Graham, 72
Human Be-In, Golden Gate Park, San Francisco (January 1967), 40–41
Humphrey, Hubert, 102
Hunt, Richard, 144
Huntington, Gloria, 62
Husted-Anderson, Ada, 116

I

IBM, 40
I Ching, 17, 58
In Praise of Hands exhibition (1974), 65
Insight '69 conference, Northeast Region of the American Craft Council (ACC), 40
Instituto Allende, San Miguel de Allende, Mexico, 112, 146
Internet, 51
"Introspection" conference (Midland Art Center, Michigan, October 1971), 117

J

Jackson, Daniel, 69, 71
Jacopetti, Alexandra, 58
Jefferson, Bob, 144
Jefferson Airplane, 41
Jennings, Lois, 39
Jerry, Michael, 28, 117
Jet, 142
Jewelry by Art Smith exhibition (Little Gallery of the Museum of Contemporary Crafts, New York, September 12–October 12, 1969), installation photograph (Fig. 5.21), 116, *116*
Jewelry by Fred Woell exhibition (Museum of Contemporary Crafts, New York City, 1967), 24
Johns, Jasper, 14, 19
Johnson, Lyndon B., 20, 52, 66, 100
Johnson Wax Company, 30
Jones, Jim, 146
Jonestown massacre, Guyana, 146, 149
Joplin, Janis, 85
Julie: Artisan Gallery, New York City, 71

K

Kansas Designer Craftsman show, 102
Kaplan, Shirley, 40
Kay, Jane Holtz, 40
Kelly, Walt, 114
Kennedy, Jacqueline, 24
Kennedy, John F., 24, 66, 100, 142
Kennedy, Robert, 24, 103
Kent State University, 105–6, 111, 117, 127
Kerouac, Jack, 76, 77, 78, 80
Khan, Hazrat Inyat, 38
Kielman, Hero, 117–18
Kimball, Richard, 73
King, Martin Luther, Jr., 24, 98, 103, 127, 142
Kington, L. Brent
  artistic philosophy of, 26
  blacksmithing conference of, 101
  exhibitions of, 29, 116
  as founder of SNAG, 28, 117
  and Richard Mawdsley, 102
  works of
    Liberty 76 on cover of *Goldsmith's Journal*, 119
    Pull Toy, no date (Fig. 1.16), *28*, 29
kitsch, 81
Knoffke, Gary, 121
Korb, Arthur
  brooch and an image of the interior of his house, published in *Craftsman Lifestyle*, 1976 (Fig. 2.1), 34, *34*
  commissions of, 34
Korean War, 56
Kramer, Hilton, 93
Kramer, Sam
  and Beat generation, 77, 79
  Cyclops broach, 1946 (front and back) (Fig. 4.1), *76*
Krassner, Paul, 114

and John Francis Putnam, *Fuck Communism!*, 1963 (Fig. 1.5), 20–21, *20*
Kriegman, Carolyn
    at the *Northeast Craft Fair 9,* American Craft Council on June 28–30, 1974, Rhinebeck, New York (Fig. 3.22), 68, *68*
    torso works of, 131
    works of, *Kinetic Necklace,* 1969 (Fig. 6.4), *130*, 131
Kriegman, Kathleen, 19
Kriegman, Sam, 131
Ku Klux Klan, 144
Kunsthaandvaerkerskolen (School of Arts and Crafts), Copenhagen, 59
Kurtzman, Harvey, 114

L

Laisner, George, 80–81
Lambda Rho Alumni Association, 119
Laos, 100, 101
LaPlantz, David
    and *Goldsmith '70* exhibition, 29
    on Vietnam War, 101
    works of, Real *American Male Pendant,* no date (Fig. 1.17), 29, *29*
Larsen, Jack Lenor, 58
Larson, Orland, 117
Leary, Timothy, 40–41, 106
Lechtzin, Stanley
    artistic philosophy of, 26, 28, 119
    electroforming technique of, 27
    exhibitions of, 116, 117
    and Helen Drutt Gallery, 72
    and Richard Mawdsley, 103
    teaching career of, 137
    works of, *Brooch 64-B3,* 1969 (Fig. 1.13), 27, *27*
Leersum, Emmy van, 72
Legion of Honor in San Francisco, 54
LePere, Leslie. *See also* Pencil Brothers
    and Ken Cory, 62, 85–87, 101
    and objects, 86–87
    and Merrily Tompkins, 92
    works of
        billboard along the highway between Pullman, Washington, and Moscow, Idaho, 1970 (Fig. 5.2), 101, *101*
        page from *Standard Objects as the Subject,* 1971 (Fig. 4.12), 86–87, *86*
Libre community, Colorado, 39
Lichtenstein, Roy, 54
Life magazine, 77, 105
Lighthouse Field, 50
Litner, Charles, 41
Lobel, Paul, 77
Loftis, N. J., 117
Lourie, Janice, 40
LSD, 34, 38, 40, 51, 106, 111

M

McCarthy, Eugene, 137
McCarthy, Joe, 114
Macchiarini, Peter, 79
McClure, Michael, 79, 80
McCord, James, Jr., 111
McCreary, Karen
    and environmental issues, 121–23
    photograph of, 1975 (Fig. 5.24), 122, *122*
    works of
        Environmentally Safe, 1980 (Fig. 5.23), *120*, 121, 123
        MAD, 1982 (Fig. 5.25), *122*, 123
McGovern, George, 137
McGuire, Elise, 41
McNeish, Ronald, 28, 117
Macumba ceremonies, 146
Mad magazine, 114
Maher, Pat, 119
Mailer, Norman, 25, 100
mainstream values, 37, 48, 58, 65–66, 76–77, 82, 127, 135–36, 156
Mann, Thomas
    in anti-war movement, 38, 100
    and counterculture, 38–39
    and craft galleries, 69
    photograph of, 1979 (Fig. 2.3), *36*
    works of, *Rainbow Winged Heart Pin,* 1974 (Fig. 2.4), *37*, 38
Manolides, Jim, 92–93
Manolides Gallery, Seattle, 92–93
March on Washington (1963), 142
marijuana, 38
Markusen, Tom, 129
Martinazzi, Bruno, 72
Marxism, 127
M.A.S.H (film), 114
Mate, Alex, photograph of (Fig. 3.24), 70, *70*, 71
Matsukata, Miye, 72, 117
Matzdorf, Kurt, 40, 117
Mawdsley, Richard
    exhibitions of, 29, 121
    narrative compositions of, 29, 102
    teaching career of, 103
    on Vietnam War, 154
    works of
        Bolting Machine, 1966, 103
        Camera, 1971 (Fig. 5.5), *104*, 105
        Gordon's Flash, no date (Fig. 1.18), 29, *29*
        The Pequod, 1971 (Fig. 5.6), *104*, 105
        The Tank, 1970 (Fig. 5.3), 102, *102*
        War Protest series of, 103, 105
        Wonder Woman in Bicentennial Finery, 1975–76 (Fig. 8.1), 154, *155*, 156
Maxwell, William, 144
Meadlo, Paul, 102
medals
    and Barry Merritt, 108
    and Don Tompkins, 19–20, 25, 85, 92, 109, 129
    and J. Fred Woell, 19
Melville, Herman, 105
Mercury Head Workshop, 50
Merritt, Barry
    and body adornment, 129
    education of, 127
    and Funk movement, 128–29
    and military medals, 108
    on Vietnam War, 100–101

and women's movement, 127, 129, 131
  works of
    Buffalo Bill Badge, 1970 (Fig. 5.11), 108, *109*, 129
    Little Orphan Annie's Secret Society Brownie Baking Badge, 129
    Nancy Drew, 129
    Torso Pieces series, 129, 131
    Wonder Woman, 1972 (Fig. 6.3), 129, *129*, 131
The Metal Experience exhibition (Oakland Museum, 1971), 54, 119
Metcalf, Bruce
  cartoons of, 107
  family background of, 106
  photograph, c. 1975 (Fig. 5.8), *107*
  and satire, 106, 113
  works of
    Epaulets, 1971 (Fig. 5.10), 108, *108*
    Waldo the Paranoid Parakeet, 1971 (Fig. 5.9), 107, *107*
    Worms from Mars Invade an Authentic New England Village & Are Attacked by the National Guard, 1971 (Fig. 5.7), 105–7, *106*, 108
Mickey Mouse (Disney character), 38, 109, 111, 113
Middle Passage, 149
Milhoan, Ron, and Summervail Workshop for Art & Critical Studies (Fig. 2.8), 42, *42*, 43–44
military-industrial complex, 19, 101–2, 103, 105
Miller, Jeffrey, 111
Miller, John Paul, 26, 102, 116, 119
Mills College Art Gallery, *California Black Craftsmen*, 1970 (Fig. 6.17), 142, *143*, 144
Minimalism, 140
Mitchell, John, 111
Mitchell, Joni, 38
Mitchell, Martha, 111
modernism, 80–81, 85
Mondale, Joan, *Politics in Art*, 109
Mondale, Walter, 109
Montgomery, Evangeline J.
  and African heritage, 142, 144
  and *California Black Craftsmen* exhibition (Fig. 6.17), *143*, 144
  works of
    Ancestor Box series, 142
    Justice for Angela, 1970 (Fig. 6.18), 142, *143*
    Marcus Garvey Box, also known as *Red, Black, Green Ancestral box*, 1973 (Fig. 6.19), 142, *145*
Montgomery Improvement Association, 142
Moody, Howard, 76
Moore, Eudorah M., 35–36, 121
Moore, Victor, 80
Morris, Robert Lee, 72
Morton, Philip, 28, 39, 117
Moty, Eleanor, 27, 43, 72
Ms. magazine, 129, 137
Muehling, Ted, 72
Mueller, Louis
  and cartoon characters, 57
  education of, 54, 57
  and Gallery of Contemporary Metalsmithing, 129
  in Morocco in a rented Volkswagen van, 1971 (Fig. 3.11), 55
  political views of, 56
  works of
    Colonial America, 1968 (Fig. 3.13), 56, *56*
    Texaco, 1967 (Fig. 3.12), 55, *56*
    Wonder Woman, 1968 (Fig. 3.14), 57, *57*
Muir Woods, 53–54
Muller-Stach, Dieter, 122
Museo del Oro (Museum of Gold), Peru, 65
Museum of Contemporary Crafts, New York, 29, 65, 70, 71, 77, 115
Museum of Modern Art, New York, 77
Museum of Non-Objective Painting (now the Guggenheim), New York, 77
music, and counterculture, 9, 38, 48, 105
My Lai massacre, 100, 102, 105

N

Nanny's Design in Jewelry, San Francisco, 69
Natalini, Bob, 69
National Conference of Artists (NCA), 144
National Council for the Education on the Ceramic Arts, 117
National Endowment for the Arts, 144
National Environmental Policy Act, 121
National Liberation Front (Vietcong), 100
National Museum, Copenhagen, 58
National Organization of Women (NOW), 126, 129
National Ring Exhibitions (University of Georgia), 121
Nation of Islam, 142
Native Americans
  beadwork of, 62, 90
  and Jim Cotter, 113
  and counterculture, 40, 58, 67, 71, 90
  jewelry forms of, 62, 137
  and Bill Reid, 53
  and Don Tompkins, 20
  and weaving, 41
  and J. Fred Woell, 19
nature. *See also* environmental issues
  and Funk movement, 95
  harmony with, 35, 37, 38, 41, 49, 50, 51, 58, 65
Neal, Frank, 78
Neal Salon, 78
Nelson, Gaylord, 121
Nelson, Mary Stephens, 119
New Age spirituality, 17
New Left politics, 48
New Tivoli Bar, San Francisco, 79
New York Amsterdam News, 142
New York Times, 53, 105
Ngo Dinh Diem, 100
Nietzsche, Friedrich, 93
Nilsson, Gladys, 81
Nivola, Ruth, 116
Nixon, Pat, 112
Nixon, Richard
  impeachment and resignation of, 42, 112, 113
  Richard Mawdsley on, 102
  on national unity, 111
  Pencil Brothers on, 89
  public opinion of, 109, 111
  and Vietnam War, 52, 100, 101, 102, 107, 109
  and Watergate scandal, 111, 112, 114, 122, 137
  Lynda Watson on, 48

Index

177

Noffke, Gary, 129
nonconformity, 65, 127
Nordness, Lee, 29, 31, 70
Northeast Craft Fair 9, American Craft Council on June 28–30, 1974, Rhinebeck, New York, Carolyn Kriegman at (Fig. 3.22), 68, *68*
Northeast Craft Fair 12, American Crafts Council on June 23–25, 1977, Rhinebeck, New York, outdoor craft displays (Fig. 3.21), 67–68, *67*
Northeast Region of the American Craft Council (ACC), Insight '69 conference, 40
Northwest Craftsman's Exhibition (Seattle, 1954), 19
Northwest Craftsman's Exhibition (Seattle, 1965), 119
Northwest Craftsman's Exhibition (Seattle, 1967), 119
Northwest Craftsman's Exhibition (Seattle, 1968), 119, 121
Northwest Craftsman's Exhibition (Seattle, 1969), 121
Northwest Craftsman's Exhibition (Seattle, 1973), 121
Northwest Indians, 62
Norton, Deborah, 129, 131
nostalgic futurism, 136
nuclear war, opposition to, 9, 123
Nutt, Jim, 81

O

Oakland Museum of California, 142
Obiko, San Francisco, 70–71
Objects: USA exhibition (National Collection of Fine Arts of the Smithsonian Institution in Washington, D.C., 1969), 29–31, 49, 62, 70, 72, 131
objects. *See also* found objects
    and Beat movement, 80
    and countercultural values, 14
    and Funk movement, 84, 95
    and Hairy Who, 81
    and Leslie LePere, 86–87
    wearable objects, 10, 17, 26, 51, 53, 58, 70, 87, 118
Ohio State National Guard, and Kent State University shootings, 105–6, 111, 117, 127
oil embargo of 1973, 137
O'Keefe, Georgia, *Sky Above Clouds IV*, 1965, 140
Oldenburg, Claus, 42, 84
Ommen, Joke van, 72
Op Art, 131
Optical Art, 36
Osborn Webb, Aileen, 65, 114, 117
Oswald, Lee Harvey, 24

P

pacifism, 38
Paley, Albert
    abstract lyricism of, 27
    exhibitions of, 117
    fibula form used by, 28
    and Helen Drutt Gallery, 72
    teaching career of, 127
    works of, *Brooch*, 1969 (Fig. 1.14), 27, *27*
Palo Alto Art Center, 54
Pardon, Earl, 26, 73, 126
Parks, Rosa, 142
Passlof, Pat, 118

Payne, Lorissa, 41
Peace Corps, 66
Pearson, Ronald Hayes, 26, 28, 69, 116, 117–18, 127
Peck, Gregory, 105
Pencil Brothers (Ken Cory and Leslie LePere)
    collaboration of, 62, 85, 86
    exhibitions of, 121, 135
    and Helen Drutt Gallery, 72
    subject matter of works, 87–89
    and Merrily Tompkins, 95
    works of
        Camel, 1971 (Fig. 4.13), 87–88, *87*
        Egypt, 1974 (Fig. 4.15), 89, *89*
Penington, Ruth, 19, 61
Penland School of Craft, Penland, North Carolina, 41
Pennington, Arthur, 112
Pennington, Ruth, 19
Pentagon Papers, 53, 105
Penzur, Linda, 69
People's Park, Berkeley, California, 52, *52*
Peoples Temple, 146
Pepsi, 17, 19
Perkins, Linn, in downtown Saratoga Springs, New York, 1970 (Fig. 6.1), *126*
Peterson, Jean, 41
Peterson, Russ, 41
Petlin, Irving, Jon Hendricks, and Frazer Dougherty, *Q. And babies? A. And babies,* 1970 (Fig. 5.4), 102, *103*
Peyton Place (television show), 17
Philadelphia Civic Center, 70
Philadelphia College of the Arts (PCA, later the University of the Arts), 26, 71, 72
Philadelphia Council of Professional Craftsmen (PCPC), 70, 71, 72
Philadelphia Museum of Art, 70
Picasso, Pablo, 72
Pine, Alvin, 119, 122
Pitchfork, Catherine, 144
Plaut, James S., 65
political and social concerns. *See also* civil rights movement; Vietnam War; women's movement
    of American jewelers, 26, 31, 35, 98–103, 105–9, 111–14, 121, 156
    and assassinations, 8, 14, 67, 98, 103, 127, 142
    and assemblage, 14–15
    collage as activist engagement, 14
    in counterculture, 9, 40, 44, 48, 118, 156
    and Robert Ebendorf, 98, 99
    and Richard Mawdsley, 102
    and music, 48
    and narrative jewelry, 121
    New Left politics, 48
    and Pencil Brothers, 88–89
    and Joyce J. Scott, 149
    and SNAG, 129, 131
    and Don Tompkins, 19, 21
    and Lynda Watson, 50
    and J. Fred Woell, 17, 19, 21, 24, 31, 100
Pollock, Jackson, 25
Pop Art, 17, 19, 36, 54, 81, 84, 117
population issues, 53, 98, 100, 127
Portable World exhibition (Museum of Contemporary Crafts, New York City, October 5, 1973 – January 1, 1974)
    back cover of the exhibition catalogue (Fig. 6.9), *135*

on mobility, 135–36
  and Mary Ann Scherr, 135
Price, Roberta, 39
Prip, John (Jack), 26, 28–29, 69, 116, 117, 119, 127
Provincetown, Massachusetts artist colony, 77
psychedelic rock, popularity of, 8
Pueblo Indians, 41
Pujol, Elliot, 121
Putnam, John Francis, and Paul Krassner, *Fuck Communism!*, 1963 (Fig. 1.5), 20–21, *20*
Putnam Country Products, New York City, 114

R

Rabanne, Paco, 58
Ramshaw, Wendy, 72
Rat Bastard Protective Association, 80
Rauschenberg, Robert, 14, 18, 19
Ray, James Earl, 24, 142
Reagan, Ronald, 48, 123
The Realist, 20
Realist, 114
Reasoner, Harry, 48
Rebajes, Frank, 77
recreational drugs, in counterculture, 9, 34, 38, 49, 54, 106
Redheart, Ellen X., 90
Reed, Gervais, 119
Reid, Bill, 53
Reifel, Stan, 70
Reinhardt, Richard, 26
religion, and J. Fred Woell, 19
Renaissance Pleasure Faire, 50–51
Renk, Merry
  Craft Horizons profile of, 117
  and Nanny's Designs in Jewelry, 69
  porch with tub, published in *Craftsman Lifestyle,* 1976 (Fig. 2.2), 34–35, *35*
  and San Francisco Metal Arts Guild, 79
Richardson, Harry S., 144
Rocca, Suellen, 81
Rochester Institute of Technology, 49, 54, 65, 69, 115, 117, 127
Roe v. Wade (1973), 127
Romero, Juan, 24
Roosevelt, Franklin D., 92
Rose, Augustus F., 39
Ross, Carol Sedestrom, 67
Ross, Linda, 121
Roszak, Theodore, 9, 48
Roth, Evelyn, 53
Roth, William, 127
Ryan, Leo, 146

S

Saar, Betye, 142
Sakata, Sandra, 70–71
San Francisco
  art and craft schools of, 78–79
  and Beat movement, 78–80
  and counterculture, 51
  and Summer of Love, 8, 51
San Francisco Art Institute, 81, 82
San Francisco Metal Arts Guild, 79
Sartor, Mary, 41
satire
  and Harriete Estel Berman, 140, 142
  and William Clark, 51
  and Jim Cotter, 113–14
  and countercultural values, 156
  and Funk movement, 82, 83
  and Barry Merritt, 108, 128–29
  and Bruce Metcalf, 106, 113
  Joan Mondale on, 109
  and Pencil Brothers, 89
  in post–World War II period, 114
  and Don Tompkins, 19, 20, 25, 111, 113
  and J. Fred Woell, 19, 24, 29, 113
Saturday Evening Post, 77
Saunders, Raymond, 142
Savio, Mario, 106
Scandinavian jewelry, 27, 58, 62, 81, 116, 127
Scavengers Protective Society, 80
Scherr, Mary Ann
  body monitors of, 132–33, 135
  design career of, 131–33, 135
  exhibitions of, 116
  and Kent State University, 105
  photograph of, c. 1970s (Fig. 6.5), *131*
  and politics of the body, 131
  teaching career of, 132
  works of
    in collaboration with Harry Hosterman, *Heart-Pulse Sensor Bracelet,* 1971 (Fig. 6.7), 133, *133*, 135
    Electronic Oxygen Belt Pendant, 1974 (Fig. 6.8), *134,* 135
    Trach Necklace, c. 1979 (Fig. 6.6), 132, *132*
Scherr, Sam, 132
School for American Crafts, Rochester Institute of Technology (RIT), New York, 54, 65, 69, 115, 117, 127
School of the Art Institute of Chicago, 81
Schopenhauer, Arthur, 80
Schor, Resia, 117
Scott, Joyce J.
  design career of, 146
  education of, 146
  exhibitions of, 144
  at Haystack, 1973 (Fig. 6.20), *146*
  works of
    The Double Cross, from the *Jonestown Massacre* series, 1980 (Fig. 6.22), 146, *148*
    For the Souls, from the *Jonestown Massacre* series, 1980 (Fig. 6.24), 149, *150*
    Jonestown Massacre series, 146, 149
    Kool-Aide Kocktail, from the *Jonestown Massacre* series, 1980 (Fig. 6.23), 146, 149, *149*
    The White Boy's Gone Crazy, from the *Jonestown Massacre* series, 1980 (Fig. 6.21), 146, *147*
Sculpture to Wear, New York City, 72
Seattle, Washington, 61
Seattle Clay Club, 119
Seattle Weavers Guild, 119
Seitz, William C., 14
self-actualization, 40
Selz, Peter, 82

Seppä, Heikki, 26, 117
sexual liberation, in counterculture, 9, 49, 92, 127, 136, 137
Shannon, Alice, 116
Sheinbaum, Betty, 70
Sheinbaum, Stanley K., 70
Sherotsky, George, 121
Shop One, Rochester, New York, 69
Sierra Club, 121
Silicon Valley, 51
Simmons, Robert, 31
Simms, Carroll Harris, 144
Sirhan, Sirhan, 24
Six Gallery, San Francisco, 78
Skoogfors, Olaf
    artistic philosophy of, 119
    Craft Horizons profile of, 117
    exhibitions of, 116
    as founder of SNAG, 28, 117
    and Helen Drutt Gallery, 71, 72
    inner circle of, 27
    and Carolyn Kriegman, 131
    and Richard Mawdsley, 103
    sculptural forms of, 26
    works of, *Brooch*, 1966 (Fig. 1.12), *26*
Slivka, Rose, editor of *Craft Horizons* magazine, 1969 (Fig. 5.19), 115–16, *115*, 117
Smith, Arthur "Art"
    and Beat movement, 77, 78
    installation photograph of *Jewelry by Art Smith* exhibition (Little Gallery of the Museum of Contemporary Crafts, New York, September 12–October 12, 1969) (Fig. 5.21), 116, *116*
    Neckpiece (Positive/Negative), 1948 (Fig. 4.2), 78, *78*
Smith, Carlyle, 102
Smith, Christina, 42
Smith, Paul J.
    as director of Museum of Contemporary Crafts in New York, 29, 115, 116
    and exhibitions, 71, 115, 116, 135
    holds Paul Stanley's boot from the rock band Kiss (Fig. 5.20), *115*
    and Richard Mawdsley, 103
    and J. Fred Woell, 31
Snyder, Gary, 42
Snyderman, Rick, 69
Snyderman, Ruth, 69
Socialism, 107
Social Realism, 14
Society of North American Goldsmiths (SNAG)
    and African American craftspeople, 144
    conferences of, 99–100, 103, 117, 118, 127–28
    conservatism of, 43
    exhibitions of, 119
    founding of, 28, 117–18, 127
    institutional politics of, 118–19
    membership criteria for, 118
    and political and social concerns, 129, 131
    as professional group for jewelers, 9, 26, 114, 128
Solar Wind Silversmiths, 39
Solberg, Ramona
    art studies of, 61
    and ethnic cultures, 61, 62
    exhibitions of, 119
    and Funk movement, 85
    and Helen Drutt Gallery, 72
    and Jim Manolides, 92
    teaching career of, 62, 85
    and Don Tompkins, 20, 85
    works of
        Ecology, 121
        Inventive Jewelry Making, 39, 62
        Mitla, c. 1951 (Fig. 3.17), 61, *61*
        Shaman's Necklace, 1968 (Fig. 3.18), 62, *63*
Soldner, Paul, 41
Sonnabend, Joan, 72
Sonnabend, Roger, 72
South Street Renaissance, Philadelphia, 69
Soviet Union, 20, 31, 53, 56, 66, 76, 100, 123
space travel, 133, 135
Sperisen, Francis, 79
spiritual practices, 38, 58
Stacey, Harold, 117
Staffel, Rudolf, 69
stagflation, 154
stand-up comedy, 114
Stanley, Linda, in downtown Saratoga Springs, New York, 1970 (Fig. 6.1), *126*
Statue of Liberty, 154, 156
Steig, Henry, 77
Steinem, Gloria, 129, 137
Stember, Jonathan, 69
Stittgen, Karl, 53
Students for a Democratic Society (SDS), 50
Summer of Love, 38, 58, 71
Summervail clowns, Summervail Workshop for Art & Critical Studies, 1976 or 1977 (Fig. 2.8), *42*, 43
Summervail Workshop for Art & Critical Studies, 42–44, 128
Surendorf, Tamara Karla
    and J. Fred Woell, 17
    works of
        Pendant, no date (Fig. 1.1), *14*
        Re-Aul, 17
        Robbery, 17
        Warf, 17
Surrealism, 14, 79, 82
Symbolism and Imagery (Central Washington University, 1975), 121
Syracuse Jewelry and Manufacturing, 137

T

technocracy, 9, 36
technology
    in counterculture, 9, 39–40, 51, 58, 65, 114
        effects on everyday lives, 135
        liquid graphics and light environments, 40
Techno-Romantic © Jewelry Objects, 39
Telleen, Daniel, 43
Tendler, Bill, 77
Texas Southern University, 144
Thomas, Richard, 117
Thoreau, Henry David, *Walden*, 15
Tohono O'odham people, 41
Tompkins, Betty, 20, 25
Tompkins, Don

countercultural values of, 25, 31
exhibitions of, 119, 121, 135
found-object assemblage of, 19, 27, 85, 99
in front of a rented storefront, 1980 (Fig. 1.11), *25*
and Helen Drutt Gallery, 72
and medals, 19–20, 25, 85, 92, 109, 129
and Richard Metcalf, 106
and Richard Nixon, 109, 111
and Ruth Penington, 61
politics of, 19, 21
and satire, 19, 20, 25, 111, 113
teaching career of, 19, 20, 85
text incorporated in work of, 19, 20, 85
trends represented by, 26
works of
    Commemorative Medals series, 19–20, 25, 85, 92, 109, 129
    Janis Joplin, from the *Commemorative Medals* series, 1970 (Fig. 4.9), *84*, 85
    Martha Mitchell, 1972 (Fig. 5.13), *110*, 111
    Nixon (Bring Us Together), c. 1970 (Fig. 5.13), 109, 111, *111*
    Patriotic (Fuck Communism), c. 1969 (Fig. 1.6), 20, 21, *21*
    Pendant, c. 1965 (Fig. 1.4), *18*
Tompkins, Merrily
   and assemblage, 92
   and Ken Cory, 90, 92–93, 95
   exhibitions of, 119, 135, 136
   family background of, 90–91
   on folk art, 91–92
   and Funk movement, 90, 92
   and Helen Drutt Gallery, 72
   photograph of, no date (Fig. 4.16), *90*
   and Don Tompkins, 25, 91
   works of
      Dad's Payday, 1968 (Fig. 4.17), *91*, 92
      Slow Boat, 1976 (Fig. 4.21), *94*, 95
      Snatch Purse, 1975 (Fig. 4.18), 92, *92*
      Thank You Hide, 1976 (Fig. 4.19), *92*, 93
      Wild Oats Sowing Kit, 1971 (Fig. 6.10), 136, *136*
Tuskegee University, 144
Twenty-Sixth Amendment, 122
Tyler School of Art, Philadelphia, 26, 27, 72, 137

U

underground media, 48
Universal Negro Improvement Association, 142
Universal Sufism, 38
Universidad de Michoacán, Morelia, 61
University of California, Berkeley Art Museum, 54
University of California, Davis, 82–83
Untracht, Oppi, 39
U.S. Constitution, 122, 154
utopian movements, 8, 41, 48, 156

V

Vecchio, Mary Ann, 111
Vierthaler, Art, 15
Vietcong, 100
Viet Minh organization, 100

Vietnam Veterans Against the War, 105
Vietnam War
   death toll of, 14
   and domino theory, 20
   and draft, 31, 38, 56, 102, 103, 122
   ending of, 122
   escalation of, 53, 100, 102, 109
   Gulf of Tonkin Resolution, 52
   industrial production for, 34
   My Lai massacre, 100, 102, 105
   opposition to, 9, 38, 51, 52, 54, 56, 98, 100–102, 105, 107, 113, 127, 128, 129, 137, 142, 154
   polarization surrounding, 107
   protests of, 8, 19, 20, 38, 40, 48, 50, 51, 52, 67, 99, 100, 103, 105, 108, 112, 117
   Senate hearings on, 19
   Tet Offensive, 100
   and U.S. reputation, 31
   veterans of, 42, 105
Vonnegut, Kurt, 21
von Neumann, Robert, 15, 16, 17, 119
voting age, 122
Voting Rights Act (1965), 142
Voulkos, Peter, 84

W

Wallace, Mike, 102
Walters, Stanley, 40
Ward, Carole Allen, 144
Warhol, Andy, 19, 54
Waroff, Deborah, 117
Washington, George, 17
Watergate scandal, 111, 112, 114, 122, 137
Watkins, David, 72
Watson, Lynda
   family background of, 48, 49
   in the jewelry lab at California State University, Long Beach, 1967 or 1968, (Fig. 3.1), *49*
   and Lee Nordness, 70
   and *Objects: USA* exhibition, 49
   and political and social issues, 50
   and Summervail Workshop for Art & Critical Studies, 43
   teaching career of, 51
   works of
      Landscape Neckpiece, 1968 (Fig. 3.2), 49, *49*
      Sheep Bracelet, 1973 (Fig. 3.3), 50, *50*
Weckström, Björn, 73
Wehrman, Richard
   house at Libre Commune, c. 1971 (Fig. 2.5), *38*
   silver jewelry of, 39
Weiner, Ed, 77, 79, 117
Weiss, Jerry, 40
Wertenberger, Kathryn, 41
West, Virginia, 40
West Coast
   American jewelers of, 78–79
   American studio craft movement in, 35
   and assemblage, 72
   Beat movement in, 78–79, 90
   Funk movement in, 90, 92, 93, 121, 128
   hot-rod and motorbike scenes, 80

Western Association of Art Museums, 142
Whitman, Walt, 80
Whitney Museum of American Art, New York, 77
Whole Earth Catalog, 39, 50, 132
Whole Earth Truck Store, 39
Wildenhain, Frans, 69
Wiley, William T., 92
    works of
        Thank You Hide, 1970–71 (Fig. 4.20), *93*, 93
Willcox, Donald, 36–37
Winston, Bob, 79, 117
Winston, Robert, 69
Winter Soldier Investigation, 105
Wirsum, Karl, 81
Woell, J. Fred
   and John Cage, 17–18
   and ceramics, 14–15
   countercultural values of, 25, 31
   Craft Horizon profile of, 117
   and Robert Ebendorf, 99–100
   elegiac subject matter of brooches, 21, 24
   exhibitions of, 116, 117, 121
   faux amateurism of, 19
   found-object assemblage of, 14, 17, 19, 21, 25, 27, 29, 31, 99, 117
   and *Goldsmith '70* exhibition, 29
   and Helen Drutt Gallery, 72
   on jewelry, 15–17, 25, 26
   and Richard Mawdsley, 102
   and metalsmithing, 14, 15–16
   and Richard Nixon, 109
   and Lee Nordness, 70
   and *Objects: USA* exhibition, 30–31
   and political and social concerns, 17, 19, 21, 24, 31, 100
   portrait from the back cover of the exhibition catalogue *Jewelry by Fred Woell* (Fig. 1.10), 24, *25*
   and rusticated look, 17, 19
   and satire, 19, 24, 29, 113
   and sculpture, 16, 17, 21
   works of
      The American Way, 1969 (Fig. 1.9), *23*, 24
      The Body Politic brooches, 117
      Come Alive, You're in the Pepsi Generation, 1966 (Fig. 1.3), *16*, 17, 19, 56, 117
      Fetish Pendant, 1966 (Fig. 1.2), *15*, 17
      The Good Guys, 1966 (Fig. 1.19), 30–31, *30*
      Mother/Family Icon, 1967 (Fig. 1.15), *28*, 29
      November 22, 1963 12:30 p.m., 1967 (Fig 1.7), *22*, 24
      Noxin, 1970 (Fig. 5.12), 109, *110*
      Requiem, 1968 (Fig. 1.8), *23*, 24
Wolf, Lam de, 72
women's movement
   and equal rights, 8, 31, 126
   Equal Rights Amendment, 117, 129, 131
   and feminism, 126–27, 128, 129, 131, 137, 140, 142, 156
   and Merrily Tompkins, 92
   and Lynda Watson, 50
Wonder Woman, as cultural symbol, 57, 129, 131, 154, 156
Woodstock Festival, 1969, 67
Worden, Nancy
   and found objects, 137
   works of
      Initiation, 1977 (Fig. 6.12), 137, *138*
      Self-Portrait, 1975 (Fig. 6.11), 137, *138*

The Works gallery, 1960s (Fig. 3.23), 69, *69*, 70
World Crafts Council (WCC), 58, 65, 72
World War II
   and Beat movement, 76, 77
   Jim Cotter on legacy of, 112
   and gender roles, 137, 140
   restrictions of, 80
   and satire, 114
   and Mary Ann Scherr, 131
   and Vietnam, 100
Wright, Donald B., 116

Y

Yakama people, 62
yin–yang symbol, 87, 95
Yost, Phillip, 119
Young, Neil, 105
Young Americans exhibitions, 115

Z

Zappa, Frank, 111
Zapruder film, 24
Zelmanoff, Marci, 71, 73
Zen, 78, 93
Zero Population Growth (ZPG), 127

In Flux: American Jewelry and the Counterculture

Authors
Susan Cummins, Damian Skinner, Cindi Strauss

Copyediting
Wendy Brouwer, Stuttgart
Heather Brand, Houston, TX

Project coordinator
Greta Garle, arnoldsche Art Publishers, Stuttgart

Graphic design
Benjamin Kivikoski and Philipp Staege,
Bureau Progressiv, Stuttgart

Offset reproductions
Paladin Design- und Werbemanufaktur, Remseck

Printed by
DZS Grafik d.o.o, Ljubljana, Slovenia

Bibliographic information published
by the Deutsche Nationalbibliothek
The Deutsche Nationalbibliothek lists this publication
in the Deutsche Nationalbibliografie; detailed
bibliographic data are available on the Internet at
www.dnb.de

© 2020 arnoldsche Art Publishers, Stuttgart,
and the authors

All rights reserved. No part of this publication may be
reproduced, stored in a retrieval system, transmitted
in any form or by any means electronic or mechanical,
including photocopying, recording or otherwise,
without prior permission from the publisher.

arnoldsche Art Publishers
Olgastrasse 137, 70180 Stuttgart, Germany
+49 (0)711 64 56 18–0
art@arnoldsche.com
www.arnoldsche.com

ISBN 978-3-89790-597-9

Cover illustrations
Front cover: J. Fred Woell, *The Good Guys*, 1966 [Fig. 1.19] /
back cover, left: Merrily Tompkins, *Snatch Purse*, 1975
[Fig. 4.18] / back cover, right: Joyce J. Scott, *The Double Cross*, from the *Jonestown Massacre* series, 1980 [Fig. 6.22]

This publication is produced with generous support from the
Art Jewelry Forum Fiscal Sponsorship program
Rotasa Fund